The
TRUE
HISTORY
of
the Caribbean Island
of
COZUMEL
Quintana Roo,
Mexico

Ric Hajovsky

ISBN 978-0-9828610-8-0

MMXV
Pan American Publishing

4th edition

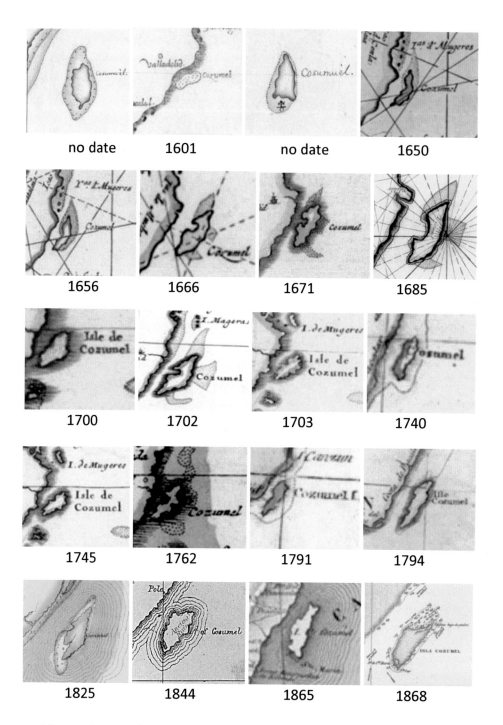

no date   1601   no date   1650

1656   1666   1671   1685

1700   1702   1703   1740

1745   1762   1791   1794

1825   1844   1865   1868

Above: Cozumel as it appeared on different maps over the years.

Table of Contents

Preface

ɔr most people, this collection of my articles on the history of Cozumel ɔntains a substantial amount of information about the past that will be ew to them. Much of that new data will contradict their long-held eliefs and traditional ways of thinking about the island's history, but ʌat is what typically happens when oral tradition is compared to written eyewitness or historical accounts; they don't always agree. Stories handed down father to son, or grandfather to grandson, have a way of morphing and mutating, like the whispered message passed along in the child's game of "telephone." By the time the message gets to the last recipient, it often no longer contains the same information that was passed from the first pair of lips to the first pair of ears. It is only the first whispered version that can be relied upon to contain the truth; oral versions of earlier oral versions are inherently unreliable and that is why original documents and eyewitness statements are so much more valuable than the third-person, or fourth-person accounts.

What is even worse than the misunderstood statements handed down by oral tradition, are the invented claims about Cozumel's history that were made with the intention to embellish its past or to cover up some uncomfortable fact. These tall-tales are now being mass marketed in the electronic social media and today's youth tend to believe them without a second thought. Today, we are being inundated with the constant postings and re-postings of these spurious accounts of Cozumel's past. Articles on history written by non-historians, or "cut & pasted" misinformation copied from other unreliable websites have multiplied a thousand-fold on the internet, newspapers, and popular books. It is not unusual to have one erroneous paragraph about Cozumel's past appear, word for word, on over one hundred other websites, Facebook pages, Wikipedia, travel guidebooks and the like. Rarely have the "authors" of these pirated, misleading articles ever bothered to look at an original 16th, 17th, or 18th century document; it is far too easy for them to simply plagiarize another plagiarist's work than it is to do any real research.

One of the reasons for this lack of serious research is the fact that f[r] many years it has been very difficult for the average historian to revie[w] the old, original documents concerning early Cozumel; most of th[e] documents and manuscripts were held in archives that were wide[ly] dispersed and difficult to access. It was not until the advent of th[e] internet and the World Wide Web that these documents could b[e] discovered and read with just a few keystrokes of the computer. No[w] universities, private foundations, and government archives are scannin[g] and uploading thousands of old documents to the internet every day[.] Thanks to them, more and more information about Cozumel's past is[s] becoming available for the first time in centuries.

It is in these digital archives that I did most of the research for this collection of articles. I did not rely on 18th, 19th, 20th, or 21st century books, articles or websites for my sources on Cozumel's early history. Nor did I rely on the previously translated versions of the source documents. I made my own translations and I was frequently surprised in the difference between my translation and a previously published translation. I often found that earlier translators had inserted words, names, or meanings into their texts that did not actually appear in the original texts. Sometimes these insertions or the manipulations of the meanings of these passages were made in order to support an author's point of view; other times they were simply unfortunate errors. Whether or not the translator intended to alter the meaning of the text is unimportant. The results were the same; the original meaning was hidden or changed and it was this new, revised content that was transmitted to the public.

For the articles covering the 18th, 19th and 20th centuries, I relied only on information gathered from letters, government reports, newspapers, travelogues, and other original documents that were generated close to the time of the events in question. A significant amount of this information was originally recorded in English by sea captains, U.S. and Texas military men, foreign government officials, and civilian visitors to the island. As a consequence, much of this English-language information has been overlooked by Spanish-speaking historians. By combining the data from Spanish, Cuban, Mexican, English, Irish, Belizean, and US records, a very different accounting of the 18th, 19th and early 20th century events on Cozumel can be reconstructed, one that is at odds with the current widely-held views.

I organized this collection of my articles more or less chronologically. Many of them were published previously in Spanish-language newspapers like the *Quintanarroense* and *Primer Mestizaje*, or Mexican magazines like *AMMJE*. Others were originally presentations I gave in Spanish at Cozumel's *Museo de la Isla* and the *Universidad de Quintana Roo*, or for the *Fundación de Parques y Museos de Cozumel*. Some articles also appeared on my website, **www.EverythingCozumel.com**. Others simply languished on my computer's hard drive, waiting for the day they could be shared with interested readers.

When I originally wrote these articles, I wrote them without footnotes due to the fact that most of the articles appeared in periodicals, newspapers, and presentations where footnotes were inappropriate. As I began to assemble and edit these articles for inclusion in this book, I realized that if I footnoted every reference to every manuscript, article, document, or digital image I consulted during my research, the footnotes would be nearly as long as the articles. That in itself was not an insurmountable problem; what made up my mind not to include footnotes were two other reasons. First, I often found that the links to web images of manuscripts or documents I consulted in the past had changed or been deleted and it would not be possible to continually update their new locations. That is not to say that the images of the manuscripts and documents in question are not still available on the World Wide Web; it is just that their location is not always permanent. All one has to do is perform either a Google, Google Books, Google Image, or Google Scholar search for them and one will find their present location on the web. That was my second reason for not including footnotes; it is so easy for the reader to simply plug in the pertinent title, author, description, or a line from a quote from my text into an on-line search, that it seemed redundant to place the same information in a footnote which would still require the reader to do the online search in order to read the original source document.

Ric Hajovsky
Isla de Cozumel, 2015

Above: Cozumel and the adjacent coast of Quintana Roo, 2001.

CHAPTER 1

The early settlement and development of Cozumel

The question often arises, "When was Cozumel first inhabited?" So far, no archaeological evidence has been uncovered that could firmly establish a date earlier than the Preclassic (or Middle Formative period) some 3,000 years ago. However, there is no reason to discount the possibility that small groups of the Paleo-Indians who had been migrating south from the Bering Strait may have visited Cozumel or even established themselves temporarily as early as 14,000 years ago. Remains of these early New-World colonizers are just now beginning to turn up in the deep cenotes of Quintana Roo. The skeleton of the Paleo-Indian "Eve of Naharon" that was recently discovered in the Naranjal cave system near Tulum has been carbon-14 dated to 11,600 B.C., over 13,600 years ago. The 10,000-year-old remains of the Paleo-Indian "Mujer de La Palma" and the child "Joven de Chan Hol" that were found near Tulum in Las Palmas cenote and Chan Hol cenote are just two of the other finds that have pushed back the timeline for the population of Quintana Roo. Bones from the extinct late Pleistocene era horse, *Equus conversidens,* around 11,000 to 12,000 years old have been discovered in Cenote Sifa in Cozumel. If a horse could make it to the island that long ago, Paleo-Indians most certainly did.

These Paleo-Indians were only the forerunners of the human migration southward in the Americas. By 8,000 years ago, Archaic period hunters and gatherers had populated Yucatán. Shortly thereafter, groups of these early settlers migrated out from northern Quintana Roo to settle the western portion of the Antilles and become the Casimiroid culture in Cuba, Puerto Rico, Hispaniola and other Antillean islands.

Around 4,500 years ago, during the Early Preclassic period (also known as the Early Formative period), the very beginnings of the Maya civilization began to coalesce and become what we now call the Proto-Maya. Within a few hundred years, these Proto-Maya begin to farm corn and their settlements become more permanent in nature.

By 1,000 B. C, or 3,000 years ago, the Maya culture had evolved into what we now call the Middle Preclassic or Middle Formative period. The earliest dateable artifacts on Cozumel are from this period.

By 2,300 years ago, the Late Preclassic (or Late Formative period) began and the Cozumel villages of Xamancab, Aguada Grande, Buenavista, San Gervasio, Oycib (Cedral) and other smaller settlements on the island were established. However, it wasn't until the Postclassic that the island became anything more than a backwater in the overall scheme of things. It was then that the Putún Maya (also known as the Chontal Maya) began to expand their sea-trade route linking their base in Tabasco with shores far and wide, including Cozumel.

Possibly the first recorded mention of these trade routes was made by Fernando Colón, Cristóbal Colón's son, in which he recounted an event from his father's fourth and last voyage in his book, _Historie del S.D.Fernando Colombo; nelle quali s'ha particolare & vera relatione della vita & de'fatti dell'Almiraglio D. Christoforo Colombo suo padre_, which Fernando wrote between 1537 y 1539 before it was published in Venice in 1571. Fernando says that in Bonacca Cay in the Bay Islands of Honduras (called Guanaja by Colón), the Spaniards ran across a canoe full of the Indian traders bringing their wares to the inhabitants of the island. Fernando was also on that voyage, so what he wrote was an eyewitness account. An English translation of this account reads: _"Having come to the island of Guanaja, the Admiral sent ashore his brother Bartholomew, with two boats... by good fortune there arrived at that time a canoe, long as a galley and eight feet wide, made of a single tree trunk like the other Indian canoes; it was freighted with merchandise... amidships it had a palm-leaf awning like that on Venetian gondolas; this gave complete protection against the rain and waves. Underneath were women and children and all the baggage and merchandise. There were twenty-five paddlers aboard, but they offered no resistance when our boats drew up to them... He then ordered that there should be taken from the canoe whatever appeared to be most attractive and valuable, such as cloths and sleeveless shirts of cotton that had been worked and dyed in different colors and designs, also pantaloons of the same workmanship with which they cover their_ *private parts, also cloth in which the Indian women of the canoe were dressed, such as the Moorish women of Granada are accustomed to wear. Also long swords of wood with a groove along each edge, wherein stone knives were set by means of fiber and pitch, cutting like steel when used on naked people; also hatchets to cut wood, like those of stone used by other Indians, save for the fact that these were of good copper, of which metal they also had bells and crucibles for smelting. For food they carried roots and grain such as they eat in Española and a certain wine made of maize, like the beer of England, and they had many of those kernels which serve as money in New Spain, which it appeared that they valued highly."* Most frequently this passage is quoted as proof that these were Maya whom Colón met in Bonacca, however, they could very well have been non-Maya Indians from that area (such as the Paya, Jicaque, or Mam) simply carrying on trade between the mainland of Honduras and the outer islands; there is no way to be sure.

Another account of the event was recorded by the early historian Peter Martyr d'Anghiera in his book *De orbe novo decades*, published in 1516. Martyr wrote that the canoe Colón saw was loaded with trade goods, like *"novaculae, cultelli, secures"* (large and small knives and cleavers) and ceramic cooking vessels.

Bartolomé de Las Casas also described Colón's encounter with the Indian traders in his book, *Historia de la Indias* written between 1527 and 1561. This is the English version of the account: *"...there came a canoe full of Indians, as long as a galley and eight feet in width; it came loaded with goods from the west and must certainly have been from the land of Yucatán, because it was close to there, a journey of 30 leagues or a little more; it was carrying in the middle of the canoe an awning of palm mats, which are called* petates *in New Spain, in and under which there came their women and children and property and goods, without the water from the sky nor the sea being able to wet the things. The goods and things that they were bringing were many cotton blankets, painted in many colors and designs, and sleeveless shirts, also painted and worked, and the* almaizares *which the men covered their private parts were also painted and worked... wood swords with grooved edges* and certain flint blades attached with pitch and thread, copper hatchets for cutting wood and bells and some crucibles and patens for casting copper; many cacao nuts, that they have for currency in New Spain and in Yucatán and elsewhere. *Their nourishment was corn bread and some edible roots that must have been those that we called* ajes *and* batatas *in Española and* camotes *in New Spain; their wine was also of corn, it looked like beer. There came in the canoe almost 25 men, and they did not venture to defend themselves nor did they flee the Christian ships...*" The fact that Las Casas added the line stating that he thought these Indian traders *"must certainly have been from the land of Yucatán"* simply because it was close by does not add any weight to that argument; it was only his personal opinion that he included in the description of the event, 25 years after in happened.

Bernal Díaz del Castillo described another group of the large Maya canoes that he saw while he was with Fernando de Córdoba on his 1517 voyage to Yucatán. In his book, *Historia Verdadera de la Conquista de la Nueva España*, Díaz says: *"On the morning of the fourth of March, five canoes came off to us. These vessels are like troughs, made of one entire tree and many of them capable of containing fifty men."*

Above: Engraving of a 54-man ocean-going canoe.

Hernán Cortés, in his 1526 "Fifth Letter" to the Spanish Crown, mentions how Spaniards in Tabasco and Xicalango were disrupting the flow of the traditional Maya sea trade routes: *"...there were certain Spaniards who did them much harm, for besides burning many villages and killing some of the inhabitants, as a result of which many of them abandoned those places and fled to the hills, they had most severely harmed the merchants and traders; for, because of them the trade which had once flourished along the coast had now ceased."*

Physical evidence of these trade routes is perhaps more reliable than these early texts. For example, a Taino Indian vomit spatula (used to induce vomiting during ritual cleansing ceremonies) was found in a Classic period grave at Altun Ha, in Belize. Since the Taino occupied the Bahamas and the Greater and Lesser Antilles and were not known as traders, one would assume a Maya trader brought the ladle back with him to Belize from a sea voyage to one of those islands. On Antigua, a cache of Maya jadeite axes, or celts, was found in the 1990s. The origin of the jadeite from which these celts were crafted was the Motagua valley in Guatemala (1,800 miles away), as ascertained by mineralogist George Harlow, of the Museum of Antigua and Barbuda in St. John's, Antigua. Another group of Maya pottery shards and obsidian implements were found on the western tip of Cuba by Maurice Ries in the 1940s. In the 1980s, I personally found a Maya celt on a small islet off Highborn Cay, Bahamas, near an early Spanish shipwreck which I was excavating with the Institute of Nautical Archaeology in the 1980s. That celt also was made from jadeite that came from Guatemala.

So, if the evidence is out there in the Caribbean that proves the Maya were trading their goods (and trade-goods they acquired elsewhere) with far-away lands, is there any physical evidence that points to Cozumel as one of their ports-of-call? There is. During archaeological excavations on Cozumel, many items that originated from distant sources have been uncovered: magnetite mirrors, gold-foil covered ceramic beads, copper bells, obsidian, flint, jade, basalt, and a wealth of ceramics imported from mainland sites.

In addition to these foreign trade items found on Cozumel, in 2013 I found two small quartzite "lightning stones" that had been eroded out of a small embankment lying only inches from one another in front of the foundation of a Postclassic Maya structure on Cozumel. Since the island is made up of limestone and has no naturally occurring quartzite, these two pebbles stood out as being obviously imported to the island.

Lightning stones are small, smooth, milky-white quartzite pebbles which, when rubbed together, produce a strong scent of ozone along with flashes of light that emanate from within the stones. This light is not produced by incandescent sparks, as when flint is struck by steel, but rather by a process known as triboluminescence. This type of luminescence is caused by the mechanoluminescent properties of quartzite, which can be activated by the mechanical forces of pressure or friction. David S. Whitley, in his 1999 article in the *Cambridge Archaeological Journal* describes triboluminescence as: *"A photon flash caused by electrons in the quartz atoms that have been ejected by gamma radiation penetrating crystal lattice defects. A small mechanical shock allows these electrons to overcome their energy barrier and to cascade down to ground state, giving off a glow as they return to their atomic orbit."*

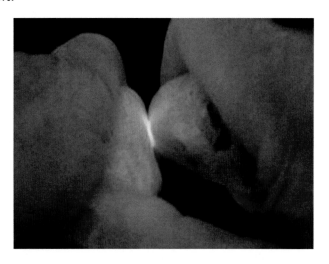

Above: Lightning stones when rubbed together emit a soft glow.

I became familiar with lightning stones in 2009, while I was writing <u>The Lost Kivas of San Lazaro</u>, my book detailing the excavation of two underground kivas in the 17th century Tano Indian pueblo of San Lazaro, near Santa Fe, New Mexico. We discovered two pairs of these quartzite pebbles cached inside of one of the kivas and subsequent research turned up several other instances where pairs of these special stones were discovered in archaeological excavations all across the American Southwest.

The Pueblo Indians of New Mexico regarded these stones as magical and used them in ceremonies related to weather. Other tribes in California and Arizona used them in a similar fashion. Archeologists have reported finding lightning stone pairs in many excavations made in the American Southwest and a pair of lightning stones discovered inside a kiva sometime during the 1930s is on exhibit in the Florence Hawley Ellis Museum at Ghost Ranch near Abiquiu, NM.

Lightning stones can be distinguished from "polishing stones," "burnishing stones," or "pebble smoothers" by their color (lightning stones must be white or translucent in order to see the faint glow), lack of exaggerated faceting, and the fact that they were cached in pairs. In all of the New Mexican pairs I have examined, the stones that made up the pair were each, more-or less, of similar size, shape and color. It is my belief that many times archeologists do not recognize the difference between lightning stones and polishing stones, and often mistake the former for the latter.

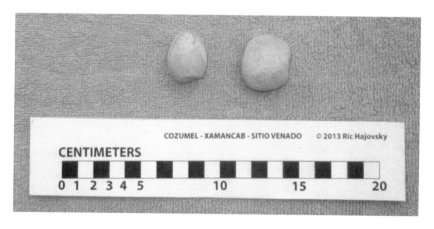

Above: Two lightning stones from Sitio Venado, Cozumel.

When I began to search the records for other mentions of lightning stones turning up in archaeological contexts in Yucatán, Quintana Roo, or anywhere else in México for that matter, I was left empty handed. There are many references to "polishing stones," "burnishing stones," or "pebble smoothers" in the literature, but no "lightning stones." Could this be an example of lightning stone pairs simply being misidentified and overlooked? I did find one report, *Classic Maya lithic artifacts from the Main Plaza of Aguateca, Guatemala* by Kazuo Aoyama that seems to hint that this may be the case. Aoyama wrote: *"Although we do not know the functions of the pebble smoothers, they may have been used as stucco smoothers. While some pebble smoothers show flat worn facets, other smoothers evidence either no usewear or have been worn smooth over their entire surface."*

Other evidence of Cozumel's role in the Maya sea trade route can be found in the Museo de la Isla on Cozumel. One can see firsthand the two Olmec objects (a carved jadeite pectoral, and a carved stone pendant) that were excavated in San Gervasio during the 1970s by Jeremy Sabloff and William Rathje's teams from Harvard and University of Arizona. Admittedly, it is possible that these items came into Quintana Roo via an overland trade-route, but the sea-trade route that followed the coast all the way from Tabasco to Cozumel makes more sense.

Above: Some of the many jadite celts and other Maya trade goods that spilled from a Maya canoe and were discovered centuries later underwater at Chen Rio on Cozumel.

Lastly, the only two known Maya shipwrecks were both discovered on Cozumel. The first was discovered by Ismay (Mary) Mykolyk (better known in Cozumel as "María la Bandida") at Chen Rio, on the eastern side of the island. While diving there in the 1970s, she noticed several jadeite celts and beads in the sand of the ocean floor. Further investigation lead to the discovery of more, embedded in the fabric of the reef. Through careful excavation, even more of the artifacts were found. Some of these are now on display in our *Museo de la Isla*.

Another Maya canoe wreck-site was discovered near a small Maya *oratorio* on the eastern side of the island. This time, it was the result of a hurricane that led to the discovery. The Maya ruin was destroyed by the storm surge, but the storm also uncovered the jadeite celts and beads that were the cargo of the wreck. Whether these canoes turned over as they were leaving Cozumel, or wrecked as they were arriving from the shores of Guatemala with jadeite celts to trans-ship from Cozumel will never be known, but they do offer positive proof that the island was once a port in the Putún (Chontal) Maya trade route.

Cozumel and the Maya salt trade

Salt is an integral part of the daily nutritional requirements that all humans need to survive, and this was equally true for the Highland Maya in pre-Columbian times. But the daily amount of salt required was impossible to satisfy by just the quantity of sodium contained in a typical Highland Maya's daily meal; a supplemental amount was needed to make up for the shortfall. Besides consuming salt as a supplement to their diet, the Highland Maya also used the mineral as a food preservative and as a mordant for textile dyes. However, the only way they had to produce salt locally was by boiling and evaporating salt-bearing water from a few saline springs or from saline lakes. This was an inefficient, labor-intensive method that required large quantities of firewood as well as specialized ceramic containers for the processing, so it is of no surprise that the main source of salt for the Highlands was from far-away coastal areas which could produce the mineral through the solar-evaporation of seawater, a much more efficient method.

Beginning in the Late Classic period, the Maya obtained their extra salt mainly from salt works located on the north shore of the Yucatán peninsula. This trade commodity was carried in canoes westward towards Veracruz as well as southward to Honduras, where it was first shipped upriver then carried overland to the Highland Maya. Belize also had salt works operating during this period, but around the end of the Classic period, the salt-making centers in Belize ceased production. The cause of this is unclear; it could have been the collapse of the nearby Maya population centers who were the consumers of this product, or it could have been due to the documented one-meter rise in sea-level around 800 A.D. to 1,000 A.D., which may have flooded the coastal salt pans and rendered them useless. Subsequently, the salt pans of northern Yucatán became the main supplier of salt for the Highlanders.

However, most archeologists believe that Cozumel was not one of these salt producing areas during the pre-Columbian and Colonial periods. Statements like *"there were important saltworks on all along the north coast of Yucatán and on the nearby Mujeres Island, but none on Cozumel..."* by archaeologist J. E. S Thompson were common, in spite of colonial documents alluding to the exportation of salt from Cozumel. Others, like archeologist Anthony Andrews, admitted that Cozumel may have exported salt, but lacked the archaeological evidence to prove it.

One mention of salt being shipped from Cozumel is in the February 2, 1549 tax list, which describes the amounts of products and labor the Yucatec Maya were required to deliver annually to their *encomenderos*, or Spanish landlords, as a tributary tax. One of the lines in this 1549 list mentions that the combined 220 tax-paying heads of households on Cozumel were required to pay Cozumel's *encomendero* Juan Nuñez "...three *fanegas* of maiz, half a *fanega* of beans, 160 Spanish chickens or local fowl as they wish, one *arroba* of honey, eight *arrobas* of bee's wax, six *fanegas* of salt, six *arrobas* of fish, and 220 cotton *mantas*, also the service of two Indians." One *fanega* was about 9.3 US gallons, so six *fanegas* amounted to about 56 gallons, the size of an oil drum. Archeologist J. Eric S. Thompson denied that the salt included in this tribute originated in Cozumel and stated in his 1970 book, Maya History and Religion: *"...but one may suppose that this was gathered elsewhere by natives of the island."*

A second mention of Cozumel salt is in Fray Francisco Morán's 1695 manuscript *Arte y vocabulario en lengua choltí*: "*xoxom, la traen de cuçumel, iucatan*" (coarse salt, they bring it from Cozumel, Yucatán). *Xoxom* means coarse salt in the Cholti (Chol) Mayan language. It is doubtful that sea-salt was still being imported from Cozumel in 1695, when the manuscript was written; Morán was probably repeating a description in Cholti that had long been attached to imported salt.

The reason that historians and archaeologists today believe that Cozumel was "salt free" is that there have never been any salt works or salt pans discovered on the island; no "smoking gun" that could prove that the Maya of Cozumel were producing the salt and not simply trans-shipping the commodity. However, after reviewing an old video that Dan Hartman took from a small airplane flying low over the northern end of Cozumel in the 1990s, I looked at the area more closely using Google Earth®. What I saw looked like the boundary walls of square salt pans, half in and half out of the water, each pan encompassing roughly 250 square meters.

Above: Google Earth image of possible saltworks near Punta Molas taken on May 8, 2012 and shown at the simulated height of 829 feet. The yellow line is for scale; it is 50.03 meters long. ©DigitalGlobe

The many lines of tightly packed stones were aligned in straight paths, and came to sharp 90-degree corners. At low tide many of the spaces contained within the boundaries of the walled areas become dry. Salt crystals could be seen clearly on some of the bedrock surfaces within the walled areas where saltwater had first pooled and then evaporated.

More of these walled areas lie underwater, one mile to the southwest, adjacent to the ruins on the small islet in Rio de la Plata and the *sacbe* that runs through the lagoon, connecting the islet to the beach berm on the north and the island's shore on the south.

Today, these possible saltworks are located in an isolated, unpopulated part of the island, but during the Classic, Postclassic and Early Colonial times, this was not the case. There were several Maya population centers close to the northern tip of the island during those periods: Aguada Grande, La Expedición, and Zuuk, which were all connected to San Gervasio by a *sacbe*, or paved roadway.

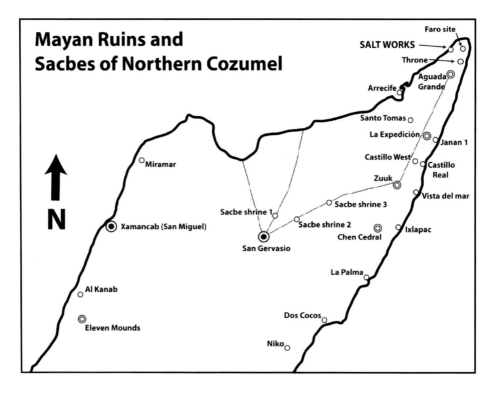

Above: Map of the Maya ruins and sacbes of northern Cozumel.

Above: Some of the walls were visible protruding from the shallow water of the lagoon. ©DigitalGlobe

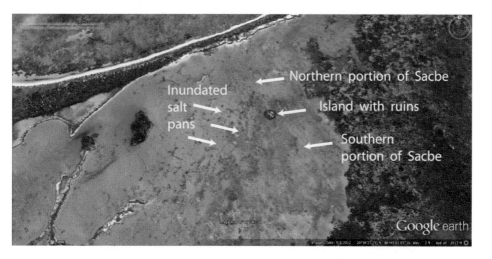

Above: The small island (known as arrecife) in a lagoon on the northern Cozumel coast, with a sacbe leading to it from the shore and also from the inland side of the lagoon. Possible inundated salt pans can be seen on the western side of this island from the air. ©DigitalGlobe

In 1895, William Henry Holmes visited the area, including the islet of Arrecife and the nearby ruins of Expedicion, Las Grecas, and Aguada Grande. As the Curator of Anthoropology of the Field Museum of Chicago, he came to Cozumel on the Allison V. Armour Expedition of 1894-5. The expedition members took several photographs of the area.

Above: One of the two small ruins on the islet of Arrecife in 1895.

Above: The sacbe leading to shore from Arrecife islet in 1895.

CHAPTER 2

Ix Chel: The Oracle of Cozumel, or a myth born of misconceptions?

Many people adamantly adhere to the belief that Cozumel was a center of worship and pilgrimage where all Maya women were required to come at least once in their lifetime to adore the goddess Ix Chel and to seek her blessings and prophecies. Many archaeologists, anthropologists, Mayanists, and historians also subscribe to this idea. But, where did this belief originate? What are its sources? Is it, in fact, even true?

Rather than taking modern-day authors, Wikipedia articles and website webmasters at their word, I went back to the original Spanish, Mayan, and Latin texts containing the earliest mentions of the religious practices of the Maya of Cozumel and read them with a fresh eye. I was dumbfounded with the differences I found in the original sixteenth-century texts and the "new, modernized, and edited" Spanish versions available to the average reader and even more dismayed by the differences between the originals and the published English translations.

After analyzing the comparisons, I came to the conclusion that the reasons many people believe in the existence of a requisite "once-in-a-lifetime pilgrimage" to the island for all Maya women and the supreme importance of the goddess and her temple to Cozumel, all had their roots in some of the documents written by early historians who paraphrased, twisted, or otherwise distorted the eyewitness accounts. Some of the misstatements made in these distorted texts eventually gave rise to a theory that was not put forward until the early twentieth century. A couple of decades later, this theory was taken up by mainstream writers and anthropologists and then regurgitated in articles and books as an iron-clad fact.

The earliest document mentioning both Ix Chel and Cozumel in the same context was written in 1579. No other mention of the two appeared linked together again in one document until the twentieth century. On the other hand, there are many other early documents that do mention Cozumel and the gods of Cozumel, but they all glaringly omit any mention of the goddess Ix Chel. If Ix Chel was as important as she is held out to be in the current popular belief and her temple was one of the three most important places in Yucatán, why then is there this lack of any other mention of her in relation to Cozumel in the early documents and eyewitness reports?

The following pages offer a new look at the roots of the myths and legends surrounding the goddess Ix Chel and her temple. After examining the original texts of the earliest documents, it seems clear that a reevaluation of the role Ix Chel actually played in the religious life of the Maya of Cozumel is needed.

First, the name Ix Chel (as well as Ixchel, Yschel, Aixchel, or Heschen) are all names given to the goddess in post-conquest documents; the name does not appear in any phonetic Mayan glyphs prior to the Spanish arrival in the New World. The earliest Mayan language document this name appears in is the 1612 document written by the *cacique* of Acalan-Tixchel in southern Campeche, Pablo Paxbolon, in Chontal Mayan. That document simply lists "Yschel" as one of the many different idols found in all the Chontal villages, and nothing more. The next earliest Mayan mention of the name Ix Chel is in the post-1779 "Ritual of the Bacabs," a Yucatec Mayan manuscript that is a collection of ritual incantations. All the other sixteenth-, seventeenth-, and eighteenth-century mentions are in Spanish language documents.

There is room for debate as to the translation or meaning of the name Ix Chel. "Ix" is clearly the Mayan indicator of the feminine sex. "Chel," could be derived from the word "Cheel" the Yucatec Mayan word for "rainbow," but nowhere in any pre-twentieth-century document or illustration is the goddess ever associated with this weather phenomenon. "Ch'el," on the other hand, is the Yucatec Maya word for "pale or fair-skinned person" an attribute that seems very appropriate to a goddess associated with the moon. "Ix Chel" is also the Yucatec Mayan name of a medicinal plant of Yucatán, but it was most likely named after the goddess of medicine, not vice versa.

Although nowhere in the Mayan glyphs that have been translated to date are there any lines that can tell us exactly who Ix Chel was or what she did, there are several images on pre-Columbian Maya vases, stone friezes, and codices that depict the goddess. One of the most frequently seen images associated with the name Ix Chel is the one below, taken from the Dresden Codex:

Above: Photo of the Dresden Codex taken by the Museum of Dresden.

The goddess pictured above is now called goddess "O" by archaeologists. She is depicted in the codex and elsewhere as an old crone with a red body, claws on her hands and feet, and crossed human bones on her skirt. Goddess "O" is identified in the Dresden Codex as "Chac Chel" (Red Chel) by the portrait-style name glyph prefixed with the "chac, or "red" glyph *(below, left)* placed close to her image. She is also identified in the same codex as "Chac Che" (Red Che) with compound phonetic name glyphs *(below right)* which also appear next to her image.

In the Madrid Codex, the aged goddess "O" is named variously "Chac-Chel-Chac" and "Ix-Kab'-Chel" in compound phonetic name glyphs. She is also depicted in that codex weaving and wearing spindles in her hair, and from that (along with her association with spiders) she is assumed to be the goddess whom the Maya believed introduced weaving to the world.

Above: Aged goddess "O" in two of her appearances in the Madrid Codex.

However, rather than Ix Chel, the depictions of aged goddess "O" most likely are meant to represent the Maya goddess known as Ixchebelyax, as there are also depictions of another goddess that the archaeologists have named goddess "I" who seems to fit the role of Ix Chel much better. In the Dresden Codex this second goddess is identified by the combination glyph meaning "Zac Ch'el" (White Ch'el) and this goddess is always depicted as a young woman. In several decorated ceramic vessels and a carved stone frieze she is shown associated with the moon and/or a rabbit, an animal the Maya also associated with the moon.

Above: The glyph for Zac Ch'el

Above: Young goddess Zac Ch'el with a rabbit, from Justin Kerr's <u>The Maya Vase Book</u>.

In the Dresden Codex, goddess "I," or "White Ch'el" is depicted multiple times on several panels which deal with diseases, strongly associating her with medicine and disease. Later Spanish texts also connect Ix Chel with medicine.

Above: Goddess "I" ("Zac Ch'el" or "White Ch'el") as she appears in the Dresden Codex.

While none of the Maya glyph texts explain in any depth exactly who Ix Chel or Ixchebelyax were and what powers they had, we do have a very few short descriptions of them in some early Colonial period documents. Their names appear in a list of goddesses in the abstract of Bishop Diego de Landa's now-lost 1566 manuscript *Relación de las cosas de Yucatán*: *"...las diosas de aquella tierra como Aixchel* [Ix Chel], *Ixchebeliax* [Ixchebelyax]*, Ixbunie, e Ixbunieta..."*

Bartolomé de Las Casas (who never set foot in Yucatán) also weighed in with some information about the goddesses Ix Chel and Ixchebelyax. In correspondence with fellow cleric Father Francisco Hernandez (who was living in Campeche) Las Casas asked Hernandez to use his Mayan linguistic skills to interview someone who might be able to tell them something about the Maya gods. Hernandez wrote back a year later that he had found a Maya elder and interviewed him. The results of the interview were recorded in Las Casas' document *Apologética historia sumaria de las Indias Occidentales*, written during the period between 1527 and 1559. In his manuscript, Las Casas states that *"...aqueste Dios era Padre e Hijo y Espiritu Sanctu. Y que el Padre se llama Içona [Itzamna], que había criado los hombres y todas las cosas; el Hijo tenía por nombre Bacab, el cual nació de un doncella siempre virgen llamada Chibirias, que está en el cielo con Dios, y la madre de Chiribias [Ixchebelyax] is called Hischen [Ix Chel]..."* (...this God was the Father and Son and Holy Spirit. And that the Father was called Izona [Itzamna], who had created mankind and all things; the Son had for his name Bacab, he who was born of a young woman who was forever a virgin named Chibirias [Ixchebelyax], who is in the heavens with God, and the mother of Chibirias is called Hischen [Ix Chel]...).

However, in the same document, Las Casas reverses the roles of Ix Chel and Ixchebelyax and says that Ix Chel was the wife of Itzamna and not his daughter: *"...antes della ni había cielo ni tierra, ni sol, ni luna, ni estrellas. Ponían que hubo un marido y una mujer divinos, que llamaron Xchel y Xtcamna. Éstos habían tenido padre y madre, los cuales engendraron trece hijos, y que el mayor, con algunos con él, se ensoberbecieron, y quiso hacer creaturas contra voluntad del padre y madre, pero no pudieron, porque lo que hicieron fueron unos vasos viles de servicio, como jarros y ollas semejantes."* (...in the beginning there were no heavens no earth, no sun, no moon, no stars. There then was a divine couple, who were called *Xchel* and *Xtcamna*. They became mother and father, who engendered thirteen children, and the oldest, with some others with him, thought of themselves better than they were and wanted to create creatures against the will of their father and mother, but they couldn't, because what they made were low quality utilitarian wares, like jars and pots and the like.) López de Cogolludo in his *Historia de Yucatán* (written around 1655 and published in 1688), says: *"the mother of Chiribias [Ixchebelyax] is called Yxchel."*

Landa also explains that Ix Chel is the goddess of childbirth and medicine, although he points out in the same sentence that the Maya had at least three other gods of medicine and then names them. Cogolludo likewise states that Ix Chel was the goddess of medicine, but just like Landa, he too points out the Maya had other gods that did the same thing.

The "Ritual of the Bacabs" is a post-1779 Yucatec Mayan manuscript containing several long incantations. In the manuscript, both red and white Ix Chels are mentioned in several places, as well as yellow and black Ix Chels. Just like the Bacabs, they took their color names from the cardinal directions they represented.

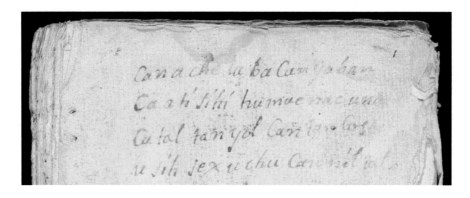

Above: A portion of the post-1779 manuscript "Ritual of the Bacabs."

There are other documents written by Maya in the 18th and 19th centuries where we can read a little more about their gods. First, there are around thirteen miscellanies that are copies of copies of copies of earlier manuscripts, each full of stories, prophecies, calendars, myths, and recipes that various Maya copyists not-too-faithfully reproduced from the previous copies. Each succeeding version was muddled by the addition of new texts and the alteration of old texts each time the scribe copied a new version. Each one of these copied manuscripts has parts of texts that appear in other versions and other parts of texts that are unique to that particular version. It is impossible to reconstruct the original root text (or texts) because of these many revisions and additions. These thirteen extant manuscripts were all produced in the 1700s and 1800s, in a mix of Spanish and Yucatec Maya with letters from the Latin alphabet. These manuscripts are collectively known as the Books of Chilam Balam. The most famous of these books was written in 1782 by Juan Josef Hoil and is now known as the *Chilam Balam de Chumayel*.

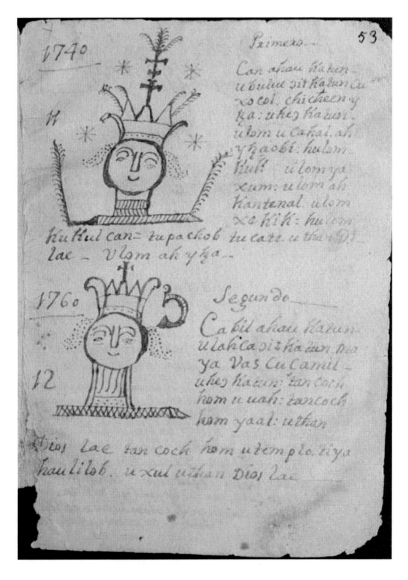

Above: Page 53 of the <u>Chilam Balam de Chumayel</u>. *To the right of the depiction of "The Lord of Cozumel" at the bottom of the page, the text reads: "1760 Second… Katun 2 Ahau was the twelfth part of the katun. Maya Cozumel was the seat of the katun. Half down was its food; half down was its water. The word of God is this: Half down is the temple, who is their lordship. The end of the word of God is this."*

Another early source that touches on the topic of Maya religion is a manuscript by Francisco Ximénez, a Spanish priest. He wrote this work in 1701, in a Mayan-language text alongside a Spanish text. Today we call this manuscript the *Popol Vuh*. This manuscript is a copy of a collection of mythical and heroic tales of the K'iche' Maya of Guatemala, and the Mayan language used by Ximenez is not Yucatec Maya, it is K'iche' Maya. The root language from which K'iche' Maya is derived (Eastern Mayan) separated from Yucatec Maya over 4,000 years ago. That is a long time for two cultures to develop independently of each other and surely the tales, fables, religion, etc., must have mutated just like the language over this period of time.

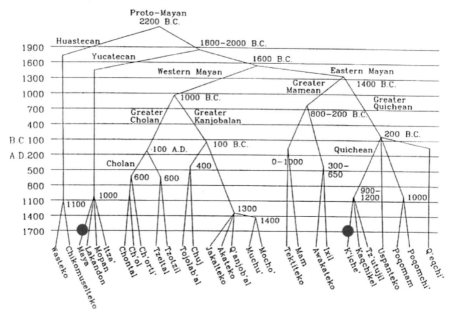

Above: Over 3,500 years of divergence separates the Maya Yucatec culture from the Maya K'iche' culture, that produced the Popol Vuh. Chart courtesy of FAMSI.org

On the first page of the *Popol Vuh* manuscript, Ximenez wrote: *"Empezan las historias del origen de los indios de esta provencia de Guatemala traduzido de la lengua Quiche en la castellana para mas comodidad de los ministros de el sto evangelio."* (Here starts the history of the origin of the Indians of this province of Guatemala, translated from the K'iche' language into Castilian for the convenience of the ministers of the Holy Gospel). On the second page, Ximenez wrote: *"Aquí escribimos y empezarémos las antiguas historias, su principio, y comienzo, de todo lo que fue hecho en el pueblo del quiche, su pueblo de los indios quiche."* (Here we write and start with the old histories; their beginnings and commencements of all that happened in the K'iche' culture, the community of the K'iche' Indians).

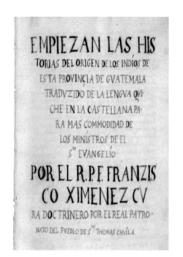

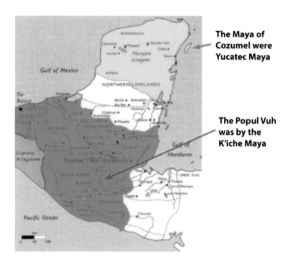

The Maya of Cozumel were Yucatec Maya

The Popul Vuh was by the K'iche Maya

Above left: The cover of the __Popol Vuh__. Above right: Territories of the K'iche Maya of the Highlands and the Yucatec Maya of the Lowlands.

So, the myths and beliefs portrayed in the *Popol Vuh* myths are not exactly the beliefs and myths of the Yucatec Maya from Cozumel, but are the beliefs of their Guatemalan neighbors in the Postclassic period, described by a Spanish priest later in the Colonial period. However, we are interested in the beliefs and gods of the Maya from Cozumel, not in the beliefs and gods of their neighbors.

Of the few early sources which deal with Maya gods and practices, very few deal with Cozumel. Reading web pages and popular books, it would seem that this is not the case, but it is the sad truth. There are very, very few early historical documents that speak of the gods and temples of Cozumel. Unfortunately, many writers have tried to fill in this gap by reading between these few lines and extrapolating and reconstructing the parts that are lacking in the originals and then publishing their reconstructed and paraphrased texts without explaining the heavy-handed manipulation to which these over-edited texts were subjected.

Of all the surviving pre-nineteenth-century documents, there are only four that specifically mention the gods of Cozumel. One appears in the book *Primera y segunda parte de la Historia General de las Indias con todo el descubrimiento, y cosas notables que han acaecido dende que se ganaron hasta el año de 1551, con la conquista de México, y de la Nueva España,* (aka *Historia General de las Indias y conquista de Mexico),* written by Francisco López de Gomara and published in 1552. In this book, Gomara says that in the island of Cozumel *"habia una cruz de cal tan alta como diez palmos, a la cual adoraban por dios de la lluvia."* (there was a stucco cross as high as ten palms [a little higher than one meter] which they adored as the god of the rain). This god of the rain was the god Chaac.

Another one of these four mentions of the gods of Cozumel can be found in the *Chilam Balam de Chumayel*: *"Kin pauahn yah kinobi, Lay mektanmail u picul katún, Cananmail ah hulneb, Tan tun Cusamil, Ah yax ac chinab, Kinich Kakmo".* (The priest Pauahn heads up an immense army, the guardians of the god Ah Hulneb, the gods Ah Yax Ac, and Chinab, and Kinich Kakmo, in front of the precious stone of Cozumel). It is very interesting to note that this list of the important gods of Cozumel in the *Chilam Balam de Chumayel* does not mention Ix Chel.

I translate the words *"tan tun Cusamil,"* as "in front of the precious stone Cozumel" and not as "in front of the flat stone Cozumel," the way in which it is translated in several popular books and web pages. *"Tan"* means "in front of" or "ahead" in Yucatec Maya. In the 1577 Motul dictionary of Yucatecan Mayan, the word *"tun"* is defined as *"piedra preciosa"* (precious stone). The word *"tun"* was also a Mayan metaphor for "altar" and at times *"tun"* was used to indicate jade. The "flat stone" translation is not correct despite being the one used on the most frequently viewed web sites.

In any event, in these lines of the *Chilam Balam de Chumayel* are found some of the few mentions of the gods of Cozumel: Ah Hulneb, which means "the Archer;" Ah Yax Ac, which I translate as "First Turtle;" Chinab, who was possibly a historical character who later became a god, and; Kinich Kakmó, which translates as "the Macaw with flaming eyes (or face) of the Sun," who was another historical figure, one of the founders of the Maya town of Izamal who later became an aspect of the god of the Sun. The historian Fray Bernardo de Lizana, who lived in Yucatán from 1606 until his death in 1631, wrote that the Maya went to the temple of Kinich-Kakmó on the north side of the square in Izamal to find cures for their diseases and to receive divinations. Sounds a bit like today's idea of the temple of Ix Chel. Kinich Kakmó is another personification of Kinich Ahau, the "God with eyes (or face) of the Sun," who, in turn, is an aspect of the God Itzamná, who Bartolomé de Las Casas says was the mate of Ixchebelyax or Ix Chel. Itzamna is also associated with the goddess in the Madrid Codex several times. It is interesting to note that James Kennedy (who was a British diplomat stationed in Havana) mentions excavating several ruins in Cozumel in 1851 and finding *"figures of divinities with hawk heads and images of tortoises."* Could these have been representations of Kinich Kakmó and Ah Yax Ac?

Above: Kinich Kakmo in the Dresden Codex.

The penultimate of the four mentions of the names of the gods of Cozumel appears in *Historia de Yucatán* written by Diego López de

Cogolludo around 1655: *"En Cozumel uno singular, que pintaban con una flecha: su nombre Ah-hulanè, ò Ah-huneb…"* (In Cozumel a singular [god], that they paint holding an arrow: his name Ah-hulanè, or Ah-huneb). Cogolludo goes on, saying: *"Reverenciaban otro ídolo de uno que decían había tenido las espinillas como una golondrina: su nombre era, Teel cuzám."* (They also revere another idol which they say had shins like a swift: his name was Teel Cuzam). So, here we have the second mention of the god Ah Hulneb, plus a sixth god, Teel Cuzám. However, still no mention whatsoever of a temple to Ix Chel on Cozumel.

The last mention containing the names of the gods of Cozumel is the 1579 testimony of Diego Contreras Duran, where he says: *"…este ídolo se llamaba Yschel, y este nombre llamaban a este ídolo. Y los indios no eran capaces de informarme lo que yschel significó, ni porqué ellos le dieron aquel nombre."* (this idol is called *Yschel,* and this is the name they call this idol. And the Indians were not capable of telling me what *yschel* meant, nor why they called it by this name). We assume by *Yschel,* Contreras meant Ix Chel.

Another god that we know was revered by the Maya on Cozumel was Kukulcán, the feathered serpent. In 1946, archaeologist Alberto Escalona Ramos, in his report of his visit to Cozumel in 1937, said that in the wall of the Cozumel public clock tower *"hay incrustada una piedra de 73 centímetros por 58 centímetros que tiene la representación de una cabeza de serpiente emplumada…"* (there is inlaid a stone 73cm by 58cm that has the image of a plumed serpent). This is the only example that I know of, in which a Maya god depicted in bas-relief in Cozumel can be identified without a doubt.

Historians and anthropologists have known about these few mentions of the gods of Cozumel for centuries. In fact, until the first quarter of the twentieth century, (before today's popular idea that the most important Maya temple on Cozumel was a temple dedicated to Ix Chel), the most widely held belief by Maya scholars was that there was a great temple dedicated to the god Teel Cuzam on the island.

Many 19th century authors quoted these passages from the early texts, but sometimes added extra words into the translation, or paraphrased the text, twisting the meaning. It is simply another example of the old childhood game of "telephone." For example, Victor Gebhardt wrote, in his 1880 book, The Gods of Greece and Rome: *"In the atrium of Teel-Cuzam, dedicated to a hero with feet of a swift, you can see a cross ten palms high, that the Indians revere and implore, even if they don't know why."* Antonio de Solís y Ribadeneyra, in his 1684 book *Historia de la conquista de Mexico, población y progresos de la América septentrional, conocida por el nombre de Nueva España*, wrote: *"A poco trecho de la costa se hallaron en el templo de aquel ídolo tan venerado, fabricado de piedra en forma cuadrada, y de no despreciable arquitectura. Era el ídolo de figura humana; pero de horrible aspecto y espantosa fiereza... dicen que se llama este ídolo Cozumel, y que dio a la isla el nombre que conserva hoy en dia..."* (Close to the shore they found in the temple of that idol that was so venerated, built in a square shape in a worthy architectural style. It was an idol in human form, but with a horrible aspect and frightening fiendishness... they say they call this idol Cozumel, and that they gave the island this name which it keeps to this day...")

In the book Fernando Cortés and the Conquest of Mexico, written by Francis Augustus MacNutt in 1909, you can read the following line, which MacNutt falsely states appears in Cogolludo's *Historia de Yucatán*: *"Cozumel was a place of pilgrimage, and in one of the great temples there stood a hollow terra-cotta statue, called Teel-Cuzam...."* Obviously, these are not the exact words of Cogolludo, who wrote his works in Spanish. They are an English paraphrase of several different parts of his book, strung together in a way they were not originally written. What Cogolludo actually wrote is the following: *"Era Cozumel el mayor santuario para los indios que había en este reino de Yucatán, y a donde recurrían en romería de todo el."* (Cozumel was the Indians' greatest sanctuary in the kingdom of Yucatán, and to where they came from all over in pilgrimage). Cogolludo went on, saying: *"la isla de Cozumel era Supremo Santuario, y como Romano de esta tierra, donde no solo los moradores de ella, pero otras tierras concurrían a la adoracion de los idolos, que en ella veneraben... para que llegan a*

Cozumel al cumplimiento de su promesas, a las ofrendas de sus sacrificios, a pedir el remedio de sus necesidades, y a la errada adoracion de sus dioses fingidos." (the island of Cozumel was the Supreme Sanctuary, like Rome is in our land, where not only the people living there, but others from other lands gather for the adoration of the idols that they venerate there... for which they go to Cozumel in fulfilment of their promises, to offer up their sacrifices, to beg help for their needs, and in the mistaken adoration of their false gods).

It is clear that in this passage Cogolludo was not speaking of one single, solitary temple that made Cozumel so important. Cogolludo said "the greatest sanctuary was Cozumel." He also said "Cozumel was the greatest sanctuary," and "Cozumel was the Supreme Sanctuary." Cogolludo made clear that the whole island was sacred, for the multitude of idols they had there; idols like Chaac, Teel Cuzam, Al Hulneb, Ah Yax Ac, Chin-ab, Kinich Kakmo, Kukulkan and Ix Chel.

Cogolludo was not the only one to write about this topic. Another source is Fray Diego de Landa, in his circa 1566 *Relación de las cosas de Yucatán*: *"Y que tienen a Cuzmil y el pozo de Chichenitzá en tanta veneración como nosotros las romerias a Hierusalén y Roma, y así les iban a visitar y ofrecer dones, principalmente a la de Cuzmil, como nosotros a lugares santos..."* (And they have Cozumel and Chichen Itza in such veneration as we do the pilgrimages to Jerusalem and Rome and so in this way they go to visit and offer their gifts, mainly at Cozumel, as we our holy sites). It should be noted, however, that Landa never mentioned any god or goddess associated with this pilgrimage, despite the fact that many modern authors have altered his original text to make it seem he associated it with Ix Chel.

Francisco Cervantes de Salazar's *Crónica de la Nueva Espana* was published in 1558. In this book (which was a compilation of data he gleaned from other sources), he says that the most important temple of Cozumel was *"un tiro de ballesta de la mar"* and *"era muy celebrado por toda aquella tierra, a causa de la mucha devocion con que a él concurrían de diversas partes en canoas, especialmente en tiempo de verano... venian y hacian allí sus oraciones, ofrecían muchas cosas a los idolos…"* (a crossbow's shot from the sea [about 50 meters]" and "was very celebrated by all the land, because of the great devotion with which they gathered around it from many diverse parts in canoes, especially in summertime… they come and make their prayers there, they offer many things to the idols). Cervantes de Salazar goes on, saying: *"era estimado este templo entre ellos que la casa de Meca entre los moros."* (this temple was esteemed by them like the house of Mecca was by the Moors). Again, we have a text which mentions idols in the plural form, but not the specific name of any god.

Bernal Díaz del Castillo also wrote of pilgrimages to Cozumel in his 1568 manuscript *La Historia Verdadera de la Conquista de Nueva España*: *"venían muchos indios en romería aquella isla de Cozumel, los cuales eran naturales de los pueblos comarcanos de la punta de Cotoche y de otras partes de tierra de Yucatán, porque según pareció había allí en Cozumel unos ídolos de muy disformes figuras, y estaban en un adoratorio en que ellos tenían."* (many Indians come in pilgrimage to that island of Cozumel, whom are residents of the bordering villages of Punta de Cotoche and other parts of the land of Yucatán, because it seems there was in Cozumel some idols with very deformed shapes and they were in an shrine that they had for them). Again, there is no mention of any god by name in this text, but it does mentions idols in the plural form.

Using the works of Diego de Landa and Bernal Díaz as a guide, Antonio de Herrera y Tordesillas wrote in his 1601 *Historia General*: *"…pero lo que más veneraban era à los Templos de la Isla de Cozumèl, i el Poço de Chichen, que era, como entre nosotros, Roma i Jerusalén, adonde iban en Romería, i se tenian por santificados los que allá havían estado; i los que no iban, embiaban sus ofrendas, i havia algunos Idolos, que daban respuestas".* (but what they venerated most was the temples of the island of Cozumel and the well at Chichen [Chichen Itzá], that were, as is with us, Rome and Jerusalem, where they went in pilgrimage and they hold holy those who have travelled there, and those who did not go sent their offerings, and they had some idols that gave answers). Again, we see the terms "idols and temples" pluralized, but no mention of a specific god.

The only early text that mentions Cozumel and the worship of Ix Chel in the same context appears in the 1579 testimony of the then *encomendero* of Cozumel, Diego Contreras Duran. Contreras wrote: *"...los yndios antiguos dellos dizen que nunca fueron sujetos a ningun señor, sino libres, y que antes todo esta tierra y yndios yvan de ordinario ala dicha ysla a adorar çierto ydolo que tenyan en çiertos edificios antiguos a quyen beneraban mucho, que yvan a la dicha ysla a adorar el dicho ydolo como si fueran a ganar perdones, porque yban desde tabasco y xicalango y chanpoton e canpeche, e de otros pueblos lexanos venyn a ber y a adorar el dicho ydolo, y en los dichos edificios a donde estava el dicho ydolo tenyan y estaba un yndio viejo que lo llamaban alquín, que quyere decir en nuestra lengua clerigo o sacerdote, y los yndios que yban a ber el ydolo hablavan con el dicho alquin y le decían a lo que venyan y lo que querian, y el dicho yndio viejo alquyn hablaba con el ydolo o con el demonio, que disen estaba dentro del, el qual le respondía a todo lo que le preguntava y sabian del todo lo que querian, y el dicho yndio viejo alquyn bolvia la respuesta que el ydolo les daba, por manera que los yndios todos desta tierra yvan a saber del ydolo todo aquello que querían, y el yndio viejo, después de aber hablado con el ydolo, les daba la respuesta y le llevan de presente de todo aquello que tenyan de sus cosechas, y este ydolo se llamaba yschel, y este nombre llamaban a este ydolo, e no me supieron dar razón los indios que quería dezir yschel y porque le llamaron asi."* (... the old Indians of there [Cozumel] say that they were never subjects of any lord, but were free men, and that <u>in the past</u> Indians from all the land around commonly <u>used to go</u> to the said island to adore a certain idol as to obtain forgiveness, because they used to go from Tabasco and Xicalango and Chanpotón and Canpeche and other far-away villages they came to see and adore the said idol, and in the said buildings where was the said idol stayed an old Indian whom they called Alquin [Ah Kin] that means to say cleric or priest in our language, and the Indians who went to see the idol spoke with the said Alquin and told him why they came and what they wanted, and the said old Indian Alquin spoke with the idol or with the demon, which they said was inside it, and he who responded to all that was asked of it and it knew all they wanted to know and the said old Indian Alquin then gave the answer that the idol gave him, by this way the Indians of all this land went to know this idol that gives the answer and they carried as offerings all that they had from their harvests, and this idol they called Yschel, and this name they called that idol. And the Indians were not able to tell me what yschel meant, nor why they gave it that name).

This unique document, the only document written before the 20th century connecting Ix Chel with Cozumel, seemed at first an anomaly to me. How is it that, unlike all the other eye-witnesses and all the early historians, Diego de Contreras is the only person to mention Ix Chel in relation with Cozumel?

This letter of Contreras was written as a response to an interrogatory sent to him by the Royal and Supreme Council of the Indies, which was asking for information regarding the Spanish territory in the New World. Contreras wrote his response to the letter while he was in Valladolid, Yucatán, where he lived. He was the son of Juan de Contreras and Beatriz Duran and had been born sometime after 1545. There are some parts of his letter that seem strange to me. First, Contreras wrote that *"que antes... los indios iban de ordinario a la dicha isla a adorar cierto ídolo,"* (In the past... Indians commonly used to go to the said island to adore a certain idol), a sentence using the past tense, which means that Contreras is reporting that the Indians were visiting this idol before 1579, when he was writing the letter, but they had ceased to visit the island by the time he wrote about it. By the time he was writing this letter, the population of Cozumel had been nearly wiped out by smallpox and the Maya traders no longer maintained the once frequent stops to the island bringing trade goods and traders. So, where did he get this information? There were monks and priests visiting Cozumel prior to 1564, when the Bishop of Yucatán, Francisco de Toral, went to the island, but they never mentioned Ix Chel or a women's pilgrimage. Toral later wrote a report saying that he *"Derroquéles todos sus templos antiguos, que era como Roma o Jerusalem entre nosotros aquella isla entre éstos...."* (I pulled down all their old temples, which were to them from that island as Rome or Jerusalem were to us). However, Toral never mentioned any pilgrimage of women or the goddess Ix Chel either.

Soon after Toral's visit to Cozumel, Fray Cristóbal de Asencio spent five months living on the island, catering to the spiritual needs of the Maya in Cozumel from the two *visita* churches that had been built in Cozumel around 1552. Fray Asencio says in his report of his visit: "*...y asi pase mis doctrinas y escuelas en cada pueblo, reformandose las iglesias, que estan como cosa de prestado.*" (and there I gave my doctrine and teachings in each village [San Miguel de Xamancab and Santa María de Oycib], renovating the churches, which were like provisional or temporary things). Does this mean that while Asencio was teaching the doctrines to the Maya in Cozumel and renovating the two sloppily-built churches in San Miguel and Cedral, there were pilgrims arriving on the island to make sacrifices in an important temple, completely unbeknownst to him? In his report, (written in 1570) Asencio lists all adults in Cozumel and says that they were no more than about 300 in San Miguel and Santa María de Oycib. Was this so many that he could not recognize a few new faces when they came on pilgrimage from the mainland? It seems to me that in his letter of 1579, Diego Contreras was repeating a story that he had been told, not something that he had seen with his own eyes. It may be that this story that was told to him was incorrect, or it may be that he misunderstood it, because if the goddess Ix Chel was so important, how is that Contreras wrote "*los indios no eran capaces de informarme lo que yschel significó, ni porqué ellos le dieron aquel nombre*"? (the Indians were incapable of telling me what *yschel* means nor why they gave it that name)? It seems that his informants were either very ill-informed or it was difficult for Contreras to understand what his informants were trying to say. It is interesting to see that Contreras does not mention Maya women or their supposed "need to visit Cozumel at least once in their lives" anywhere in his letter.

So, why is the story of a pilgrimage of women to the temple of the Ix Chel in Cozumel so engrained in the minds of people today, when there is a not a single mention of a pilgrimage of Maya women to Cozumel in any of the archives, in any of the codices, or any of the Mayan inscriptions? And why is Ix Chel so bound up with this imaginary pilgrimage of women when there is only one, single mention of Ix Chel in relation to a pilgrimage to Cozumel (which does not address the gender of the pilgrims) and more than <u>ten</u> that speak of a pilgrimage to Cozumel to make human sacrifices to the gods, using the <u>plural</u> of the word gods?

The association of the temple *"a un tiro de ballesta de la mar"* (a crossbow shot from the sea) in San Miguel de Xamancab with Ix Chel (instead of Teel Cuzam) began in 1924, when Samuel Kirkland Lothrop wrote something about Ix Chel in his book <u>Tulum</u>. *"To her shrine on Cozumel pilgrims flocked from all parts of Yucatán and even from distant Tabasco,"* Lothrop boldly stated. We assume that he took the idea that this temple belonged to Ix Chel from the 1579 testimony of Contreras, but we do not know for sure; Lothrop did not quote his source for this tidbit. In 1939, the archaeologist Sir John Eric J. Thompson published a scholarly article in which he put forward the same theory that the temple *"a un tiro de ballesta de la mar,"* was the temple of Ix Chel and a pilgrimage destination. However, Thompson used only the Contreras letter as support, along with a quote from the book of López de Cogolludo, in which Thompson inserted the name "Ix Chel," into a line of text, when that name did not appear in Cogolludo's original text.

Another theory of Thompson's was that Mayan glyphs had no phonetic element to them and that they only represented complete ideas. This theory was disproved after his death, like many of Thompson's other theories which were based on his own misinterpretations of Mayan glyphs. Even so, for many years most archeologists and writers accepted Thompson's and Lothrop's theories as facts and began to repeat them in their own books and reports. In 1970, Thompson published a popular book, <u>Maya History and Religion</u>. The book was translated into Spanish and sold like hotcakes. In the book, his old theory was presented as fact. From that moment on and with the help of dozens of writers including American and Mexican archaeologists once again using modern texts like Thompson and Lothrop as a guide instead of the original historical texts, Ix Chel would be linked firmly in the collective memory with a pilgrimage to a temple erected for her in Cozumel.

So, if Thompson and Lothrop are the sources of the theory that the temple where Cortés destroyed the Maya idols was the Temple of Ix Chel, where did the belief originate that holds that all Maya women were required to make a pilgrimage to the said temple at least once in their lifetime? The idea comes from badly paraphrased texts, or intentionally distorted lines in papers and books written during the 20th and 21st centuries. They do not come from any historical text. For example, here is a quote from the paper *Religious resistance and persistence on Cozumel Island,* written by Shankari Patel: *"Ethnohistorical sources note that Maya women traveled to Ix Chel's shrine at Cozumel at least once in their lifetimes."* Patel says this information came from the book of Arthur G. Miller, <u>On the edge of the Sea; Mural paintings at Tancah-Tulum</u>, published in 1982. But is that information actually contained in Miller's book? When we read Miller's book, we see that it is <u>not</u> what Miller wrote. Miller says nothing about *"Maya women traveled to Ix Chel's shrine at Cozumel at least once in their lifetimes."* What Miller <u>did</u> write was: *"A major shrine to Ix Chel, where pregnant women consulted a famous idol of this goddess, is well documented on Cozumel."*

So, even though Miller never wrote the phrase *"at least once in their lifetimes,"* he does repeat the old theory of Thompson's as if it were a fact, reinforcing that idea in the collective memory of the general public. And what "well documented" ethno-historic archive did Miller read to know *"pregnant women consulted a famous idol of this goddess?"* We don't know; Miller doesn't tell us. He has all of his historical sources listed in the bibliography of his book, but there is <u>not</u> <u>one</u> source listed that contains this statement. This is because **there is no document written before the twentieth century that says this**. In other words, this statement by Miller, as well as the one by Patel, are unreliable.

There are several early descriptions of the interior of a certain temple that was close to the beach at Xamancab. One of the earliest is repeated in a Spanish <u>translation</u> of a <u>summary</u>, made by Gonzalo Fernández de Oviedo of an <u>appendix</u> of the eighth edition of the 1522 Italian book *Itinerario de Ludovico de Varthema, Bolognese nello Egitto, nella Soria nella Arabia deserta y feliz, nella Persia, nella India & nella Ethyopia* that was printed from the <u>draft</u> of the Italian <u>translation</u>, of the scribe's <u>copy</u> in <u>Spanish</u>, of the report written by Benito Martín, in which Martín <u>redacted</u> and <u>paraphrased</u> Juan Díaz' original 1518 eyewitness report of the events that took place on Cozumel in that year.

The Italian book that contains this translated, abridged version of a synopsis of a summary says that inside the temple in Xamancab of San Miguel Cozumel, the Maya *"teniua certe figure de ossi & de cenise de idoli che sono qlli che adorauano loro"* (had certain figures of bones and of *cenise* that are the idols that they adore). This is all that this report says of the items in the interior of the temple and the idol. Nothing more. But, there are some very interesting words in this text.

One of these words is *"cenise."* This word is most frequently translated as "ashes," as if it was written "cenizas," the Spanish word for ashes. However, the word *cenise* is actually a sixteenth-century misspelling of the word *cemís*, a word from the language of the Taino Indians who lived in Cuba, Hispaniola, Jamaica, Puerto Rico and other Caribbean islands from the fifth to sixteenth-centuries. *Cemís* are idols or relics that contain the spirit of a powerful ancestor. This spirit (contained in the bones or ashes of the deceased ancestor) can be kept in a basket, terracotta urn, hollow wooden sculpture, or terracotta sculpture, (all of which could be the "figures of bones" the *Itinerario* referred to) but often the ancestor's whole head was saved as *cemí*. His head was mummified, covered in mud or resin and housed inside a bundle or anthropomorphic reliquary package, which served as a link for the living to communicate with the spirit of the deceased chieftain. Before their trip to Cozumel, Bernal Díaz and his companions interacted frequently with the Tainos on Cuba and probably saw many of these *cemís* during the years they were there. Several of Bernal's companions also learned the Taino language during their stay on Cuba, so it is not surprising that they used a familiar Taino word to describe a Maya reliquary bundle.

The first mention of a *cemí* can be found in Bartolomé de Las Casas' summary of the *Diario de abordo* (ship's log) that Cristóbal Colón made during his first voyage to the new world. Later, in 1498, Fray Ramón Pane wrote about *cemís* in his manuscript *Relación acerca de las antigüedades de los indios*. Peter Martyr, someone who spoke with Colón and Cortés personally and someone who had access to their documents regarding their discoveries, also wrote extensively about *cemís* in his book *Décadas de Orbe Novo*, published in 1516 and 1521.

Diego de Landa, in his manuscript *Relación de las cosas de Yucatán*, mentions that the Maya also made this kind of reliquary. *"A los antiguos señores Cocom, habían cortado las cabezas cuando murieron, y cocidas las limpiaron de la carne y después aserraron la mitad de la coronilla para atrás, dejando lo de adelante con las quijadas y dientes. A estas medias calaveras suplieron lo que de carne les faltaba con cierto betún y les dieron la perfección muy al propio de cuyas eran, y las tenían con las estatuas de las cenizas, todo lo cual tenían en los oratorios..."* (the old Cocom [Cocom Maya] lords had their heads cut off after they died, which were then boiled and cleaned of flesh and later sawn in half from the crown back, leaving the front part and the jaw and teeth. To these half-skulls they replaced the missing flesh with a certain tar and they did it to perfection so it was very similar to how they once looked, and they kept them with the statues of the ashes, all of which they kept in the shrines). In this text Landa states that the *cemís* were stored together with the hollow "statues of the ashes" that they kept in the oratorios. Landa explains that cremation was reserved for the most important persons and then continued, saying: *"echaban las cenizas en estatuas huecas de barro, cuando eran muy señores"* (they place the ashes in hollow statues of baked clay, when [the dead] are very noble) and *"guardaban estas estatuas con mucha reverencia entre sus ídolos"* (they keep these statues with much reverence among their idols). Landa also says they kept these hollow statues *"en muy gran reverencia y acatamiento, y todos los días de sus fiestas y regocijos les hacían ofrendas de sus comidas para que no les faltase en la otra vida donde pensaban sus almas descansaban..."* (in very high reverence and respect, and on every holy day and day of rejoycing they gave them offerings of their food so that they do not lack it in the other life where they believe their souls rest).

Above: Photos of the front and back of a 16ᵗʰ century cemí from the island of Hispaniola, covered with cotton cord and beads made from fish bones and red shells. Both the front and back of this cemí have faces. The face on the front side is made of resin applied over the skull of a Taino Indian. Image from, <u>Taino</u>, edited by Fatima Bercht, et al.

These small, hollow, clay statues were made specifically as containers to hold the ashes of deceased chieftains, not as something for someone to hide inside of and imitate a god's voice. In the 1535 *Historia General y Natural de las Indias* by Gonzalo Fernández de Oviedo y Valdés, there is mention of the *cemí* in the temple on Cozumel: *"Tienen allí ciertas esteras de palma hechas líos e unos huesos que dixeron que eran de un señor calachuni muy principal."* (They have there [in the temple] certain woven palm mats made into bundles and some bones that they say were of a very important *halach uinic.*)

There are some *cemís*, says Fray Pane, *"...que hablan, otros que causan crecer las plantas, otros que traen lluvia, otros que hacen que los vientos soplen... y otros que ayudan a las mujeres en el parto."* (that talk, others that cause the plants to grow, others that bring the rain, others that make the winds blow... and others that assist women in birthing). This last sentence sounds very much like one of the functions attributed to Ix Chel.

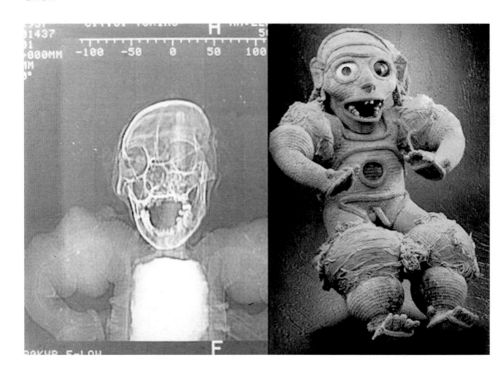

Above left: An x-ray image of a Taino cemí (above right) made of cotton cord and a human skull discovered in a cave in Dominican Republic. Image from L'Art Taino by Jacques Kerchache.

In his *Historia*, Oviedo also wrote how the Maya chieftains used the cemís to control and manipulate their subjects: *"se anunciaban como dimandos de un oráculo, o de un Cemí, a quien hacían hablar lo que quierian por medio de los agoreros o médicos, que exercian las funciones de ministre del ídolo. Estos se ocultaban detrás de la estatua del Cemí: declaraban la guerra y la paz, arreglaban las estaciones; concedían el sol, la lluvia, y cuanto convenía según las necesidades lo exigían, o el antojo del Cacique lo dictaba..."* (they make pronouncements like they were the outpourings from the oracle, or from the *Cemí*, which says what they want it to say by means of the priests or attendants who take care of the idol. These hide behind the statue of the *Cemí:* they declare war and peace, regulate the seasons, grant sunlight, rain, and whatever suits according to the needs at the time, or whatever the whim of the *cacique* dictates). In another part of his book, Oviedo says: *"fuera de sus pueblos tenían un adoratorio grande en donde tenían al cemí tutelar. Allí concurria el cacique y los sacerdotes, que se ocultaban a las espaldas del ídolo y hablaban por su boca cuanto el Cacique les surgería. En las funciones que celebran, llevaban de comer al Ídolo, y sus ministros se regalaban con las ofrendas."* (outside of their towns they have a big shrine where they keep the tutelary *cemí*. There the *cacique* and priests gather, who hide behind the idol's back and spoke as if with its own voice whatever the *cacique* suggested to them. During the events when they celebrate, they brought food to the idol, and the priests availed themselves of the offerings.)

In his book *Historia de la Indias*, Fray Bartolomé de Las Casas also wrote about the consultations with the *cemís*, saying that the Maya priests spoke with the *cemís* and then transmitted the message to the other Indians. The son of Cristóbal Colón, Fernando Colón, wrote in his book, *Historie del S.D.Fernando Colombo; nelle s'ha particolare et vera relatione della vita e de fatti dell'Almiraglio D. Christoforo Colombo suo padre*, that the admiral described how the Spaniards uncovered the way the *cemís* functioned: *"entraron los cristianos con ellos en la dicha casa, y de súbito, el cemí gritó fuerte y habló en su lengua, por lo que se descubrió que era fabricado con artificio: porque siendo hueco, tenía en la parte inferior acomodada una cerbatana o trompa que iba a un lado oscuro de la casa, cubierto de follaje, donde había una persona que hablaba lo que el cacique quería que dijese, cuanto se puede hablar con una cerbatana. Por lo que los nuestros, sospechando lo que podía ser, dieron con el pie al cemí y hallaron lo que hemos contado. El cacique, viendo que habíamos descubierto aquello, les rogó con gran instancia que no dijesen cosa alguna a los indios sus vasallos, ni a otros, porque con aquella astucia tenían a todos a su obediencia."* (The Christians went inside the said house, and suddenly, the *cemí* shouted loudly and spoke in its language, because what we found was that it was an artifice: because it was hollow, a blowgun or tube could be fitted into it lower part and then stretched to a dark part of the house, covered with fronds, where there was a person who spoke whatever the *cacique* wanted it to say, by speaking through the blowgun. So our people, suspecting just what it could be, kicked the *cemí* and found what we just described. The *cacique*, seeing that we had exposed it, begged with great insistence that we not say a thing to the other Indians, his vassals, nor to others, because through that trick he kept all of them in obedience).

In his *Crónica*, Francisco Cervantes de Salazar cites the words supposedly spoken by Hernán Cortés to the Maya of Cozumel, when Cortés was on the island destroying the idols there: *"quiéros descubrir una maldad con que hasta ahora os han engañado los ministros del demonio, perseguidor vuestro, y es que esas figuras son huecas por de dentro, métese un indio por debajo y por una cerbatana habla y da respuesta, fingiendo que las figuras hablan; y porque no penséis que os engaño, delante de vosotros derribaré un ídolo y hare que los sacerdotes confiesen ser así lo que digo."* (you need to know about an evil that until now the priests of the demon, our persecutor, has tricked you with, and it is that these figures are hollow inside, and they put an Indian below and by way of a blowgun he speaks and gives answers, making it seem like the figures speak themselves; and so you will not think we are tricking you, I will knock down an idol in front of you and make the priests confess it to be as I say). Notice the plural use of the word "figures" in this text. Cortés was not speaking of only one hollow idol, but several.

So, if the idols were not large enough so that the priest could enter into them, why were they hollow? Landa says: *"A los señores y gente de mucha valía quemaban los cuerpos y... echaban las cenizas en estatuas huecas, hechas de barro, cuando los muertos eran muy señores."* (they cremated the bodies of the nobles and the very influential people and... placed their ashes in hollow statues, made of clay, when the dead were very noble). These hollow ossuary statues would have been the *"figure de ossi"* (figures of bones) that were mentioned in the *Itinerario* of Grijalva's vistit to Cozumel in 1518. It is also interesting to read that the priests used a hollow wooden tube as a megaphone, located on the back of the hollow idol to make them "speak." Which makes perfect sense, because it is difficult to imagine an idol of earthenware made in Cozumel that was large enough for a priest to enter, since there is simply no example or report of any artifact made of baked clay by the Maya that was of that extreme size. In addition, the Maya of Cozumel imported almost all their ceramics from the coast, or farther afield, since the island does not have the appropriate clay with which to make strong pottery.

Andrés de Tapia, who was with Cortés in Cozumel in 1519, wrote in his 1539 report that in Cozumel "*Adoraban la gente della en ídolos, a los cuales hacían sacrificio, especial a uno que estaba en la costa de la mar en una torre alta. Este ídolo era de barro cocido e hueco, pegado con cal a una pared, e por detrás de la pared había una entrada secreta por do parecie que un hombre podía entrar y envestirse el dicho ídolo, e así debie ser, porque los indios decían, segund después se entendió, que aquel ídolo hablaba.*" (The people there adored idols, to which they made sacrifices, especially one that was on the coast in a high tower. That idol was of baked clay and hollow, stuck to a wall with plaster, and behind the wall was a secret entrance with which it seemed a man could enter and empower the said idol, and that is as it was, because the Indians said, according to what I could understand, that that idol talked). The word *envestirse* in this text does not mean that the priests "entered" the idol. The word *envestirse* means that they invested, granted, or conferred power to the idol. The poor interpretation of the word *envestirse* has caused innumerable historians and writers to believe, incorrectly, that the statue was large enough for priests to enter into it; but this is not the case. The text says nothing of the idol's size; it simply explains that the priest could enter the secret room behind the idol and "empower" it by making it seem as if the statue was speaking.

Antonio de Herrera y Tordesillas' wrote in his book *Historial General*, that in Cozumel, the Spaniards: "*Vieron algunos adoratorios y templos y uno en particular cuya forma era de una torre cuadrada ancha de pie y hueco en lo alto, con cuatro grandes ventanas, con sus corredores y en lo hueco que era Capilla estaban ídolos y a las espaldas estaba un sacristía a donde se guardaban las cosas del servicio del templo.*" (Saw some shrines and temples and one in particular whose form was a square tower, wide at the bottom and hollow at the top, with four large windows, with its corridors, and in the cavity that was like a chapel there were idols and behind the back was a sacristy where they kept the accouterments for the service of the temple). In this text, the room behind the back wall of the front room of the temple was described as a sacristy, where the priests kept their religious paraphernalia. Also note that Herrera did not write that there was only one idol in the temple, but he used the term _idolos_, plural.

In his _Historia de Yucatán,_ Cogolludo combined and embellished the reports of the earlier writers such as Tapia, which were written 136 years earlier. The result was a mish-mash of bits and pieces of the original texts, cut and pasted together in sequences different from the originals with new descriptive words and phrases thrown in for good measure. In his re-crafted version of history, Cogolludo wrote: _"La singularidad de un ídolo, que había en aquel templo, y por cuya causa era tan visitada de peregrinos aquella isla... Estaba este ídolo en el templo cuadrado... era muy diverso y extraño demás. Su materia era barro cocido, la figura grande y hueca, pegada a la pared con cal. Había a las espaldas una como sacristía, y en ella tenían los sacerdotes una puerta pequeña oculta abierta a las espaldas del ídolo, por donde uno de los sacerdotes entraba, y de allí respondía a las demandas.... Creían los miserables engañados, que su ídolo les hablaba, y creían lo que decía, y así le veneraban más que a los otros con diversas ofrendas, sacrificios de sangre, aves, perros, y aun a veces de hombres. Como este siempre su parecer les hablaba, era tan grande concurso de todas partes a consultarle y solicitar remedio a sus cuidados."_ (the extraordinary nature of an idol, that was in that temple, and for whose cause the island was so visited by pilgrims... this idol was in the square temple... it was very strange and different from the rest. Its material was baked clay, the figure large and hollow, stuck to the wall with plaster. Behind its back was something like a sacristy, and in that the priests had a small hidden door opening behind the back of the idol, by which one of the priests could enter, and from there respond to the petitions... The miserable fools believed it, that their idol talked to them, and they believed what it said, and so they venerated it more than the others with sundry offerings, sacrifices of blood, birds, dogs, and even at times men. The gatherings from all over to consult and petition remedy and help were so large because it always appeared to them that it spoke to them).

This text, pieced together from earlier texts and twisted as it is, still does not say the priests entered <u>into</u> the idol, it says the priest entered into the <u>sacristy</u>, behind the idol, and spoke to the people from a small door behind the idol. It looks like the story of the huge, hollow idol of Ix Chel in Cozumel began when the early writers began copying and altering the text slightly with each rendition, just like the game of "telephone."

In 1552, Francisco López de Gomara's *Historia General de las Indias* was published and his is the text that many archeologists, historians, and writers cite when they write about "the giant, hollow statue of Ix Chel." The problem is, Gomara had never been to Cozumel, nor to the New World for that matter and he only edited and rewrote reports of others (like Cortés and Tapia), adding words and lines here and there that the originals did not have and deleting others that the originals did contain. It was exactly this kind of sloppy and twisted writing that caused an eyewitness to the events on Cozumel, Bernal Díaz de Castillo, to criticize Gomara so severely in his own book, *La Historia Verdadera de la Conquista de Nueva España*. Díaz wrote that he felt he was forced to write *La Historia Verdadera* in order to counter *Historia General de las Indias* because Gomara's work was so bad, so full of errors, and so slanted, that he could not bear to let it go unchallenged. Here, then, is the pertinent part of Gomara's text: *"Los sacerdotes tenían una puerta secreta y chica hecha en la pared á par del ídolo. Por allí entraba uno de ellos, Embutiase en el hueco del bulto, y hablaba y respondía á los que venían en devoción y con demandas."* (The priests had a secret and small door made in the wall near the idol. From there one of them would enter, squeezing into the hollow of the statue, and spoke and responded to those who came in devotion and with petitions).

In this text of Gomara's, one can see the traces of other writer's words, but with more details and additions that did not appear in the original works. Gomara often alters a word here and there and changes the message, as in his use of the word *embutiase* (to squeeze into a small or tight space), instead of *envestirse* (confer power), which is the word the eyewitness Tapia used to describe the act. Once again, an example of the old game of "telephone!"

So, exactly what do we know for sure about the temple where Cortés destroyed the idols on Cozumel and ordered the wooden cross and an image or statue of the Virgin to be placed?

- That it held the bones of an important chieftain, guarded inside what the Spaniard's called a *cemí*.
- That it had <u>several</u> small, hollow idols holding the ashes of other dead chieftains and the priests used a long, hollow wooden tube to speak through and simulate the voice of the gods, while standing or crouching in the small sacristy behind these idols.
- That the "talking idol" was not large enough for a priest to enter inside and hide.
- That there is no document written before the 20th century that mentions any relationship between Ix Chel and the temple near the beach where Cortés destroyed the idols.

Given all the early documents that place the temple where Cortés pulled down a talking idol on Cozumel within fifty yards of the edge of the sea, why then, is the pyramid in San Gervasio with the remnants of a temple on top (structure C22-41-a, or Ka'na Nah) also called the "Temple of Ix Chel" in today's guidebooks and webpages? It is because the archeologist David A. Freidel put forth that theory when he wrote chapter nine of the preliminary report of the two seasons of fieldwork which the University of Arizona and Harvard University made in San Gervasio during 1972 and 1973. The report, entitled <u>Changing pre-Columbian Commercial Systems</u>, was published in 1975. In his chapter, Freidel made it clear that he relied on the writings of modern historians and the English translations of the historical sources and not the original Spanish accounts when he was searching for references to a temple dedicated to Ix Chel on Cozumel. With these poorly-done English translations as his foundation, Freidel arrived at the same erroneous conclusion that many others made before him; that the temple in Xamancab where Cortés destroyed the idols had a giant, hollow statue with a doorway in its back that a priest could use to climb inside of the statue.

Freidel says he first drew a floor plan of how he believed the Temple of Ix Chel would have looked. He then decided that if he found a ruin that conformed to this plan, that is to say, a temple on a pyramid with two rooms and a small doorway in the wall separating the front room from the rear room and two other doors on each side of that wall, that ruin would be the Temple of Ix Chel. He felt he needed no other proof to identify the temple, such as pieces of the giant statue, identifying glyphs, or murals showing Ix Chel; just a temple that matched his drawing.

Figure 24. Probable plan of the Ix Chel temple which was situated on Cozumel.

Above: The plan that Freidel drew of how he imagined the "Temple of Ix Chel" would have looked, based on its description in English translations of the early sources <u>prior</u> to his first visit to Cozumel.

In the summary of the chapter, Freidel wrote: *"In conclusion, we have discovered a structure on Cozumel that bears a strong resemblance to the Temple of Ix Chel as described by Spanish observers at the time of contact. It has been argued that this similarity of form indicates a similarity in function."* And that was his whole argument for identifying the temple at San Gervasio as the Temple of Ix Chel: *"a strong resemblance to the Temple of Ix Chel as described by Spanish observers at the time of contact."* However, it appears Freidel never actually read the original documents that described the temple. His citations shows he only read English versions of how the temple in Xamancab appeared. Worse yet, when he was unable to locate an important temple on top of a pyramid near the beach at Xamancab, where the original sources indicated it had been when Cortés arrived, Freidel decided that since the temple in San Gervasio "more of less" matched his idea of how the

Temple of Ix Chel must have looked, there must have been <u>two</u> big temples dedicated to Ix Chel, with <u>two</u> big hollow idols of the goddess; one located by the beach in Xamancab and one far inland in San Gervasio.

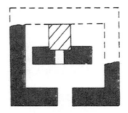

Above: Plan of structure C22-41-a, or Ka'na Nah in San Gervasio.

In 1984, archeologists Wiliam Rathje and Jeremy Sabloff published their book, <u>Cozumel, Late Maya Settlement Patterns</u>. This was the final report of the 1972-73 field seasons in San Gervasio. In this book, Rathje and Sabloff wrote: *"We have identified a structure in Cozumel as similar to the structure described by López de Gomara,"* speaking of structure C22-41-a. From these two statements, one published by Freidel and the other published by Rathje and Sabloff, sprang the belief that is so widely held today: That structure C22-41-a in San Gervasio, also known as Ka'na Nah, was the Temple of Ix Chel. And, there has been no other information, proofs, or data put forth since then to support this theory.

Above: Structure C22-41-a, or Ka'na Nah in San Gervasio.

What about the current and popularly-held idea that Ix Chel is the goddess of love and fertility? Where did that come from? Again, it comes from twentieth-century "spin-doctors" who base their belief on their ethnocentric interpretation of the few lines of texts we have that touch on the powers of Ix Chel. One of the mentions is in Lopez de Cogolludo's _Historia de Yucatán_, published in 1688. In that book, Cogolludo wrote: _"como tambien á otro de otra grande Hechizera que dezian inuentò ò hallò entre ellos la medicina, y la llamaban Yxchel, aunque tenian Dios de la medicina, nombrado Citbolontun."_ (There is also another important sorceress who they say invented or brought medicine to them, and they call her _Yxchel_, although they have a god of medicine named _Citbolontun_.)

Another mention of Ix Chel's powers comes from Bishop Diego de Landa in his circa-1566 manuscript, _Relación de las cosas de Yucatán_: _"Al día siguiente se juntavan los medicos y hechizeros en casa de uno de ellos, con sus mugeres, y los sacerdotes echavan el demonio; lo qual hecho, sacavan los enboltorios de sus medicina en que traían muchas niñerias y sendos dollillos [idolillos] de la diosa de la medicina que llamavan Ixchel, y así a esta fiesta llamavan Ihcil-Ixchel, y unas pedrezuelas de las suertes que echavan y llamavan Am, y con su mucha devoción invocavan con oraciones a los dioses de la medicina que dezian Yzamna, Citbolontum, y Ahau-Chamahez..."_ (The next day the doctors and sorcerers gathered in one of their houses with the women and the priests cast out the demon; having done so, they pulled out their medicine bags which contained many childish things and some small idols of the goddess of medicine they call _Ixchel_, and so they call this celebration _Ihcil-Ixchel_, and they cast some lucky pebbles they call _Am_, and with a lot of devotion they invoke the gods of medicine whom they call _Izamná, Citbolontun, y Ahau Chamahez..._")

Landa's second mention of Ix Chel is also from his _Relación de las cosas de Yucatán_: _"para sus partos acudían a las hechiceras, las quales las hazian creer de sus mentiras, y las ponian debaxo de la cama un ídolo de un demonio llamado Ixchel, que dezian era la diosa de hacer las criaturas."_ (The sorceresses, who made them believe their lies, attended the women during childbirth, and they put under the bed an idol of a demon named *Ixchel*, who they say was the goddess of childbirth.)

Most commonly, the last phrase of this passage, *"la diosa de hacer las criaturas,"* is translated as "the goddess of fertility." However, Bishop Landa did not write *"la diosa de fertilidad;"* he used a very arcane twist of the phrase in old Spanish *(de hacer las criaturas)* to indicate the specialty of the goddess Ix Chel. *"De hacer las criaturas"* in this case does not mean "makes the children." In this case, the phrase *"De hacer las…"* has the same connotation as it does in the saying *"de hacer las tripas,"* which means "to make a bowel movement." The correct connotation of *"de hacer las criaturas"* in this passage is "childbirth." The notion of childbirth is very different from the concepts of either conception or fertility.

So, it appears that Ix Chel was actually the goddess of <u>childbirth</u>, not the goddess of <u>fertility</u>. Why does it matter? It matters because the ancient Maya (as well as all other early Mesoamerican cultures) viewed the act of childbirth in a <u>very</u> different light than we do today. It was not seen as a joyous event that women prayed for, but rather an event that women must face and struggle with, much like being called on to go to war. In fact, in Mayan and Aztec texts women going into childbirth are often referred to as a women going into "battle." And, those women who did not survive this traumatic event were considered as holy and special as a male warrior who died in battle.

Mexica, Toltec, and Maya each had their own patron goddesses of childbirth. For the Toltec, the goddess Cihuacoatl (Snake Woman) was the homologue of Ix Chel; she was the Toltec goddess of midwives and women who died in childbirth. Toltec women who died in childbirth were buried in the courtyard of Cihuacoatl's temple. These burials had to be guarded for several days, as the warrior class believed the fingers, hands, arms, and hair taken from the body of a woman who died in childbirth would afford the warrior supernatural protection in battles and these fellows would eagerly dig up the body to procure these magic bits and pieces, if they could.

Cihuacoatl was also a very demanding goddess. Historian Fray Bernardino Sahagún wrote in his circa 1540 codex *Historia general de las cosas de Nueva España*, that when she wanted another child sacrifice, her priests would leave an obsidian knife in an empty cradle in the marketplace as a sign of her impatience.

A homologue of both Cihuacoatl and Ix Chel was the goddess Coatlicue (Snake Skirt) of the Mexica people. The Tlaxcalans knew her as Chimalman, the mother of Quetzalcoatl, the Toltec leader who later became a god. Coatlicue was depicted by the Mexica to be an old woman with claws on her hands and feet wearing a skirt of writhing snakes and a necklace of severed human hands, human skulls and human hearts. Coatlicue was also held by them to be a goddess of medicine and to be a virgin who gave birth, similar to Ix Chel.

Today, a few "new-age" believers carry flowers to structure C22-41-a, thinking that they are repeating a traditional act; making offerings to a goddess. It is difficult to imagine what the gods might make of this new kind of offering, but in times long past, flowers were not the gods' preferred gift. Diego de Landa mentions several kinds of animals sacrificed by the Maya, including dogs and deer. Furthermore, he describes human sacrifices which the pilgrims performed when they went to Cozumel: *"tenian aquellos dos descomulgados sanctuarios de Chichen-itza y Cuzmil donde infinitos pobres enviaban a sacrificar o despeñar al uno y al otro a sacar los corazones."* (they have two unholy shrines of Chichen-itzá and Cuzmil where they send an infinite number of unfortunates to be sacrificed or thrown from a height in one [Chichen Itzá] and the other [Cozumel] to have their hearts ripped out). Landa describes the human sacrifice thusly: *"llegava al saion nacon con un navajon de piedra y davale con mucha destreza y crueldad una cuchillada entre las costillas del lado izquierdo, debaxo de la tetilla y acudíale allí luego con la mano y echava la mano del corazón como rabioso tigre arancavaselo vivo, y puesto en un plato lo dava al sacerdote, el cual iva muy a prisa y untava a los ídolos los rostros con aquella sangre fresca."* (The executioner priest arrived with a large stone knife and with practiced cruelty made a slash between the ribs, on the left side, under the nipple and then stuck his hand inside and tearing the heart out alive like a rabid tiger, and gave to it to the priest on a plate, who then hurried and uncted the idols' faces with that fresh blood.) Landa continues, saying: *"...estos sacrificados comúnmente solian enterrar en el patio del templo, o sino, <u>comianseles</u>, repartiendo por los que alcançavan y los señores, y los manos y pies y cabeça eran del sacerdote y oficiales..."* (these sacrificial victims were commonly buried in the courtyard of the temple, or if they were not, they ate them, dividing them between the nobles and those who there was enough left over for).

Does this mean that the Maya of Cozumel offered bloody, beating, living hearts to Ix Chel and later ate the bodies of the sacrificed victims? This grisly image does not square well with the sweet image of Ix Chel that many people have today; a goddess whose areas of interest are purported to be sex, love, fertility, medicine, and weaving. Or, maybe it does, if your idea of Ix Chel is the image in the Dresden Codex of the goddess with claws instead of fingers and human bones festooning her skirt.

Guillermo de Anda, an archaeologist of the Autonomous University of Yucatán, performed an inventory of the bones of the victims of Maya sacrifices found submerged in the cenotes of Yucatán. He found that most of the skeletons were incomplete and disarticulated. He also stated that that most of those bones had butcher marks, pointing to the fact that the Maya ate the flesh of many of these victims. Some of these bones were also semi-carbonized, as if they had been roasted in a fire.

Above: Bone of a sacrificial victim of the Maya, showing butcher marks where the meat was cut off the bone with obsidian knives.

There is a Spanish eyewitness to the cannibalism that the Maya practiced. Jerónimo de Aguilar, one of the survivors of the 1511 shipwreck on the Quintana Roo coast, reported that the Maya sacrificed four other of his fellow survivors and ate them. Díaz Bernal de Castillo also reported that Cozumel Maya sacrificed ten of the eleven Taino Indians who shipwrecked on Cozumel after their canoe washed up during a storm.

In _Crónica de la Nueva España_, Francisco Cervantes de Salazar says that the Maya on Cozumel "_ofrecían muchas cosas a los idolos, haciendoles muy grandes y solemnos sacrificios, no solamente de brutos animales, sino de hombres y mujeres, niños, viejos, niñas, y viejas..._" (offered many things to the idols, making very grand and solemn sacrifices, not only of brute animals, but <u>also of men and women, young boys, old men, young girls, and old women</u>).

Peter Martyr wrote that the Indians of Cozumel: "_Inmolan niños y niñas a los zemes que son simulacros que ellos veneran..._" (They immolated boys and girls to the cemís which are the idols that they venerate). He went on saying: "_los morcillos de los brazos y de los muslos y las pulpas de las pantorrillas se los comen..._" (they ate the upper arms and thighs and the muscular part of the calf).

Above: Dining on the leftovers. From Fray Bernardino Sahagún's
Historia general de las cosas de Nueva España, 1540-1585

The charred bones of children found by archaeologist Anda attest to this macabre Maya version of BBQ. We know that the sacrifices of children and babies were a very common kind of sacrifice in Yucatán. Anda says of 2,500 bones taken from the sacred cenote of Chichen Itzá, seventy-nine percent were children who were between three and eleven years of age when they were killed. In 2010, archeologist Steven Houston of Brown University found a Maya tomb of a *halach uinic* with the remains of six children who had been sacrificed and buried with him. The children were all under two years of age. Next to the chieftain was a bowl with the charred skeletal remains of a baby. Another funeral of a Maya chieftain in Northern Belize had the remains of five slaughtered children, ranging from newly-born to eight-years-of-age.

Above: A scene from a Maya vessel, illustrating a small child being sacrificed from Justin Kerr's The Maya Vase Book.

Bernal Díaz del Castillo speaks of religious pilgrimages and sacrifices in Cozumel in his 1568 book, _La Historia Verdadera de la Conquista de Nueva España_. He wrote: _"había allí en Cozumel unos ídolos de muy disformes figuras, y estaban en un adoratorio en que ellos tenían por costumbre en aquella tierra, por aquel tiempo, de sacrificar."_ (There were some idols with very deformed features in Cozumel and they were in a shrine that they customarily used in that time and place to slaughter). Cogolludo wrote: _"llegan a Cozumel al cumplimiento de su promesas, a las ofrendas de sus sacrificios"_ (they arrived in Cozumel in completion of their promises, for the offering of their sacrifices).

Above: A scene painted on a ceramic vessel depicting a Maya sacrifice, from Justin Kerr's **The Maya Vase Book**.

But where did the Maya of Cozumel make their human sacrifices? In this temple _"a crossbow's shot from the sea?"_ If so, exactly where was this temple located? One possible location was mentioned by Alberto Escalona Ramos in his 1946 report of his visit to Cozumel with the Mexican Scientific Expedition in 1937. He wrote that he found a group of four mounds one kilometer north of the clock tower in the square, less than half a kilometer from the sea. Escalona said that the citizens of San Miguel had looted most of the stones from the site to build the Municipal Pier.

There is another possibility; the Temple of Miramar, or Santa Pilar, which was located a little to the north of the yacht basin, _Puerto de_

Abrigo. This temple was far enough away from the village of San Miguel to escape the looting that Escalona said had happened in the sites closer to town. That is, at least until the 1950s; that was when a group of students and teachers from the Benito Juárez School decided to dismantle the shrine and take the central column to the museum that was located in the main square at that time.

Above: A photo of the Maya temple at Santa Pilar taken by the Allison V. Armour expedition en 1895.

Archeaologist William Henry Holmes described the temple he as he found it in 1895: *"The terrace on which the temple stands is four or five feet high and twenty feet in length from north to south, and, as nearly as can be ascertained by present exposures, about twenty feet wide. The facing has been of hewn, or partially hewn stone, somewhat irregular in form but well laid in mortar. No trace of a stairway is visible. The temple was perhaps not over sixteen feet square, and contained an outer room or corridor ten feet in length by four in width, and two small chambers back of it. The distinguishing feature of this little temple is a remarkable column which has sculptured upon its front a large, ape-*

visaged figure. The sculptured figure is much weather-beaten, and apparently battered, especially about the head and face, and seems to have been intended for a human creature than an ape. The hands are held in front, apparently grasping the folds of a garment. So far as I can see, no particular significance can be attributed t the position. The figure is that of a female.... Originally the surface was covered with plaster and paint. In parts protected from the weather as many as six successive layers of plaster are seen, each application in turn having received a coat of red, blue or green paint... Encircling the front of the column over the sculptured head are painted or imprinted four red hands, a feature occurring with considerable frequency in ancient Maya structures."

Today, the central column of this temple is in the Museo de la Isla. It no longer has the remains of the layers of plaster, nor the green paint that it had on its legs in 1895 and its capital is now under its feet instead of on the top of its head. There are many people who say that this is a statue of Ix Chel, but there is no way to tell if that is the case. The archaeologists did not report any glyphs associated with the temple when it was found and there is no statue or drawing of Ix Chel that resembles the posture of the figure depicted by this column. Yes, it seems that it represents a woman giving birth, but this does not mean that it was Ix Chel: There is no other stone idol, nor ceramic vessel, nor murals, nor a single piece of jade or bone engraved with a representation of Ix Chel in this position. That is also the problem with all the Maya ruins in Cozumel: There are no legible glyphs or murals left associated with them that could identify which temple was of what god.

It seems clear that today's mythology surrounding the goddess Ix Chel and the island of Cozumel is far from the truth of the matter. Did the Maya of Cozumel worship the goddess Ix Chel? Most probably, but there is no evidence that she was the most important deity and there is plenty of evidence that there were other gods that the Maya of Cozumel worshiped in addition to her.

Did the Maya of Cozumel perceive her to be the sweet goddess of love that she is so often portrayed to be today? Surely not. As a homolog of the fearsome, clawed, snake-skirt-wearing, human-bone-bedecked, Mexica goddess Cihuacoatl, it seems unlikely that the Maya believed the goddess Ix Chel would be someone who preferred flowers over beating, bloody hearts as gifts.

Was there a main temple on Cozumel, a temple that was dedicated solely to Ix Chel? Although some early writers speak of a uniquely important temple on Cozumel, none save Contreras link it to Ix Chel and many others say it was filled with the statues of several different gods.

Were all Maya women required to make a pilgrimage to a temple dedicated to Ix Chel on Cozumel at least once in their lives? No. There is no document written prior to the twentieth century putting forward this idea and the vision of hundreds of thousands of Maya women trying to make their way across Campeche, Yucatán, Quintana Roo, Honduras, Guatemala and Belize to complete this pilgrimage is absurd. To imagine <u>pregnant</u> women made this trek and canoe voyage is even more far-fetched.

Was there a giant, hollow, pottery statue of Ix Chel that was large enough for a priest to enter and imitate the voice of the goddess for the visiting pilgrims? No. "Talking idols" were not giant hollow phone-booths. They were small, hollow, anthropomorphic urns that held the ashes of important personages.   From their descriptions in various documents it is clear that the priest was hidden by a wall or screen <u>behind</u> the small statue and used a hollow wooden trumpet to throw his voice in imitation of the spirit residing in it.

Is structure C22-41-a, also known as *Ka'na Nah* in San Gervasio the temple of Ix Chel? While there may have been several temples dedicated to Ix Chel on Cozumel, there are no early documents saying that this was the case, and even if there were, there is no proof that this temple was one of them.

Will this article convince people to abandon their old beliefs regarding the goddess Ix Chel? Probably not. As the saying goes, *"it is easier to fool people than it is to convince them that they have been fooled."*

CHAPTER 3

The first Europeans to visit Yucatán

Contrary to popular belief, the survivors of the 1511 Valdivia shipwreck were not the first European visitors to land in Yucatán, nor was Francisco Hernández de Córdoba the first European to claim Yucatán for Spain, nor was Juan de Grijalva the first to discover Cozumel. The first Europeans to visit Yucatán were <u>Portuguese</u> explorers. Just as the discovery and settlement by the Vikings of L'Anse aux Meadows in Newfoundland was overlooked in the history books, most books on the history of the discovery of México do not include all the data now known to historians. The Portuguese were sending out their own explorers for decades before Cristóbal Colón set off on his first voyage of discovery in 1492. Portuguese maps made as early as 1424 show the parts of the New World that these early explorers were discovering.

In 1424, Giovanni (Zuane) Pizzigano, an Italian working in Portugal for the Portuguese King, made a chart of Western Europe and the Atlantic Ocean. Shown on the chart are a group of islands, including one called *Antilia,* which may be the earliest portrayal of the Antilles in the western Atlantic. This chart (shown below) is in the James Bell Ford collection, in the University of Minnesota.

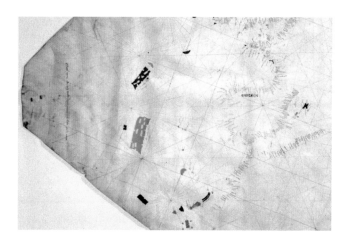

In 1474, Portuguese King Alfonso V heard about a theory put forward by Paulo dal Pozzo Toscanelli (an Italian spice trader and geographer) that set out the idea one could sail westward from Europe to the Spice Islands. The King directed a confidant of his, Canon Fernando Martínez de Roritz to write the Italian and ask for more information. In a responding letter from Toscanelli, dated June 25, 1474, Toscanelli refers to the island of Antilia in a set of sailing directions he outlined for a proposed western route to the spice islands: *"desde la isla de Antilia que ya conoceis y nombrais Sette-Citá, hasta la famosa isla de Cipango, hay diez espacios, que hacen 2,500 millas, o 225 leguas."* (from the island of Antilia which you know and you call Seven Cities, to the famous island of Cipango, there are 2,500 miles, or 225 leagues). When Cristóbal Colón heard about Toscanelli's letter to Martínez, he began a correspondence with Toscanelli as well, and the Italian geographer sent him a copy of a map he made earlier showing Antilia and the route he had proposed to the King of Portugal.

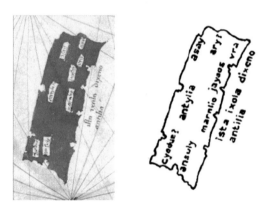

Above Left: Enlarged view of "Antylia" or "Antilia" island from the Pizzigano map. Above right: A black and white rendition of the original showing the seven towns on the island.

The Portuguese did not sail only to the Caribbean prior to Cristóbal Colón. They also were visiting the mainland of Canada as early as 1472, when the João vaz Côrte-Real expedition laid claim to a portion of it, naming the new land *"Terra dos Bacalhaus"* and later *"Terra dos Corte Reais."* This land is now known as Newfoundland and Labrador and is also the site of the Viking settlement of L'Anse aux Meadows, whose founding dates to 1000 A. D.

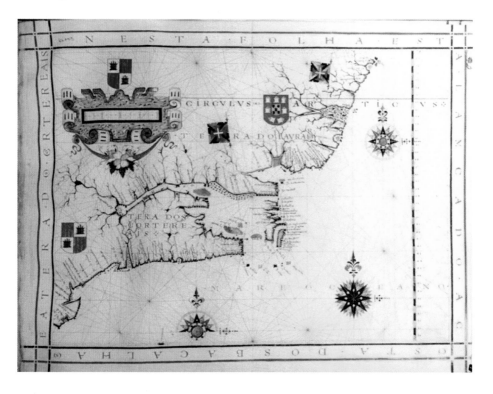

Above: The "Land of Corte Reais," or Newfoundland and Labrador, was discovered and named in 1472 by João vaz Côrte-Real.

After Cristóbal Colón's first voyage to the New World in 1492 was made public in 1493, the rush to claim parts of the New World began in earnest. Official and unofficial exploratory expeditions were departing Spain and Portugal one right after the other. In 1493, the Pope ruled that all newly discovered land over the ocean should be divided between Spain and Portugal and then chose a meridian 370 degrees west of the Cape Verde Islands as the dividing line separating the Spanish territories from the Portuguese territories. In 1494, the line of demarcation was moved slightly westward, which allowed Portugal to claim Brazil when they discovered it six years later, in 1500. Any Portuguese trespass east of this line of demarcation (a line which set all of North America, México, and Central America firmly under the ownership of Spain) would be severely punished. By 1500, the Spaniard

Juan de la Cosa had mapped much of the east coast of North and South America as well as the Caribbean, showing these new lands Spain now claimed.

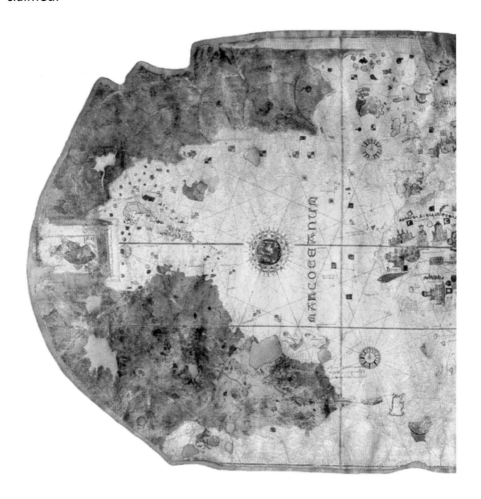

Above: The Juan de la Cosa map of 1500.

Consequently, all Portuguese voyages that were undertaken to these prohibited Spanish-owned areas were top secret. It must have been a very similar situation to when the US sent U-2 spy-plane flights over Russia during the Cold War. The US felt compelled to see what was going on in their enemy's camp and tried hard not to get caught doing it; the Portuguese were up to the same thing with the Spanish. Although they were somewhat successful at keeping their incursions secret from Spain, there remains solid evidence of these Portuguese intrusions into Spanish New World territory in the form of the official government-sponsored maps the explorers helped make for the Portuguese King once they returned from their secret voyages. One such map was drawn by a Portuguese mapmaker and smuggled out to Italy by the spy/diplomat Alberto Cantino in 1502. Cantino was working for the Italian Duke of Ferrara, who was trying to circumvent a loss of income from his spice trade that would result if Portugal or Spain found a route to the Spice Islands via a westward route.

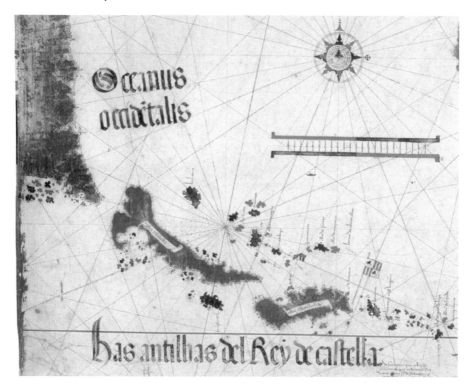

Above: Portion of a map drawn by a Portuguese mapmaker prior to 1502 and now known as the Cantino Planisphere, showing Yucatán, Cuba, and Hispaniola.

Sometime between 1504 and 1505, the Genoese cartographer Nicolo Caveri made another world map showing the Antilles, the north coast of South America, Honduras, Belize, and Yucatán. Today, this map (known as the *Planisferio de Caveri*) is kept in the Bibliothèque Nationale de France in Paris.

Above: The 1504-5 map drawn by Genoese mapmaker Nicolo Caveri (also known as Nicolo Canerio) showing the Portuguese discoveries on Yucatán and the north coast of South America.

Above: Part of the Universalis Cosmographia *drawn by Johann Ruysch, in 1507, 10 years before the Córdoba expedition.*

Johann Ruysch's map of 1507 is also very interesting. The map shows *Terranova* (Newfoundland) but none of the rest of North America except for Yucatán and the Antilles; since the portions of North America that lay between Newfoundland and the Gulf of Mexico were still unknown, Ruysch placed Yucatán and the Antilles (Hispaniola, Monserrat, Virgin Islands, and Dominica) directly south of Newfoundland. Over the portion of land that represented Yucatán, the mapmaker placed a scroll with the Latin text that reads *"The ships of King Ferdinand of Spain never reached here."* The name *Contil* appears on the map where *Conil* is actually located on the Yucatán coast.

Martin Waldseemüller was a German cartographer who published a world map in 1507 called *Universalis Cosmographia,* which was the first map to ever use the word "America." He also included the Antilles and the Yucatán Peninsula on the map. Yucatán had twenty different named locations labeled by Waldseemüller, one of them being "Rio de los Lagartos," a name the location is still known by today. This map pre-dates the Francisco Hernández de Córdoba expedition of 1517 by ten years.

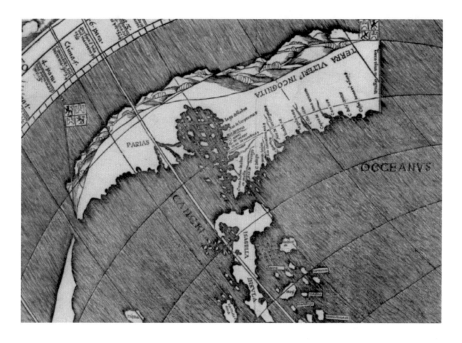

Above: The 1507 map by Martin Waldseemüller.

Above: A close up of the part of Waldseemüller's map showing Yucatán, rotated 180 degrees from the original. Rio de los Lagartos is also shown and labeled on the coast of Yucatán.

But the Portuguese were not the only ones to visit Yucatán before Córdoba and Grijalva. Andrés de Morales, who accompanied Cristóbal Colón on his third voyage and took part in the expedition of Juan de la Cosa and Rodrigo de Bastidas to the coast of the New World in 1500, drew a map of the Caribbean in 1509. It was printed by Peter Martyr in April, 1511, and was included in the first edition of his work, <u>De Orbe Novo Decades</u>. The legend on the northern part of the Yucatán peninsula reads *"Baya de lagartos"* (*Bahía de Lagartos*). Three small Islands (Contoy, Isla Mujeres and Cozumel?) are shown just off the coast nearest Cuba, more unidentified cays are drawn near Belize, and the Bay Islands of Honduras are shown and labeled *Guanaia* (Guanaja), just west of the Cape labeled *Gracias de Dios*.

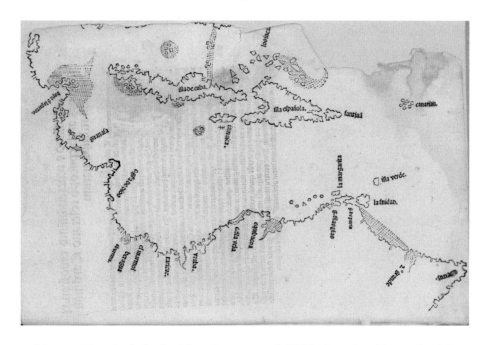

Above: The Andrés de Morales map of 1509 showing Yucatán, Isla Mujeres, Cozumel, the Cays of Belize, and the Bay Islands to the south.

There was also a well-documented expedition to Yucatán in 1508, when Vicente Yañez Pinzon (as captain of the 84-ton *San Benito* with Gonzalo Ruiz as the ship's Master) and Juan Díaz de Solis (as captain of the *Magdalena* with Pedro de Ledesma as the ship's Pilot) sailed from Spain to Yucatán in 1508 on their voyage of discovery. Ledesma had been on Cristóbal Colón's voyage to the Bay Islands of Honduras in 1502, so he was familiar with the coast of Honduras and with just how far north Colón had sailed on that trip. A Spanish royal decree was issued in March 23, 1508, granting Pinzon y Solis the rights *"sigais la navegación para descubrir aquel canal o mar abierto que principalmente is a buscar e que yo quiero que se busque"* (navigate to discover the strait or open sea that is your main goal to find and that I want you to find). By this, the King meant he wanted the expedition to find the strait or seaway that they believed would take them through the New World and into the China Sea and the Spice Islands, which was where the Europeans felt the real wealth lay for their taking. The King's edict went on to say:

"mandado van en dos carauelas Viceyntyañes Pinçon e Juan de Solis, nuestros pilotos, por capitanes dellas a descubrir a la parte del Norte."

(I have ordered Vicente Yañes Pinzon and Juan de Solis, our pilots, to go as captains in two caravels to discover the Northern part). That is to say, that they were mandated to search out the lands to the north of the areas discovered by Cristóbal Colón in his fourth voyage in 1502. With that authorization in hand, Pinzon and Solis sailed from Sanlúcar de Barrameda, Spain on June 29, 1508 and returned 14 months later, on August 29, 1509.

Another source of information regarding this voyage can be found in the court testimony of Pinzon at the trial of Solis. Pinzon stated: *"Yo y Solis fueron por mandato de su alteza y descubrieron toda la tierra que hasta ahora está descubierta luego hacia el Oriente en otra provincia de Camarona; yendo la costa luego hacia el oriente en otra provincia se llaman Chabanin, que descubrieron una gran bahía llamada Gran Bahía de Navidad. A estas provincias nunca el dicho Colón llego."* (I and Solis went by the order of Your Highness and we discovered all the land that up until now has been discovered, and then to the east to another province of Camarona; following the coast to the east to another province called Chabanin, where we discovered a great bay called Gran Bahía de Navidad. Colón never reached these provinces.)

Six other witnesses at the trial who had been on the voyage also testified that they had discovered the Yucatán Peninsula and then travelled as far as 23 ½ degrees, or the Tropic of Cancer (in other words, a little north of Tampico) before the leaders of the expedition decided to return to Spain, arriving back to the Iberian Peninsula in 1509. Indeed, the historian Fray Bernardino Sahagún, wrote in 1585 that the Indians of Pánuco remembered Solis and Pinzon's visit prior to that of Cortés.

Another text detailing the 1508 expedition is in Fernando Colón's book, *Historie del S.D.Fernando Colombo; nelle quali s'ha particolare & vera relatione della vita & de'fatti dell'Almiraglio D. Christoforo Colombo suo padre.* Fernando, the son of Cristóbal Colón, wrote in the book: *"que habían navegado hacia el Poniente, desde los Guanajes, y debieron llegar en paraje del Golfo Dulce, aunque no lo vieron porque estaba escondido, sino que vieron la entrada que hace la mar entre le tierra que contiene el Golfo Dulce y la de Yucatán, que es como una gran ensenada, o bahía grande... Así como vieron aquel rincón grande que hace la mar entre dos tierras, la una que está a la mano izquierda, teniendo las espaldas al Oriente, y está es la costa que contiene el puerto de Ceballos y adelante dél el Golfo Dulce y la otra de la mano derecha, que es la costa del reino de Yucatán, parescióles gran bahía... y por esto parece sin duda descubrieron entonces mucha parte del reino de Yucatán."* (that they had sailed to the West, from the *Guanajes*, and had come to rest in the *Golfo Dulce*, although they did not see it because it was hidden, but they looked at the entrance which the sea makes between the land that makes up the *Golfo Dulce* and the Yucatán, which is like a large cove, or large bay... And so they saw that big corner which the sea makes between the two lands, the one that is on the left hand, which backs to the East, and this is the coast containing the port of *Ceballos* and farther on the *Golfo Dulce* and the other on the right hand, which is the coast of the realm of Yucatán, which seemed to them great bay... and it seems without doubt that they then discovered the large part of the Kingdom of Yucatán.)

Bartolomé de las Casas in his *Historia de las indias*, wrote that Pinzon and Solis: *"Llegaron a la costa de Caray, y pasaron cerca del Cabo Gracias a Dios hasta la punta de Caxinas, que ellos llamaron de Honduras; y las dichas islas llamaron Guanajas, dando, como hemos dicho, el nombre de la principal a todas. De aquí pasaron mas adelante, y no quisieron confesar que el Almirante [Colón] hubiese estado en ninguna de dichas partes, para atribuirse ellos aquel descubrimiento y mostrar que habían encontrado un gran país."* (arrived at the coast of *Caray*, and passed near cape *Gracias a Dios* to *Caxinas* point, which they called Honduras; and these islands called *Guanajas*, giving them, as we have said, the name of the main one. From here they went farther on, and did not want to admit that the Admiral [Colón] had been in any of such parts, so that the discovery could be attributed to them and to show that they had found a great country.)

If this is true, you ask, why haven't you heard anything else about this before? Why aren't Pinzon and Solis listed as the discoverers in history books other than the books of Las Casas and Colón? Because something happened during the expedition that caused the two leaders to have a major falling out and by the time they got back to Spain, the argument had become an outright war between the two. Whatever the problem was about, it greatly displeased the King, who threw Solis in prison and issued a royal Spanish decree in November, 1512 taking away the rights of both Pinzon and Solis to the land they found north of Cristóbal Colón's earlier landfall in Honduras. The King then granted the privilege instead to Diego Colón.

Above left: Vicente Yañez Pinzon. Above right: Juan Díaz de Solis.

So, if Pinzon and Solis (and several others prior to their expedition) landed in México years before Francisco Hernández de Córdoba found it, should we really believe the oft-repeated story that the first Catholic Mass in México was said on Cozumel, on top of a Maya temple somewhere near Playa Las Casitas in 1518 by Juan Díaz, the chaplain on the Juan de Grijalva expedition? What is the source of that statement?

The one and only source that this story is based upon is what is purported to be the *itinerario* (route report) that Fray Juan Díaz wrote for the Governor of Cuba, Diego Velázquez. This report is supposed to have said: *"Thursday, the sixth day of the month of May... [we saw] a turret which had eighteen steps high, with a solid base, with a circumference of one hundred and eighty feet. On top of it there was a turret of the height of two men, one on top of another and inside it had some figures of bones and* cenise, *which are the idols they worshiped...shortly the tower was put in order and Mass was said."* The problem is, this report of Juan Diaz no longer exists and nobody but Grijalva, Díaz, Governor of Cuba Diego Velázquez and his cleric Benito Martín ever saw it before it was destroyed in 1519.

Here's what happened: Juan Díaz, was the chaplain on Juan de Grijalva's expedition that landed in Cozumel in 1518. Díaz wrote a report detailing the events that occurred during the expedition and gave it to Cuba's governor Diego Velázquez. Velázquez knew he had to pass the report on to the King of Spain, but he did not like the contents of the report for some reason. Whether it put the Governor in a bad light, or omitted mentioning things the expedition was supposed to have done (such as, officially claiming the new land for the King, or saying a Mass on their arrival), we will never know. To make it more to his liking, Velazquez had his minion, the cleric Benito Martín, <u>rewrite</u> the report, omitting the parts the Governor was unhappy with and adding others. After that, the original report by Juan Díaz was destroyed. Velázquez then ordered Martín to take his newly redacted copy of the report to Spain in May 1519 and present it to the King. When Martín got to Spain, a copy was made of the redacted report before it was given to the King and that copy was given to a translator. Using the new copy of the redacted version of Juan Diaz' original report, Martín had it translated into Italian, which is a good thing, because the Spanish copy of Martín's handwritten redacted report based on Juan Díaz' original report, as well as Martín's copy of his redacted report that he gave the King were subsequently lost and have never reappeared. A typesetter in Italy then used the Italian translation of the Spanish copy of Martín's redacted version of Juan Díaz' original report to set movable lead type and printed it in the appendix of a book in Italian. Thirteen years later, Gonzalo Fernández de Oviedo made a redacted and shortened version of the appendix of this Italian book and translated it back into Spanish. Later a typesetter set Oviedo's words into type and printed his book *Historia general y natural de las Indias*. Today, the closest thing we have to the original text of Juan Díaz' original report is the Italian book containing the Italian translation of the copy of Benito Martín's redacted copy of the original report, entitled *Itinerario de Ludovico de Varthema, Bolognese nello Egitto, nella Soria nella Arabia deserta y feliz, nella Persia, nella la India & nella Ethyopia* published in 1522. If you are reading the Spanish text provided by Oviedo, you are probably also reading a "modernized" and edited version of the old Spanish text of Oviedo's abstract of the Italian appendix. If you are reading an English version, you are at least eight generations and two languages away from the original.

But what about the report of Grijalva's landing on Cozumel written by Bernal Díaz del Castillo? True, Díaz was on that expedition when it came to the island and he <u>did</u> write about that experience in his manuscript, *Historia verdadera de la conquista de la Nueva-España*. However, Díaz did not finish writing his manuscript until 1568; fifty years after the events took place on Cozumel. He was 76 years old when he finished writing. His memory of specific events that happened half a century earlier when he was just 20 must have been somewhat blurry by then, but interestingly, Díaz makes <u>no mention</u> in his own book of <u>any</u> Mass being said on Cozumel, let alone where it was supposed to have taken place. He makes many detailed descriptions of what happened on Cozumel during his stay, but not one word about a Mass.

Antonio de Herrera's book, *Historia general de los hechos de los castellanos en las islas y tierra-firme de el mar occeano*, was published in 1601, eighty three years after the supposed Mass of Grijalva. The words he used to describe the event in his book were very brief and said nothing about a temple. Herrera simply wrote: *"Grijalva mando que se dijese misa."* (Grijalva ordered that a Mass be said.) It is assumed he got this bit of information from Oviedo's book.

Fray Diego López de Cogolludo copied parts of the manuscript of Bernal Díaz, almost word for word, around 1655 in his *Historia de Yucatán*, 137 years after the events took place. However, the only thing Cogolludo had to say about Grijalva ordering a Mass on Cozumel was: *"Aunque Herrera dice que se dijese misa, no hace mención de esto Bernal Díaz."* (Although Herrera says that a Mass was said, Bernal Díaz makes no mention of it.)

But even if Grijalva did order a Mass said on Cozumel, it could not have been the first Catholic Mass said in México. Francisco Hernández de Córdoba brought a priest named Alonso González along with him on his visit to Yucatán in 1517. The historian Antonio de Herrera y Tordesillas wrote in his *Historial General de los hechos de los castellanos de las islas, y terra-firme de el mar occeano,* that before leaving Cuba, Córdoba sailed from Santiago to San Cristobal de la Habana, *"...y rogaron a Alonso González, Clérigo que se embarcase con ellos por llevar algún sacerdote que les dijese Misa y administrarse los sacramentos."* (...and begged Alonso González, clergyman, to embark with them so they would have a priest to say Mass and administer the sacraments.) We also know that Father González said a Mass for the crew just before he set sail with them from Cuba. Bernal Díaz del Castillo confirms these two statements. Surely Padre González would have said at least <u>one</u> Mass during the several weeks the expedition was in México. As a matter of fact, in the old convent of San Francisco in Campeche there is plaque repeating the tradition that says that the first mass in México was said on that spot by González. Obviously, there is no way of knowing that this spot was where a Mass was said by González, but it stands to reason he would have said one somewhere on the Mexican mainland during his visit in 1517. However, even if Father González did not say a Mass in México, one would think Pinzon and Solis must have ordered one said during their visit in 1508. They were in México for several months, after all; they must have attended at least one Mass in all that time.

How Yucatán got its name

There are several different stories about how Yucatán got its name and each one has its own share of websites and books claiming that it is the one, true version. Some are clearly apocryphal and are often repeated simply because they make a good story. Others have their credibility bolstered by the fact they were cited in the early historical accounts that were written shortly after the Spanish first came to Yucatán. A few have a ring of logic, but have no historical mention. Some are based on erroneous etymological origins, which sound good at first, but do not stand up to close scrutiny.

One story of the origin of the name Yucatán is that the name is derived from the Nahuatl word *"Yokatlān,"* meaning "place of richness." The two words are markedly similar, but since Nahuatl is an Aztec language and the first Spanish to land in Yucatán only encountered Maya, the chance the Maya used an Aztec term to describe their homeland is highly improbable. It would be like a Frenchman going into a Texan BBQ joint and asking a likely looking Texan (in French) *"what do you call this meat?"* and the Texan replying (in Japanese) *"the best food there is."* The bullet that really puts a hole in this theory of *Yokatlān = Yucatán* is that there is no such word as *Yokatlān* in Nahuatl, according to the department of Nahua Language and Culture of the University of Zacatecas! It seems an author once tried to put two Nahua words together to make a compound word sounding like "Yucatán" in a book about the origins of place names, but one of the two words he chose *(yoka)* is not possible to pair with *"tlan"* in that language, nor does it mean "richness."

Another frequently heard version of where Yucatán got its name states that when Francisco Hernández de Córdoba first arrived in 1517 at Cabo Catoche, Yucatán, he asked the first Maya he encountered *"what do you call this place?"* The Maya was supposed to have responded with something that sounded like *"Yucatán,"* allegedly meaning *"I don't understand what you are saying."*

The first one to point out that Yucatán was not the correct name for the peninsula may have been Hernán Cortés, in his first letter to the Spanish Crown on July 10, 1519. In the letter, Cortés writes about his voyage to México earlier that same year and points out to the King and Queen that the name they know Yucatán by is not its real name. Cortés refers to Francisco Hernández de Córdoba's voyage to Yucatán two years earlier and wrote: *"al principio fue intitulado por nombre Cozumel, y después la nombranon Yucatán, sin ser lo uno ni lo otro..."* (at first it was called by the name of Cozumel, and later they named it Yucatán, without it being one or the other). Fray Toribio de Benavente (also known as Motolinia) tells his version of why the name was not actually Yucatán in his 1541 *Historia de los indios de la Nueva España*: *"...mas tal nombre no se hallará en todas estas tierras, sino que los españoles se engañaron cuando allí llegaron: porque hablando con aquellos indios de aquella costa, a lo que los españoles preguntaban los indios respondían: 'Tectelán, tectelán', que quiere decir, 'No te entiendo, no te entiendo', los cristianos corrompieron el vocablo y no entendiendo lo que los indios decían, dijeron; 'Yucatán, se llama esta tierra'."* (further, that name was never found in all of these lands, but the Spaniards were fooled when they arrived, because speaking with those Indians of that coast, the Spaniards asked and the Indians responded: *'Tectelán, Tectelán,'* which means to say 'I don't understand, I don't understand,' the Christians corrupted the word and didn't understand what the Indians said, and they said *'Yucatan* is what they call this land.')

Francisco López de Gomara, in his 1552 work *Primera y segunda parte de la historia general de las Indias con todo el descubrimiento, y cosas notables que han acaecido donde que se ganaron hasta el año de 1551, con la conquista de México, y de la Nueva España,* repeats this version: *"preguntados cómo se llamaba un gran pueblo allí cerca, dijeron tectetan, tectetan, que vale por no te entiendo. Pensaron los españoles que llamaba así, y, corrompiendo el vocablo, llamaron siempre Yucatán, y nunca se le caerá tal nombre."*

This version, where the Maya reply with ""*I don't understand*" and the misunderstood phrase becoming the peninsula's name for all time, makes a fun story, but there is no clear 16th century Yucatec Mayan cognate which matches the phonology of "Yucatán." *"T'an"* and *"t'aan"* are root words in Mayan meaning "language," "speech," or "words," but *"Yuca t'an"* is Mayan gibberish.

It has also been suggested in certain books and websites that Yucatán is a derivation of the Chontal Tabascan word *"yokatan,"* meaning "language," or "the region where the language is spoken." Again the notion seems tempting; *"yokatan"* is very similar sounding to "Yucatán." However, the Chontal word postulated here is actually written *"yokot'an"* and it does not mean language, but rather "speaker of *yoko ochoco,"* with *yoko ochoco* being the language of the Chontal Maya of Tabasco. But, why would the Yucatec Maya who Córdoba had encountered in 1517 reply with the Chontal *yoko ochoco* words meaning *"Chontal speaker"* when asked "what do you call this place?"

The Chontal Maya were well known to the Yucatec Maya and there had been substantial intercourse between the two groups over the centuries, so there would have been no way the Yucatec Maya would mistake the Spanish visitors for Chontal Maya. Given the fact the Yucatec Maya couldn't even understand Córdoba's question (phrased in Spanish as it was), this theory makes no sense.

Another often quoted version of the origin story comes from William Gate's 1937 English translation of Fray Diego de Landa's 1566 document *Relación de las cosas de Yucatán*. The English translation reads: *"When Francisco Hernández de Córdoba came to this country and landed at the point he called Cape Cotoch, he met certain Indian fisherfolk…. When he then by signs asked them how the land was theirs, they replied Ci uthan, meaning 'they say it,' and from that the Spaniards gave the name Yucatán. This was learned from one of the early conquerors, Blas Hernández, who came here with the admiral on the first occasion."*

The words the Spaniards were supposed to have misunderstood for "Yucatán" are actually spelled *"ci u than,"* Mayan for "they say that." The problem with this story is, it presupposes the Maya could understand the rather abstract question put to them in Spanish of "How is this your land?" when they supposedly replied "so say they." Try asking someone who only speaks Chinese this question in Greek and see how far you get.

Another origin story points to an early use of the word "Yucatán" in the Mayan manuscript called the *Chilam Balam de Chumayel*. This is one of 13 known versions of the *Chilam Balam*, which were 18th century manuscripts written in Mayan using the Latin alphabet. In the text of the Chumayel version, there is a line that reads *"uay ti luum Yucal Peten, Yucatán tu than maya ah Itzaob lae"* ("here in the land Yucal Peten, Yucatán in the Mayan language of the Itzas"). That seems pretty definitive, until you realize the text was written down at least 200 years after the place was first called Yucatán by the Spaniards, a name which by that time was used by everyone, including the Yucatec Maya.

A similar problem is encountered when one tries to pin down the origin of the name Yucatán to the 1506 report Bartolomé Colón (Cristóbal

Colón's brother) wrote regarding Colón's fourth voyage to the New world in 1502. As participant in this expedition, Bartolomé's eyewitness account should be deemed fairly reliable. The translation of the report that is most often quoted as the first use of the word Yucatán is: *"In this place they seized a canoe of theirs loaded with merchandise and wares which they say comes from a certain province called* Maia *or* Yuncatan..." Unfortunately, the line in the original Italian manuscript (located in the National Library of Florence, Italy) actually reads *"In questo loco pigliorono una Nave loro carica di mercantia et merce la quale dicevono veniva da una cierta provintia chiamata Maiam vel Iuncatam..."* The word often transcribed as "Yuncatan" or "Yucatán" is actually written in the manuscript as *"Iuncatam."* Not only that, but the real nail in this story's coffin is that this word *"Iuncatam"* is superscribed over the word *"Maiam"* in a later, differently colored ink in order to correct and update the report by changing the word *"Maiam"* in the original manuscript to a term more closely approximating the name "Yucatán" that was in common use when the correction was made.

Many historians have tried to read the word "Maya" into the word *"Maiam"* that was written in the original of this Italian report. However, it most likely refers to the people from the area on the Honduran mainland called "Maia" by Pedro de Ledesma, the pilot of the *Vizcaino* and an eyewitness to the event. In the *Probanzas* of Diego Colón, Ledesma testified that *"doze leguas ántes que fallasen la tierra firme, fallaron vna ysla en la mar que se dize Guanasa en lengua de indios la qual puso el Almirante la isla de Pinos e saltaron en ella en tierra é platicaron con un señor que se decía Yunbe e que de allí travesaron fasya la tierra firme que se dize tierra de Maia en lengua de yndios, e que de ahí corrieron la costa adelante en el leueste fasta hasta vn cabo que el le puso por nombre el dicho Christoual el cabo de Gracias á Dios."* (twelve leagues before the mainland they found an island that the Indians called Guanasa in the language of the Indians which the Admiral named Isla de Pinos and they landed there on it on land and talked with a man who they called Yunbe and from here they crossed over toward the mainland which is called the land of Maia in the language of the Indians and from here to the coast ahead as far as a cape which the Admiral called Gracias a Dios.) Peter Martyr, in his book

De Orbe Novo, says of the Atlantic coast of Honduras: *"This vast region is divided into two parts, one called Taia and the other called Maia."*

The last contender for the origin of the name "Yucatán" is found in the account written by Bernal Díaz de Castillo, the soldier who had traveled widely in the new world on several expeditions before arriving at Cabo Catoche with Córdoba in 1517. Díaz always recorded his first hand accounts better and with less fanciful additions to the narrative than the other historians of the day. He wrote in his account, *La Historia Verdadera de la Conquista de la Nueva España*, that when Córdoba and his group began to try to speak with the first Maya they encountered, there was a lot of confusion and misinterpretation. Díaz, who was present at the time the two groups were trying to communicate with one another, later wrote that through signs and pantomime the Spaniards tried to get information from the Maya, such as "was there gold to be found nearby?" and "were there gold mines in this country?" The Maya, Díaz wrote, answered with signs in the affirmative, but began to show the Spaniards how to plant in the ground. This, one assumes, was through a misinterpretation of the pantomime of mining for that of planting. The Spaniards, Díaz wrote, quickly understood that the Maya were indicating how to plant crops in a field, rather than the act of mining gold, so they asked if the Maya had manioc, or *yuca*, as the tuber was called in Cuba by the Caribe Indians who used it to make cassava bread. Since the Spaniards were in need of fresh provisions and this was the type of bread they were accustomed to eating in Cuba where they had been living for the past ten years, the question makes sense. Díaz wrote that the Spaniards kept repeating the word *yuca* as they pantomimed and the Maya kept saying the world *tlatli*, or earth, as they pantomimed planting. Díaz wrote that one Spaniard in the group, Blas Hernández, must have remembered the two words *yuca* and *tlatli* and then fused them together into the word *Yucatán* by mistake. When the expedition returned to Cuba, Díaz said Hernández was the person responsible for telling Governor Velázquez that the Indians they encountered on their expedition with Córdoba called their land *Yucatán*. Governor Velázquez, in turn, reported this exotic name "Yucatán" in his account to the King and Queen of Spain, resulting in the name catching on and becoming irrevocably tied to the peninsula.

But, once again, there is the problem of a Nahuatl word *(tlatli,* or "land") being used by a Maya to describe something to a Spaniard who only speaks Spanish. How could that be? I believe in this case it was by Díaz misremembering the word he heard that the Maya were saying to indicate "dirt" or "earth." Díaz was only in Yucatán for a few weeks, all told, but he was later to travel with Hernán Cortés on the conquistador's famous expedition and war against the Aztecs two years later. By the time Díaz got around to writing his *Historia Verdadera*, he must have been at least partially fluent in Nahuatl, judging by the many definitions of Nahuatl words contained in his book. It is easy to mistake an unfamiliar foreign word for one you are familiar with and I believe this is why Díaz later recalled the word he heard as *"tlatli"* instead of whatever word the Maya were actually saying.

Regardless of however the name "Yucatán" came to be, Córdoba himself never used it to refer to the peninsula. When he first landed and encountered the Yucatec Maya, he had a scribe write out a *Requerimiento,* or document which formally claimed the land for the Spanish Crown, and gave the peninsula the official name of "Santa María de los Remedios." The *Requerimiento* was read out to the assembled Maya and then witnessed and signed by the scribe. The Yucatec Maya, however, continued to call their land *"u luumil cutz yetel ceh,"* or "land of turkeys and deer."

How Cozumel got its name

Almost every story of how Cozumel got its name agrees that it was based on some sort of combination of the Mayan word *cuzam* for swallow and the Mayan suffix *luumil,* meaning "land of." Sometimes they also add the Mayan word *peten,* or island, to this combination. That may be correct; then again, maybe not. People have been trying for over one hundred years to make that theory fit, but there could be another root for the name Cozumel.

The 19th century Mayanist, Juan Pío Pérez Bermón, was probably the first one who tried to paste together those three words he found in the *Calepino de Motul* to come up with an equivalent of "Cozumel Island."

His manuscript (which he wrote in the first half of the 1800s) was later finished by others and published as the *Diccionario de la Lengua Maya* in 1877. The finished work says: *"golondrina, en la acepción de cuzam ó cuzmin. así la isla de cozumel, tiene este nombre que significa lo mismo que 'isla de golondrinas': u peten cuzam, y que desde la conquista degeneró por un vicio de pronunciación en cozumel; debe ser cuzamil como decían los indios, derivándolo de cuzam."* (Swallow, in the sense of cuzam *or* cuzmin. *Also the island of Cozumel has this name that means the same as 'island of swallows:'* u peten cuzam, *and since the conquest degenerated by poor pronunciation to* cozumel; *it should be* cuzamil, *as the Indians say, deriving it from* cuzam.*"*

However, Juan Pío Pérez Bermón's source for this tidbit, the *Calepino de Motul,* (otherwise known as the "Motul Mayan-Spanish Dictionary") written in the years between 1580 and 1610 by Fray Antonio de Ciudad Real, actually does not say that. What happened was that Pérez simply took three different entries from three different pages of the Motul dictionary and stuck them together to invent his Mayan equivalent of "Cozumel Island." In the *calepinio,* Ciudad Real defines *"peten"* as *"ysla o prouincia o region o comarca"* (island, or province or region or district), *"ah cuzam"* as *"golondrina"* (swallow), and *"luumil,"* as "land or country where one is born."

The truth may be the name of the island was derived from the name of the god of Cozumel, *Teel Cuzam,* who Diego López de Cogolludo (in his 1688 book, *Historia de Yucatán*) says *"había tenido las espinillas como una golondrina"* (has shins like that of a swallow). In any event, the early sources in which the name of the island first appears are a varied lot and may not help much in determining the origin:

Coçumel in a Spanish royal decree dated 1518
Açuçamil in Francisco López de Gomara's 1552 Historia General de las Indias y conquista de México
Cuzmil in Fray Diego de Landa's circa 1566 *Relación de las cosas de Yucatán*
Cu Camil and *Cusamil* in Juan Josef Hoil's 1781 *Chilam Balam de Chumayel*

How Flemish almost became the official language of Cozumel

During the 1517 Córdoba expedition, the Spaniards captured two Maya near Cabo Catoche and later brought them back to Cuba to learn Spanish so they could act as interpreters on future voyages to the peninsula. These two Maya lived in Cuba for a year and as they learned the language, they began to tell the Spanish about the lands from which they were taken. One of the things they explained to the Spanish was that the most important place (in their way of thinking) in the land of the Maya was the Island of Cozumel.

The Spanish King Ferdinand died only a year earlier, in 1516, and after a brief interlude the 16-year-old Flemish Archduke Charles was crowned Charles I, King of Spain. It is clear that this report made by the Maya interpreters reached the ears of King Charles, as Cozumel was explicitly named *(Ysla de Coçumel)* in a royal decree dated March 29, 1518, a full month before Juan de Grijalva's April 1518 voyage that resulted in the actual <u>recorded</u> discovery of the island of Cozumel. Due to the interpreters' description of the island as being the most important place in Yucatán, Grijalva made it his first landfall and claimed Cozumel for the Spanish Crown.

But, though Charles was King of Spain and all her colonies, he was also Flemish and ruler of the "Seventeen Provinces," an assortment of principalities and enclaves that today makes up Netherlands, Belgium, Luxembourg, a good part of the North of France, and a small part of Western Germany. His loyalties were with his kinsmen, not with the Spanish Court. One such kinsman, Laurent de Gorrevod, Charles' Flemish cousin and later his *majordomo mayor*, had gained Charles' confidence as a loyal advisor. As a token of his esteem, the young King granted Laurent de Gorrevod the rights in the royal decree to *"rule Cuba for the rest of your life"* and to *"conquer the Island of Cozumel so that you can rule it and possess it now and forever, and pass it down to your descendants."* On April 1, 1518, Charles sent a letter to the current Governor of Cuba, Diego Velázquez, ordering him to send no more ships to Yucatán and Cozumel as he was reserving the land for Gorrevod.

It was Gorrevod's plan to use Flemish soldiers to conquer the island and then settle it with more Flemish-speaking colonists from his homeland of Flanders. There were two things standing in his way. One was a lawsuit Cristóbal Colón's family had pending against the Spanish Crown, which they filed after the monarchy had taken away Colón's rights to rule all the lands he found on the voyages of discovery, originally granted to him on April 30, 1492. The lawsuit brought up the good point that it was illegal for the Crown to revoke a hereditary right, such as the one granted to Colón. The other impediment to Gorrevod getting his hands on Cuba, Cozumel, and Yucatán was that Spanish law did not allow foreigners to rule Spanish land, and Gorrevod was Flemish, not Spanish.

After a failed attempt to circumvent the law, Gorrevod agreed to exchange his newly granted right to rule Cuba, Yucatán and Cozumel for the royal license to ship 4,000 black slaves to Cuba and sell them to the colonists there. Thus, Cozumel avoided the fate of becoming a Flemish-speaking colony of Belgium.

However, Belgium never lost its lust for Cozumel. In 1840, Baron Félix de Norman was sent by the Belgian government to México to feel out the possibilities of purchasing the island from the Mexican government. México was very hard up for funds at the time and seriously considered the idea. In 1841, they responded with a demand of six fully-equipped warships (two brigs, two small steamboats, and two gun-boats) and 500 rifles in exchange for the island. The British government, however, was opposed to the idea of a Belgian controlled port in the Caribbean and sent its minister, Richard Pakenham, to do his best to wreck the deal, which he was eventually able to do. The idea was resurrected by Belgium in 1843, when Martial Cloquet prepared to lead an expedition to Cozumel with the aim of surveying the island, but Belgium's efforts were again derailed, and the attempt to acquire the island were abandoned.

CHAPTER 4

Re-examining the Gonzalo Guerrero story

After Cristóbal Colón returned to Spain at the end of his fourth voyage, he was a broken and dishonored man. In the Spanish Crown's eyes, he had failed miserably to find a way to Cathay, to establish any viable colonies in the newly discovered lands, or even to find any sources of the small amounts of gold he brought back to Spain. To add insult to injury, when he lost all four of his ships on his last voyage to the wood boring *teredo* worms, he had to pay for a ride back to Spain from Cuba on another ship. The Spanish King stripped Colón of his rights to govern the lands he had discovered during his four voyages and gave that authority to several other people in the Admiral's stead. Two of these new governors were Alonso de Hojeda and Diego de Nicuesa.

Diego de Nicuesa had traveled with Colón on his second and third voyages and had come to know many of the islands in the Caribbean, but he had not been with Colón when the old explorer had discovered the coast of Panamá on his last voyage. It may have been a surprise to Nicuesa then, when in 1508, King Ferdinand awarded him with the right to govern a land he had never seen. At the same time that Nicuesa was given his new fiefdom, King Ferdinand also gave Alonso de Hojeda the right to govern a contiguous part of the Panamanian and Colombian coast farther to the east. The two men began recruiting colonists, soldiers, and seamen (some of whom also had been on some of Colón's previous voyages) to make the journey to the new lands. Once fully staffed, they agreed to have their fleets meet up in the Bay of Cartagena, Colombia, and go their separate ways from there. Nicuesa's fleet of twelve ships left shortly after Hojeda's in 1509 with seven hundred and eighty-five men and one pregnant mare.

When Nicuesa met up with Hojeda's fleet in the Colombian bay several weeks later, he found the other governor's men licking their wounds from a fierce battle they just lost with the local Indians. It seems that upon his arrival at the bay, Hojeda sent a group of his men ashore to reprovision with fresh water and game, when they were attacked. The Indians peppered the Spaniards with poison darts shot from blowguns and over a hundred of Hojeda's men died from the festering wounds these darts caused, including Juan de la Cosa, the pilot and map maker who helped guide Colón's fleets on earlier voyages. Now reinforced by Nicuesa's contingent, Hojeda plotted his revenge and the next morning they launched a surprise attack on the Indian village, killing all the men, women, and children except for seven young adolescents he spared to use as interpreters.

Having done what he considered more than his fair share to help out Hojeda, Nicuesa took his fleet westward towards the coast of Panamá to find and settle the lands that he had been given by the King. His fleet was comprised of large and small vessels; some of them big, lumbering *naos*, or cargo ships, a couple of *bergantines* that had two rows of oars as well as sails, and two of the faster, shallow-draft ships called *caravelas*. Impatient to set sight on his new lands, Nicuesa divided his fleet into two parts; he would go ahead in one of the fast *caravelas* accompanied by two *bergantines,* while the rest of the fleet would meet them on the Veraguas coast as soon as the slower *naos* could make it. This decision proved to be a disastrous one, since almost all of the men who had visited the Veraguas coast previously with Colón were on the trailing ships and not aboard the *caravela* with Nicuesa to give him the benefit of their experience and advice.

Nicuesa and his three ships sailed westward for a few days, until one night near Isla Grande the two *bergantines* were separated from the faster *caravela.* In the morning, the lookouts saw no sign of Nicuesa and his flagship. The captains of the two *bergantines* talked the situation over and decided to turn back and reunite with the rest of the fleet. They sailed back to the mouth of the Chagres River, where they found the crews busy unloading the two *naos* of all their cargo and bringing it ashore. Just as Colón before them, the men had found the hulls of their ships were being eaten away by teredos and the ships were sinking beneath their feet. One of the captains of the two *bergantines,* Lopez de Olano, took control of the situation and had the men distribute the cargo between the ships that were still seaworthy and then abandoned the *naos* to sink at anchor. He then ordered the remaining ships to set sail for Rio Belén, where he intended to meet up with Nicuesa.

After several days of sailing, they spied Rio Belén. Standing offshore, Olano saw that the water over the sandbar in front of the river's mouth was very shallow. The sea was running high and huge waves were breaking at the entrance, making it too dangerous to try to sail the larger vessels into the protected bay that was just inside the bar. He ordered a longboat lowered and he and a small contingent of his crew rowed towards the bar to reconnoiter the bay. They didn't make it; the longboat turned turtle in the breakers and fourteen men were drowned. Olano and a few others managed to swim to shore safely, where they found themselves stranded without food. Sodden by a constant rain, the small group huddled under make-shift palm-frond shelters as they waited for four days for the seas to subside enough so that one of the other ships could send another longboat to pick them up. When the seas calmed, a group of colonists tried to enter the river mouth once more, this time with more success. They brought food to Olano and his stranded companions and set up stronger huts so they could shelter from the incessant rain. Unknown to them, this part of the Veraguas coast gets more precipitation per year than any other part of the western hemisphere, sometimes measuring over ten feet of rain a year.

After finally getting something to eat and resting a few days in the muddy, dripping lean-tos, Olano and the others hunkered down to wait for Nicuesa. Three weeks later, they came to the conclusion that his ship must have sunk and he wasn't coming back. As the highest ranking member left in the fleet, Olano assumed Nicuesa's position as governor. One of his first official acts was to direct that a portion of the colonists would stay and continue to improve the settlement at Belén, while he took the ships and a few other colonists over to neighboring Rio Veraguas to look for signs of gold. The colonists who were left behind soon found their food supplies had become wet and were starting to spoil and before long they were as hungry as Olano had been. To add to their discomfort, hordes of mosquitoes drove the Belén colonists wild, keeping them from sleeping at night while small, biting, black flies pestered them during the day. The nearly one-hundred-percent humidity facilitated the rampant spread of skin fungi and the constant rain kept any cut or scrape wet and open to infection. Soon colonists were dying not only of hunger and exhaustion, but septicemia. At low tide, the living would drag the dead out to the beach and bury them in shallow sandy graves, being too exhausted to clear trees to make a proper cemetery. One night, a huge storm blew up and the pounding waves began to erode away the beach where the bodies had been buried. The putrid corpses of the shallowly interred Spaniards began to wash out to sea. Little by little, the water's edge crept closer and closer to the colonists' flimsy huts, until at last the shelters had to be abandoned to the sea as it ate away the sand beneath them. The men retreated back into the jungle, and huddled together in misery until the morning light, when they could rebuild their camp farther away from the crashing waves.

Olano, in the meantime, was not having a much better time of it. He made it to Rio Veraguas, where he pitched camp and began sending small scouting parties up into the hills to look for signs of gold. Every day the recon parties slogged through the swamps, streams, rivers, and over the hills covered with dense rainforest vegetation looking for indications that gold could be found there, but even when the men saw signs of the precious metal, they told Olano they hadn't. They wanted to get away from this godforsaken coast and sail back to Hispaniola, where they knew other Spaniards had established a thriving colony, and they believed that if they told their leader about the signs of gold, he would want to stay and make a permanent settlement. After weeks of hearing discouraging reports from his scouts, Olano decided to give it up, and believing there was no gold to be found, loaded everyone aboard and weighed anchors for Belén, unknowingly leaving behind one of the richest gold-producing areas in Panamá.

He arrived back in Belén just in time. The surviving colonists had finished off the last of their rotten rations a week earlier, and had just eaten the foal that Olano's mare had given birth to, as well as its afterbirth. The meager food supplies that Olano had aboard would now need to be divided amongst the larger combined group and each man's daily ration would be miniscule. One preserved olive each morning and evening and half a dried biscuit every other day was augmented by lizards, snails and worms that the men scavenged around camp.

Nicuesa, it turned out, had not shipwrecked; at least not right away. After he was separated from Olano's two ships, he had sailed right by the mouths of both the Belén and Veraguas Rivers and was well on his way to the coast of present day Costa Rica before one of the sailors aboard told him he had sailed too far westward and needed to turn around. Nicuesa, a man known for his abundant pride and inability to admit mistakes, didn't take this advice kindly. He chose to ignore the sailor and ordered the *caravela* to keep sailing westward. Spying a large river he took to be Rio Belén, Nicuesa sailed his ship into it and anchored a little way into its mouth. He didn't realize that the river was not normally that wide, but was only temporarily swollen from the heavy rains the night before. He and the crew were shocked when they felt the bottom of their ship knocking on the river bottom that night as the level of the river receded. Before they could haul up the anchor, the *caravela* grounded and began to heel over. A crewman grabbed a line and tried to swim to shore where he could tie off to a tree and the men on board could haul the ship back upright before the water poured into their hold and sank them, but he was swept away by the current. A second seaman managed to make it ashore with the line, and tying it off, found that it was too late; the ship was on its side and filling up with water. Nicuesa and the rest of the crew pulled themselves hand-over-hand along the rope to safety, just as the timbers of the ship began to crack apart and the whole thing was washed out to sea by the river's strong current.

The next morning found the men wet, nearly naked, and bereft of provisions. The only bright spot was that they found their longboat washed up on the beach, its oars still tied down inside. The shipwrecked men stayed at the river mouth for some time, hoping that the trailing ships would pass by and rescue them, but days and then weeks passed with no sign of sails on the horizon. Eventually, Nicuesa realized the other ships weren't coming and if they wanted to reunite with the rest of his men, they would have to do it themselves. He assembled the men and began to march them westward toward where he thought Veraguas lay. He had four men board the longboat and follow their fellow colonists' slow, painful progress on land by rowing along with them a few hundred meters off shore. When the weary group walking along the beach came to a river or bay too deep to ford, the longboat ferried the men across so they could continue their march ever westward. Most of Nicuesa's men were now barefoot, and all were starving. Over the weeks, the hostile environment began to take its toll and the men began to die from the lack of food and the onerous marching conditions.

More than a month into their trek, the group came to a large body of water, too deep and wide to wade, and after being ferried across it by the longboat, they discovered it wasn't the other side of the river or bay at all; they had crossed over to an island. It happened that the sailor who had warned Nicuesa earlier that he had passed Veraguas was one of the four men assigned to row the boat, and when he saw what had happened, he knew that this was his chance. Now that Nicuesa and his group were isolated on the island, the sailor convinced his other three companions that they should leave them there and go for help. He knew that they had been rowing in the wrong direction for weeks, away from Veraguas and any chance of meeting up with the rest of the fleet. If they wanted to survive, they needed to turn the longboat around and row back eastward to meet up with their companions, who he believed had already reached Veraguas and were probably waiting there, as ordered, for Nicuesa to show up. If they could make it back to Veraguas, the sailor reasoned, they could get help to come back with a ship and retrieve the rest of their colleagues on the island. And so, in full view of the astonished and furious Nicuesa, the men in little longboat reversed their course and began rowing back from the direction they had come and eventually disappeared from sight, leaving their fellow colonists marooned. The four men rowed for all they were worth, and three months after they had first set out, nearly dead from overwork, lack of food, and exposure, they reached the mouth of the

Belén River. There, they encountered Olano and the rest of the colonists who had settled down and made camp months before.

Like Colón's fleet six years earlier, the hulls of the ships that Nicuesa's colonists had anchored offshore were slowly being eaten away by teredo worms. The leaks produced by the boring worms finally got so bad that all but two of their ships, a *caravela* and a *bergantín* they had managed to keep afloat with new planks they had cut in Belén, had both been scuttled and abandoned to the waves. It was in the little *caravela* that a small group of the colonists set out to find and rescue Nicuesa and his party from the island where the longboat crew left them stranded.

The *caravela* sailed westward and within the week found the remnants of Nicuesa's party, sick, starving, and on the verge of giving up any hope of survival. The rescue party shared with the emaciated men what little food they had and then brought them back to Belén, where Nicuesa's tattered group soon realized they were out of the kettle and into the fire. Of the seven hundred and eighty-five men that began the voyage of colonization, there were now only a couple of hundred left, and more were dying every day. Nicuesa re-assumed the reins of governorship and immediately ordered Olano to be arrested, accusing the man of not searching for him when he did not arrive in Belén and purposefully abandoning him so that he could become Governor. The men rebelled at this, saying that it was Olano who had saved Nicuesa; how could he be so ungrateful? Seeing he was greatly outnumbered, Nicuesa relented and let Olano keep his freedom, but remained convinced that all his problems were Olano's fault.

Next, Nicuesa organized the colonists into groups of thirty to forty and sent each party in different directions with orders to find any Indians living nearby, kill them, and bring back all the food they could find in the Indians' huts. The worn-out, weary men obeyed and went out on several raids, but the few Indians that could be found had no food to steal and were simply killed and left to rot. After days of not finding any food, some of the men returned to a spot where they left a dead Indian a few days before and consumed his putrefying body. They all died shortly thereafter from massive infections. Finally recognizing the desperate situation they were in, Nicuesa capitulated and allowed as many of his remaining colonists that could fit in the *bergantín* and the *caravela* to climb aboard, and they set sail back towards Colombia to try to find Alonso Hojeda's colony. The men who could not fit aboard the ships were left to fend for themselves at Belén.

The two ships sailed eastward for days, eventually reaching a safe-looking bay where they disembarked and made camp. They named the bay *Nombre de Dios*. Of the 785 men that had started on the expedition, now there were only 60 left alive. After building a small palisade fort, Nicuesa sent the *bergantín* back to Belén to retrieve the men and the mare that had been left there and then the camp at Rio Belén was abandoned. (As a side note, while working at Rio Belén with the Institute of Nautical Archaeology in 1988, I found one of Nicuesa's mare's two bronze stirrups. It is now on display at the Panamanian National Museum of History.)

During the time Nicuesa had been traipsing up and down the coast, Hojeda had been up to his neck in his own problems. He had attempted to settle on the part of the north coast of South America that was assigned to him by the King, but the constant attacks by the Indians surrounding his camp was taking its toll. When a ship captained by Hojeda's friend, Fernández de Enciso, arrived from Spain carrying fresh supplies (as well as a stow-away named Vasco Núñez de Balboa), Enciso and Hojeda talked it over and decided to move the camp to the other side of the Gulf of Uruba, where there were fewer Indians. This new location was part of the territory that the King had awarded to Nicuesa, but they didn't care. It was more important to get farther away from the hostile Indians than to be picky about borders.

After they set up the new camp, christened Santa María la Antigua, there was a new round of Indian attacks and Hojeda was shot in the leg with a poison arrow. Before returning to Santo Domingo to recover, Hojeda appointed his friend Enciso as provisional governor of the colony. Enciso, however, proved to be a harsh leader and after several weeks of abuse, the colonists rebelled and put Balboa in charge. Balboa turned out to be the first effective leader this rag-tag group ever had. Soon the colony was thriving and amassing large amounts of gold they panned from the nearby rivers.

When one of Nicuesa's ships that had been sent out by Nicuesa from Nombre de Dios to look for help finally arrived in Santa María, the ship's captain was upset to find Hojeda's colony had set up camp on land that was assigned to Nicuesa. Knowing that the best defense is a good offense, Balboa had already given orders to arrest Nicuesa on sight if he showed up, and when Nicuesa landed with the rest of his men on the second ship arriving from Nombre de Dios, he was slapped in chains, put back on the leaky *bergantín,* and sent off towards Hispaniola. The rest of the men were invited to stay and join Balboa's colony. That was the last anyone ever heard of Nicuesa and it is assumed the *bergantín* sank before it made Hispaniola.

By now the gold had piled up at the new colony in an amount that was enough to warrant sending the King his share, the *Quinto Real* or Royal Fifth. Balboa wrote a letter to the governor of Hispaniola, Diego Colón, requesting the gold he was sending be forwarded to the King in Spain. He also sent back a large group of Indian slaves they had captured and appended a long list of supplies he would like Colón to send the colony in return for them. He chose Juan de Valdivia to captain the ship carrying the gold, slaves, and letters. Valdivia, in turn, chose a hardy fellow who was one of the sixty survivors of the Nicuesa expedition to go along on the voyage. That man was later to become known as Gonzalo Guerrero.

Unfortunately, the ship carrying Valdivia and his crew never made it to Hispaniola. It hit a reef during a storm just south of Jamaica and sank, with all but twenty of the Spaniards drowning during the wrecking event. While these twenty survivors drifted in a salvaged longboat, eight more died of dehydration. Their bodies were eaten by their fellow crewmembers. The remaining twelve of the shipwreck survivors came to shore two weeks later on the Quintana Roo coast, where they were found and taken captive by the Maya. There, five of the Spaniards, including Valdivia, were sacrificed to the gods, after which their bodies were roasted and eaten. Seeing their fate, the seven remaining Spaniards managed to escape, including "Gonzalo" and a deacon named Jerónimo de Aguilar. Their freedom did not last long, however, and they were taken captive once more, this time by a different group of Maya. The seven were taken to Xamanzamá (present day Tancah) a village located just to the north of Tulum. One by one the Spaniards began to die from overwork and abuse. After a couple of years, only "Gonzalo" and Jerónimo were left alive.

Up to this point in our story, the facts are ironclad and supported by the testimony of eyewitnesses recorded in early documents; there is no doubt about the events that led to the Spaniards being shipwrecked on Yucatán's coast. However, from the point the last two survivors were separated, the "history" that has been handed down to us has been so adulterated with embellishments and flights of fantasy, that it is nearly impossible to distinguish the truth from wishful thinking and outright propaganda put forth by writers with an agenda that is clearly designed to put the survivor known as "Gonzalo Guerrero" in a positive light.

This effort to manipulate "Gonzalo Guerrero's" public image had its beginnings in an effort to portray his motives for staying behind with his family and ignoring Cortés' offer to be rescued in the account given by Gonzalo Fernández de Oviedo y Valdés in his 1535 book, *Historia General y Natural de las Indias, islas tierra firme y mar océano*. Oviedo pushed the idea that "Gonzalo" was a Spanish nobleman who stayed with his Maya family for the most altruistic of reasons; his love of his family. The myth grew from there, and over the centuries ripened to a legend that fit very nicely with Mexican President Luis Echeverría Álvarez and his populist program to rekindle ethnic pride, and its emphasis on *"Mexicanidad"* and *"Mestizaje."* This federally funded program funneled state monies to help disseminate this rehabilitated image of "Gonzalo Guerrero," subsidizing numerous statues, murals, revisionist novels, and questionable "investigations" that turned up the shipwreck-survivor's supposed "long lost" diaries as well as other works purportedly written during his lifetime.

One manifestation of this federal program to turn "Gonzalo" into a national hero is the statue of the shipwrecked-Spaniard standing with his wife and children on the *malecón* of Cozumel. This statue is one of several similar to the first one that Pablo Bush commissioned artist Rául Ayala Arellano to make in 1974 for the *Club de Deportes Aquaticos de México (CEDAM)* headquarters in Akumal. Other versions of this statue can be found in Mérida and Mexico City. It is a powerful image of the man who has become an icon of the blending of the Spanish and indigenous New World cultures, a process called *mestizaje* in Spanish. "Gonzalo" himself has become known as the *"Padre del Mestizaje."* But, for all the fame and honor heaped upon his shoulders, what do we know about the man?

The legend most people are familiar with is that after he was shipwrecked in Yucatán in 1511, he was enslaved by the Maya, along with fellow survivor Jerónimo de Aguilar. "Gonzalo" was supposed to have worked his way up from this lowly position to the second highest in the land, that of *nacom*, or war chief, second only to the *batab*, or high chief of the Maya town of Ichpaatún. And, as in all good fairytales, our hero supposedly married a Maya princess. The legend also says when Gonzalo was approached by fellow shipwreck survivor Jerónimo Aguilar with a letter that Hernán Cortés had sent from Cozumel in 1519, offering to rescue them, he refused the offer and chose instead to stay with his family and fight against his former countrymen. Later, he was supposedly killed by a Spaniard in a battle in Honduras.

But what is the truth? What are the sources for this incredible story?

First, it is important to know that the name "Gonzalo Guerrero" <u>never</u> appeared in any written document until Francisco López de Gomara published his *Primera parte de la Historia General de las Indias con todo el descubrimiento, y cosas notables que han acaecido donde que se ganaron hasta el año de 1551, con la conquista de México, y de la Nueva España*, (also known as *Historia General de las Indias y conquista de México*) in 1552. The first mention of the shipwreck survivors was in the orders from the Governor of Cuba that Hernán Cortés had with him when he set off on his expedition in 1519. When Julián and Melchor, the two Maya who Francisco Hernández de Córdoba had captured in 1517 were taken to Cuba in that year, they told the Spanish of the castaways' existence and that the men were being held by the Maya as slaves. Cortés was ordered by Cuban Governor Diego de Velázquez to sail by the coast of *"Yucatán Santa María de los Remedios where there were some Christians being held by caciques who Melchor knows."* The second mention of "Gonzalo" was likewise not by name, but by inference only, in a letter Hernán Cortés sent to Spain dated July 10, 1519. In the letter, Cortés seems to refute the much later story put forth by others that "Gonzalo" refused to be rescued and instead he says it simply was not convenient for the expedition to waste much time in a search for the shipwrecked sailor. The letter states, in part: *"By this Jerónimo de Aguilar we were informed that there were other Spaniards in that caravel that sank and that they were spread out far and wide across the land, which, he informed us, was very large and it was impossible for us to be able to gather them up without wasting a lot of time."*

Andrés de Tapia, the Spaniard who first talked to Aguilar on Cozumel in 1519, stated in his 1539 account of the meeting that the shipwreck survivor had told him *"otro español habie tomado por mujer a una señora india, e que a los demás los indios los habien muerto; e que él sintió del otro su compañero que no quería venir, por otras veces que le habie hablado, diciendo que tenía horadadas las narices y orejas, e pintado el rostro y las manos; e por esto no lo llamó cuando se vino."* (the other Spaniard had taken an Indian woman as a wife, and the Indians had killed all the other Spaniards; and he thought that other one, his companion, did not want to come because other times he had talked to him he said he had pierced his ears and nose and tattooed his face and hands, and for that reason he didn't ask him when they came.) Again, it seems that "Gonzalo" was never actually asked by Aguilar if he wanted to be rescued or not.

Cortés did not write again about "Gonzalo" until 1534, in an interrogatory he submitted during a court case. In the document, Cortés states he was told by Jerónimo de Aguilar *"que muchos de los naufragos habian muerto en la travesia y que ocho o nueve liegaron a Yucatan pero en tan malas condiciones que si los yndios no los remediaran, no escapara nenguno; e ansi murieron todos, ecebto dos"* (that many of the shipwrecked sailors who survived the wrecking event later died, and only eight or nine made it to Yucatán, but in very poor condition... and if it hadn't been for the Indians capturing them, they would have all died. Regardless, all except two died anyway.) These two survivors, Cortés wrote *"...eran Geronimo de Aguilar, el uno, y el otro, un Morales, el qual no abia querido venir, porque ternia ya oradadas las orexas, y estaba pintado como yndio, e casado con una yndia, y ternia hixos con ella."* (were one Jerónimo de Aguilar and the other one a **Morales**, who did not want to come because he had pierced his ears, was painted [tattooed] like an Indian, had married an Indian, and had children with her.) Francisco Cervantes de Salazar, a good friend and confidant of Cortés, also refers to the second shipwreck survivor as "*Fulano* [guy; fellow] *de Morales*" in his recounting of the tale in his *Crónica de la Nueva España,* published in 1558.

In 1536, a letter from the *Contador de Honduras-Higueras*, Andrés de Cerezada, tells of finding the body of a Spaniard who died on the battlefield in 1534 in the Uluá River valley, but he too gives the man a name other than Gonzalo Guerrero: *"the Spanish Christian, **Gonzalo Aroça**, who had been with the Indians in Yucatán twenty years now died by an arquebus shot."* The original of this letter says nothing of how the man was dressed or how his body looked; the description of a Spaniard *"almost naked, dressed like an Indian and tattooed"* came from an invented description that appeared in Robert Chamberlain's 1948 book, The Conquest and Colonization of Yucatán.

When Gonzalo Fernández Oviedo y Valdés published his *Historia general y natural de las Indias* in 1535, he avoided the thorny problem of Gonzalo's last name entirely, by simply calling him *"Gonzalo, a sailor."* Regardless, Oviedo decided to embellish the story by adding many details that had not been recorded previously by anyone else. It was in this book that the legend of "Gonzalo Guerrero" was born. He was a *"son of a Hidalgo,"* wrote Oviedo, and went on to say that Francisco Montejo the *Adelantado* had sent Gonzalo a letter in 1527, offering to make him the highest ranking Spaniard in Yucatán, if he would only leave the Indians and join the Spanish. Gonzalo was supposed to had replied by means of a note written on the back of the letter, which Oviedo quotes: *"Sir, I kiss you Excellency's hand, but as I am a slave, I am not free, even though I am married and have a wife and children, I believe in God and you and the Spanish can always count on my friendship."*

Using this embellished story of Oviedo's as a starting point, Francisco López de Gomara wrote about Gonzalo in his 1552 *Historia General de las Indias y conquista de Mexico,* adding many more details about the man and solidifying the mythological image of Gonzalo as a warrior. Gomara also attached the last name of **Guerrero** to him for the first time, eschewing either **Morales** or **Aroça**, the names he was identified by in earlier records (although Gomara also referred to him twice as Gonzalo **Herrero,** earlier in his writings). Gomara wrote (33 years after the fact) that *"Gonzalo **Herrero**, sailor, was with Nachanchán, the lord of Chectemal, and he married a rich lady of that town, and he had children, and he was the war captain of Nachanchán, and was held in high esteem for the victories he had during the wars with neighboring kingdoms."* Gómara also combined Tapia's description of Gonzalo with that of Cortés', adding that it was either for the shame of the way he now looked or the shame of being married to an Indian or the love of his children that he refused to rejoin the Spanish. In addition, many more elements were added to the story that had never appeared before, such as the entire, word-for-word text of the letter Cortés wrote to Aguilar, the idea that the letter was hidden in the hair of the messenger, and the word-for-word recital of the conversation between Aguilar and Andrés de Tapia in Cozumel. A very curious side note is that Gomara included a short mention of Aguilar's mother, who, he states, upon hearing her son had been captured by cannibals in Yucatán, went insane, and every time she saw roasted meat, she would exclaim *"That is my son!"*

Fray Diego de Landa added more details to the story in his 1566 manuscript *Relación de cosas de Yucatán*, and repeated Cortés and Tapia's statements that Aguilar was never able to go and see Gonzalo, as he was living too far away. He also repeated Oviedo's statement that Gonzalo was a war captain in Chectemal, married a woman there, had children, pierced his ears, and added the new bit that Gonzalo taught the Maya the Spanish style of warfare.

In the late 1560s, Bernal Díaz del Castillo wrote his *Historia Verdadera de la Conquista de la Nueva España,* in which he actually <u>quoted</u> (supposedly from memory, even though he wasn't present at the time) what Gonzalo was to have said to Aguilar in 1519, over 45 years earlier. The fabricated conversation reads: *"Brother Aguilar, I am married, I have three children, they have made me war captain in time of war; you go with God's blessing, I have my face tattooed and my ears pierced. What would they think of me if the Spanish saw me like this? And I have my beautiful children. For their sake, leave me theses green beads that you bring, and I will give them to my children, and tell them my brothers sent them from my land."* At this, Díaz del Castillo says Gonzalo's wife interrupted and sent Aguilar away. This story, copied from Díaz del Castillo's work, was repeated in Diego López de Cogolludo's 1688 book, *Historia de Yucatán.*

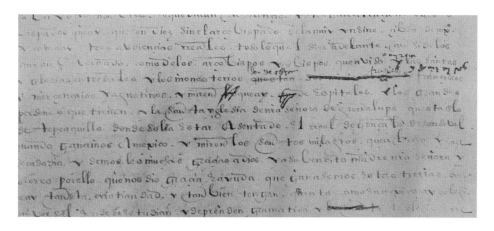

Above: A section of Bernal Díaz del Castillo's manuscript <u>Historia Verdadera de la Conquista de la Nueva España</u>.

Antonio de Solis y Ribadeneyra piled on more fabrication in his 1684 book *Historia de la conquista de México, población y progresos de la América septentrional, conocida por el nombre de Nueva España,* raising the number of Gonzalo's children to *"three or four,"* and attributing the real reason for him refusing to join Cortés was his love for his Indian wife.

In 1974, Mario Aguirre Rosas, a writer for the Mexico City newspaper *El Universal,* published what he described as Gonzalo Guerrero's diary, supposedly written on deerskin velum and sheets of 16th century European paper. However, no one except Aguirre was able to examine the original manuscript, which Aguirre said belonged to a private collector named José López Pérez who would let no one else see it. This purported autobiography of Gonzalo, parts of which Aguirre later published in his newspaper, was full of fabricated details, which have been repeated *ad nauseam* by uninformed, amateur historians who read the mendacious tale and believed it to be authentic. It is in this fairy-tale invented by Aguirre that the myth Gonzalo's wife was a princess named Zazil first started, as well as many other details about the man that are patently false. In 1975, two thousand copies of *Gonzalo de Guerrero: Padre del mestizaje iberoamericano* by Aguirre were printed in Mexico City by Editorial Jus. The book was simply a rehash of his newspaper articles about his spurious autobiographical document of Gonzalo Guerrero.

Much later, in 1994, a mysterious manuscript appeared in Mexico City that was claimed to be written by Fray San Buenaventura of Mérida in 1724, purportedly describing a manuscript in the priest's possession written partially on paper and partially on deerskin by none other than Gonzalo Guerrero, in which he tells the story of his life. The Buenaventura document has been discredited; an invention connected to Aguirre's work and made in order to deceive. It was written on paper of a later manufacture and containing many passages copied from earlier historical works, but it was published nevertheless in 1994 as *Historias de la conquista del Mayab, 1511-1697 de Fray Joseph de San Buenaventura* by the Universidad Autónoma de Yucatán.

So, just what do we know for certain about Gonzalo, the shipwrecked Spaniard? We know that he was in Panamá with Diego de Nicuesa and later with Nuñez de Balboa, when he was sent on a fateful voyage that ended abruptly off the shores of Jamaica, resulting in him being cast-away on the coast of Yucatán. We know that he lived the rest of his life with the Maya, married, had children, and acquired some kind of body modification as adornment. But, that is it; that is all we know for sure. All other details above and beyond these scant facts are fabrications. We do not even know his real name.

CHAPTER 5

Cozumel from 1518 to 1527

Juan de Grijalva

The conquistador turned author, Bernal Díaz de Castillo, tells in his book, *Historia Verdadera de la conquista de Nueva España*, that he went along on the Francisco Hernández de Córdoba expedition in 1517. Díaz also states that when the Cuban Governor, Diego Velázquez, sent his nephew, Juan de Grijalva, on a follow-up expedition to Yucatán in 1518, he was a member of that trip as well. The Grijalva expedition was comprised of somewhere between 170 and 300 men spread out over four ships, two of them captained by Pedro de Alvarado and Alonso Dávila, men who had been to Yucatán before with Córdoba. Another ship was captained by Francisco de Montejo. Grijalva, the expedition's leader, was in charge of the fourth. The pilot of the expedition was Antón de Alaminos, who had also sailed with Cristóbal Colón on his third and fourth voyages, with Ponce de Leon on his voyage of discovery of Florida in 1513, and with the Córdoba expedition in 1517. Juan Díaz was the expedition's chaplain. Julián and Melchor, the two Maya captured by Córdoba and taken back by him to Cuba, served as the expedition's interpreters.

The expedition left Cuba and arrived a few days later on the northeastern shore of Cozumel on May 3, 1518. Just how long they stayed on the island is in doubt. Díaz says they left on May 9, sailed to Bahía de la Ascensión, then returned to Cozumel on May 19 for water. Gonzalo Fernández de Oviedo y Valdés, in his 1535 *Historia general y natural de las Indias* says they left Cozumel on May 7, but then immediately returned for water. He then says they again departed Cozumel on May 11 and never returned. Reading both accounts one is tempted to favor that of Díaz over Oviedo, as the former was actually on the voyage and the latter was simply recording hearsay.

Upon sailing close to the northern tip of Cozumel, Grijalva named the island Santa Cruz, (as recorded by the expedition's *escribano*, Diego de Godoy) in honor of the Feast of the Finding of the Holy Cross, which is celebrated on May 3. Two canoes approached the ships and the Maya invited the Spaniards to come ashore the next morning, after they could notify their *Halach Uinik*. The ships then followed the eastern shore southward, rounded the southern tip of the island, and landed on the south-western shore, where they found Maya buildings and named the place "San Felipe y Santiago," after the two apostles whose holy days are celebrated together, on May 3 as well. The inhabitants of the village they found there fled at the sight of the expedition's approach, except for a couple of old men who were hiding in a cornfield. They gave the old men gifts and asked them to go tell the rest of the village that they meant no harm and it was safe to come out of the woods, but the men left with the gifts and did not return. Later, they were approached by a woman speaking Taino, a language many of the Spaniards were familiar. She told them she was from Jamaica and had been on a fishing trip with her husband and nine other men when their canoe was driven to Cozumel with the wind and currents. When they landed on the island, the Maya of Cozumel had sacrificed the ten men and made her a slave. The Spaniards sent this woman back into the woods to try to coax the Maya out, but she returned saying they still refused to come. Grijalva decided to take her along as another interpreter, so she boarded his ship and the Spaniards sailed northwards to the village of Xamancab (the site of today's San Miguel de Cozumel), arriving there on May 6. The *Halach Uinik* of Xamancab boarded Grijalva's ship and greeted them, assuring the Spaniards that they were welcome to come ashore. Grijalva named the town San Juan Ante Portam Latinam, or "Saint John before the Latin Gate," after the Apostle Saint John, whose holy day was celebrated on that day. The *Itinerario de Juan de Grijalva* (a document that is only a copy of an Italian translation of a redacted copy of a Spanish copy of the original) says that there they found a small pyramid with a temple on top containing ossuary idols and *cemís*. Atop the pyramid, the Maya priest recited a long incantation and burned copal in front of the idols before sitting down with the Spaniards and smoking some kind of herb with them. It was the first time the Spaniards had tried it, but they said they found it had a delicate aroma. The *Itinerario* also says that the Spaniards "put the temple in order" and held a Mass there. Later, they read a proclamation claiming the island for the King of Spain, exchanging gifts with the Indians afterwards. The Indians had prepared a meal for the occasion, so the Spaniards joined them in the home of the *Halach Unik* for the repast. During the Córdoba expedition, two of the wounded crew were captured by the Maya, so Grijalva took the opportunity to ask the *Halach Unik* if he had any news of the men. The Chief replied that one had died of his wounds, but the other still lived. What ever became of this fellow is not recorded. Curiously, the subject of the Valdivia shipwreck survivors never appeared to come up during the conversation between Grijalva and the chief, even though Melchor and the Chief were both well aware of their existence on the mainland.

Above: The name "St. John before the Latin Gate" and the holy day refers to the legend of the miraculous survival of the Apostle St. John, who it was said the Romans tried to boil in oil in front of a gate to the city of Rome.

After Grijalva left Cozumel, he traveled up the coast of Yucatán and Campeche, battling Indians along the way until he reached San Juan de Ulúa on June 24. There, he gathered his wounded soldiers together with what little gold they had managed to acquire and sent them back to Cuba in the ship under the command of Pedro de Alvarado. When Alvarado reached Cuba, he gave the Cuban Governor, Diego Velazquez, a highly unflattering report of Grijalva's leadership abilities, painting a picture of an inept incompetent. Velazquez began to worry that his fool nephew (or *"bobo,"* as he called him) was lost, so he dispatched Cristóbal de Olid in a single ship to go find Grijalva and bring him back. Olid sailed first to Cozumel and, not knowing that Grijalva had already been there, claimed it once more in the name of Spain before continuing on along the coast of Yucatán on his search for the overdue expedition. He never found them and returned to Cuba just a week before Grijalva did.

Hernán Cortés

The next group of Spaniards to land on Cozumel was the Cortés expedition, which left Cuba with Antón de Alaminos, the pilot who had guided both Córdoba and Grijalva on their previous trips to Yucatán. The expedition consisted of eleven vessels, of which only three were of any real size: Cortés' flagship was a 100-ton *nao*, or slow-moving cargo vessel; two of the others were eighty- and seventy-ton vessels and the rest were small, open, un-decked vessels and *bergantines*. They had 200 Cuban Indians as porters, a few black slaves, 16 horses, around 100 sailors and 508 other Spaniards who would make up the army. This group of fighters included 13 musketeers, 32 crossbowmen, and 5 artillerymen. They also had Melchor, one of the two Maya men captured by Córdoba the year earlier who acted as their interpreter. Cortés divided the group into eleven companies and placed a captain in charge of each one. One of the captains was Francisco de Montejo, who along with his son and nephew, were later to subdue the Yucatán Peninsula for Spain. Cristóbal de Olid, who had just returned from Cozumel and Alonso Dávila, who had been with both Córdoba and Grijalva, was another.

The expedition departed Cuba (according to Bernal Díaz del Castillo) on February 10, 1519 and the ten captains were instructed to keep Cortés' flagship in sight at all times, so that they could all arrive in Cozumel together. However, the group became separated from one another after the first night and they all reached Cozumel independently, (except for one, which was lost for several more days and never reached Cozumel) with Pedro de Alvarado's ship arriving first and Cortés arriving last, two days later. Díaz was aboard Alvarado's ship and he writes that when they got to "the town" (Xamancab) on Cozumel, it was deserted, so they sailed about a league to "another town" (Oycib) which they also found deserted. The Spaniards gathered up forty domesticated fowls there and took them back to the ship. Upon inspecting a temple in the town, they discovered ornaments, cloth, small chests containing diadems, idols, beads, and pendants made of poor quality gold, so they seized those as well. Díaz writes that when they found an Indian woman and two men hiding nearby, they captured them and took them aboard their ship and sailed back to the town (Xamancab) where they had first landed.

When Cortés finally landed, he immediately reprimanded Alvarado and made the men return all the belongings they stole, and then gave the captured Indian woman gifts to placate her. When Cortés' private chaplain, Francisco López de Gomara, retold this account in his 1552 *Historia General de las Indias y conquista de Mexico,* the captured Indian woman was the wife of the *Halach Uinik,* and the two other captives were her children. He goes on to say Cortés put her at ease and gave her a mirror and a pair of scissors and then gave some beads to her children. They then sent one of the male children back to go get his father and bring him to Xamancab.

The *Halach Uinik* returned to Xamancab with the rest of his people and met with the Spaniards as if nothing had ever happened. Gifts were exchanged and Cortés inquired about the Spanish shipwreck survivors that Melchor had told them about. The *Halach Uinik* explained that as far as he knew there were still two alive living as slaves on the mainland and that he could send a message to them, if Cortés wished. He also suggested sending a gift for their masters along with the message.

Cortés wrote a letter to the shipwrecked Spaniards, telling them he would send a boat for them, but it would only wait for eight days before returning to Cozumel. He then dispatched two ships to the mainland. One ship was to carry the two Maya who would deliver the letter and the gift of glass beads and then stay at anchor to wait for a response from the men they were trying to rescue. The other ship was to shuttle back and forth with any news.

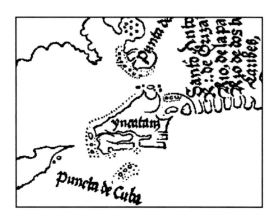

Above: A portion of the map Cortés drew of Yucatán in 1519.

When the Indians carrying the messages and beads found Jerónimo de Aguilar, he read the letter and then presented the beads to his Maya master, asking for and receiving his permission to go to Cozumel to rejoin his countrymen. Unfortunately, he did not make it back to the ships within the allotted eight days, so they returned to Cozumel without him. In Bernal Díaz' telling of this event, he says Aguilar walked five leagues (about 13 miles) south to confer with the other shipwreck survivor and that is why he did not get to the boat in time. This statement does not add up, because it would have been very easy to walk that short distance and back in the amount of time given. In actuality, the other survivor was in Chetumal, over 160 miles farther south. It is very unlikely that Aguilar would have attempted to walk over 320 miles round-trip and be back within the eight-day period given in the letter. More likely, it was just another embellishment of the story, just like the inclusion, word-for-word, of the conversation the two survivors had regarding their rejoining the Spaniards. That conversation was added to the story Díaz told for effect and did not actually happen.

During the time they were waiting for word from the two ships they had sent to the mainland for the survivors, Cortés and his men got to visit Xamancab. One morning, they happened to witness a Maya priest officiating at a ceremony atop one of the small pyramids and asked Melchor to interpret what the priest was saying. Upon hearing the translation of the Mayan "sermon," Cortés sent for the *Halach Uinik*. He then lectured the chief with a long-winded explanation of the wickedness of their ways and how the only true religion was the Catholic religion. To add emphasis to this statement, Cortés ordered his men to break up the idols in the temple atop the pyramid and that carpenters Alonzo Yáñez and Alvaro López erect a wooden cross in their place. After that was done, the chaplain Juan Díaz, who had visited Cozumel with Grijalva, said a Mass in the room at the top of the pyramid. Cortés also gave an image of the Virgin Mary to the Maya and told them to honor her. For the Maya, there was no problem at all with adding another god to their pantheon, so they agreed to revere this new god and his mother, bringing a couple of fowl for the Spaniards to offer up to these two new gods as a sacrifice. Cortés, however, understood these to be gifts, so he accepted them as such.

The expedition set sail again around the first of March, but did not get very far before the ship that was carrying most of their food supplies began taking on water. They quickly returned to the island and repaired the ship, which was a good thing for Aguilar, who managed to find a canoe, paddle across the channel, and rejoin his fellow Spaniards. After conversing with the *Halach Uinik* in Mayan, Aguilar asked Cortés to write a letter of recommendation for the fellow so that any future Spaniard visiting would know that he was a friend. That being done, the expedition again departed Cozumel for Veracruz on the fourth of March, 1519.

Four months after Hernán Cortés arrived in Veracruz, on the road to conquer the Aztec capital of Tenochtitlan, he sent a shipload of pillaged loot back to Spain, part of which was the "Royal Fifth," or the 20% share of the plunder taken during the conquest that was owed as tax to the Spanish Crown. Along with the plunder, Cortés sent a letter from Veracruz dated July 10, 1519; a letter now known as his *"Primera carta de relación."* In the missive, Cortés lists in detail all of the items he was sending back to the royal court, including *"dos libros de los que acá tienen los indios"* or *"two books of the kind the Indians here have."*

Although this is the first ever mention of pre-Colombian codices, there were more to come. *Hispania Victrix: segunda parte de la historia general de las Indias* is the book Francisco López de Gomara, Hernando Cortés' private secretary, published in 1552 detailing Cortés' conquest of México. In his account, Gomara describes in great detail the collection of gold, silver, and art that comprised the Royal Fifth shipment of 1519, and also mentions that a group of six captive Indians from the Totonac capital Cempoala were sent along as well. But, most interestingly, Gomara says that the shipment also included *"algunos libros de figuras por letras, que usan los mexicanos, codigos como paños, escritos por todas partes. Unos eran de algodón y engrudo, y otros de hojas de metl, que sirven de papel..."* (some books containing figures as letters, used by the Mexicans, cryptographs on canvass, with writings all over. Some were made of cotton and paste, and others of agave leaves that served as paper).

Gomara's description of the materials used in the construction of some of the books was somewhat confused; the folded panels were actually made of the processed bark of the *ficus* tree (a paper the Maya called *kopó*) rather than cotton fiber, and the surface treatment was gesso, not starch paste. The Maya called these screen-folded books *hu'un*. Regardless of the slight errors in his description of the books, it is very clear that what Gomara was describing were accordion-folded, Maya codices.

After being inventoried at *Casa de Contratación* in Sevilla, the loot (including the codices and the captured nobles) was moved to the royal court in Valladolid. There, in March of 1520, Pietro Martire de'Anghiera (who is known as Peter Martyr in English) examined the codices, along with Giovanni Ruffo a Forli, who was the archbishop of Cosenza and the Pope's representative in Valladolid. Although Martyr did not write about the codices until a few years later, Archbishop Ruffo did, in a letter he immediately fired off to Francesco Chieragati of Rome, dated March 7, 1520. In the letter, the Archbishop says *"Hauía allí tanbién que me oluidava de dezir unos quadros de menos de un palmo todos juntos que se plegavan y juntavan en forma de un libro y desplegado alargávase. Estavan en los quadritos figuras y signos a forma de letras arábicas y egiptiacas que acá an interpretado que sean letras dellos y los indios no supieron dar buena razón qué cosa fuese aquella."* (I had forgotten to say that there were some paintings less than a palm's span in height that were folded into the form of a book, which when unfolded, stretched out. In these little books, figures and signs in the form of Arabic and Egyptian letters have been interpreted to be their letters, and the Indians had no idea what they meant.)

The Indians who the Archbishop said had no idea what the books contained, were the six Indian nobles who had been captured by the Totonacs of Cempoala and turned over to Cortés, who had then sent them to Valladolid as part of the Royal Fifth. It was no surprise that they couldn't read the glyphs in the texts; these Indian nobles were from the central part of México and were only familiar with deerskin codices illustrating Aztec, Mexica, Totonac, Chinantec, or Zapotec mythology written and illustrated by scribes of that area; the screen-folded *kopó* codices that formed part of the Royal Fifth were written in Maya glyphs and dealt with Maya mythologies and Maya astronomical calculations, something these fellows knew nothing about.

The notion that the codices in the Royal Fifth were made by the Maya is supported by the later writings of Peter Martyr. As the historian for King Ferdinand and Queen Isabella, Martyr proved his worth when he interviewed Cristóbal Colón and several of his crew and recorded what the explorers experienced during the first voyages to the New World in his book *De Orbe Novo*, which details the earliest years of the Spanish exploration of America. Martyr later added five additional chapters, or *Decades*, to that book, chapters dealing with the history of the Spanish conquest of the New World. In Decade Four, Martyr describes what Hernán Cortés and his expedition found when they set foot on Mexican soil for the first time when the landed on Cozumel in February of 1519:

tíbus . Quía plana quínqz tantum ,& ǵdragínta leucarum ſpacio ambítur. Aufugunt incolæ
ad ſiluas nemoroſas , oppída deſerǔt præ tímore , vacuas domos íngrediuntur noſtrí, patt iis
fruuntur cíbís, domorum ornatus varíorum colorum, aulea , veſtesqȝ, ac lodíces . Amaccas
appellant , ex goſampio natiuo reperíunt. E n pater Sanǎe libros etíam ínnumeros de hís vnǐ
cum cæterís ad nouǔ Cæſarc noſtrum adueǎís ,late ínfra dícemǫ. Perluſtrǎt vníuerſam nſ i mí

Or, in English: *"Our people found themselves among various unoccupied
houses, and availed themselves of the food of the land, and found
adornments of various colors in the houses, tapestries, clothing, and
coverlets of rustic cotton that they call Amaccas. They also have, O Holy
Father, innumerable books. Of these and the other things which they
brought to our new Caesar [King Charles] we shall tell of further on."*

As promised, later in the book Martyr describes the codices: *"En lo que
ellos escriben son unas hojas de cierta delgada corteza interior de los
árboles que se cría debajo de la corteza superior; creo que se llama
philira; conforme lo vemos, no en el sauce u olmo, sino en la de los
palmitos que se comen, que hay una tela dura que separa las hojas
exteriores, á modo de las redes con agujeros y mallas estrechas, y las
embetunan con unto fuerte. Cuando están blandas, les dan la forma que
quieren y la extienden a su arbitrio, y luego de endurecida la
embutunan, se supone que con yeso o con alguna materia parecida."*
(What they write upon are some sheets of a certain thin inner tree bark
which grows underneath the outer bark... where there is a hard cloth
that separates the layers... when they are soft, they give them the form
that they desire and spread them out at their discretion, and then to
harden them they coat them, one supposes with plaster or some similar
material.)

Martyr goes on to add: *"Not only do they bind their books, but they also
stretch out this material many cubits, and reduce it to square sections,
not loose, but so united... [so that] whenever one looks at an open book,
the two written faces are displayed; two pages appear, and under these
are hidden another two as it is not stretched out at length, but
underneath one folio are many other joined folios."*

Peter Martyr had never been to the New World and the Indian captives
he interviewed at Valladolid couldn't tell him anything about the books.
So, how could he go into such detail about their manufacture and the

materials of which they were made? The answer is that when Cortés sent the Royal Fifth back to Spain in 1519, it was accompanied by one of the conquistador's men, Francisco de Montejo, who had been to Yucatán earlier with Francisco Hernández de Córdoba in 1517 and to Cozumel with Juan de Grijalva in 1518. Montejo was surely familiar with the Maya use and manufacture of *ficus*-bark codices, and it is known for certain that Martyr interviewed him at length during the four years Montejo remained in Valladolid. Now, the next question is, if the codices that were shipped to Spain as part of the Royal Fifth were Maya in origin, where in the Maya realm did Cortés get them? The most plausible answer is Cozumel.

Cortés' expedition came to the island directly from Cuba in February of 1519 and stayed on Cozumel for several days, interacting peacefully with the Maya there and exchanging many gifts with them. When he left the island on his way to Veracruz, his second landing in México was at Isla Mujeres, which expedition member Bernal Díaz de Castillo said they found abandoned. López de Gomara wrote that in Isla Mujeres *"surgió Cortés para ver a la disposición de la tierra y el aspecto de la gente. Mas no le agrado."* ("Cortés landed to ascertain the lay of the land and the disposition of the people, but he didn't like it much.") They then said a Mass on Isla Mujeres before sailing away.

The third stop was in the anchorage in front of Campeche, but Gomara and Díaz both say that they did not go ashore there and had no interaction with the Maya. Later, they moved on to *"una gran cala que ahora llaman puerto escondido"* ("a large bay that is now known as Puerto Escondido") where they hunted rabbits but found no Indians with whom they could trade. The expedition's next stop was Potonchán at the mouth of Rio Tabasco, (not Champotón, Campeche, as often reported), where they fought with the Indians they encountered there. Gomara says that after the battle the Indians gifted the Spaniards with food, 400 pesos worth of small jewelry, some small pieces of low quality turquoise, and twenty slaves. But in any regard, Potonchán was a city of the Chontal Maya, not the Yucatec Maya. These two groups speak different languages and have different customs, and the images, glyphs, and rituals in the Dresden Codex are all typical of the Yucatec Maya. All the expedition's stops after Potonchán were in territories that belonged to non-Maya Indians, so it is doubtful that a Maya codex would have been acquired in any of those areas, either.

Could one of the Maya codices that Cortés sent back as part of the Royal Fifth have been the very same now known as the Dresden Codex?

The Dresden Codex is a pre-Columbian Mayan document that is 3.56-meters-long and made up of 74 pages, each 20.5 centimeters high with glyphs and drawings on each side. The document contains various almanacs, divination calendars, astronomical tables, ritual regulations, and numerous representations of Maya gods. It is a Late Postclassic period (1200 AD-1517 AD) copy of an earlier work that had been crafted between 934 AD and 1052 AD (during the Early Postclassic period), according to the dates that can be derived from the astronomical calculations contained on pages 46 through 50 and 61 through 64.

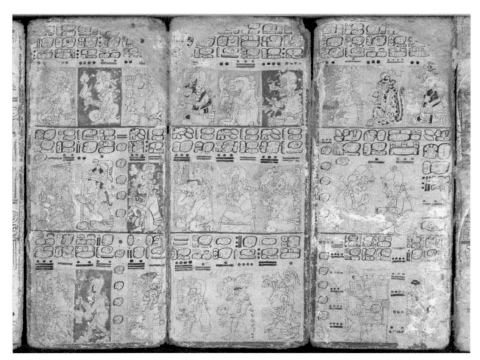

Above: Pages 6-8 of the Dresden Codex.

Many archaeologists and ethnologists have noted the similarity between the styles of the drawings and glyphs in the Dresden Codex and those appearing in the murals in the Late Postclassic Maya ruins at

Playa del Carmen, Tulum, and Tancah, three Maya cities that had very close political and religious ties with pre-Columbian Cozumel. Many have gone as far as to hypothesize that the Dresden Codex was created in one of these locations, based upon these similarities. Unfortunately, no Maya temple murals have survived on Cozumel, but there is no reason to believe they would not be similar, if not identical, to those of the cities on the adjacent mainland, and by corollary, to the Dresden Codex.

So, if the Dresden Codex was indeed one of the codices included in the Royal Fifth of 1519, it seems clear that it had to have come from Cozumel. But, how did it end up in Dresden? We do not know the whole story. There is a 220-year-long gap in the ownership records of the Dresden Codex from 1519, when it arrived in Valladolid, and the year 1739, when it was purchased from a Viennese book collector by Johann Christian Götze. At the time the codex arrived in Spain, Vienna was also a part of the Holy Roman Empire, but how the codex moved from Valladolid to Vienna is still a mystery. After purchasing the codex, Götze became director of the Dresden Royal Library and later gifted the book to the library in 1744. The library is now known as the *Sächsische Landesbibliothek* and still houses the codex.

Pánfilo de Narváez and Alonso de Parada

On March 5, 1520, another expedition, headed by Pánfilo de Narváez, left Cuba with 11 large ships and 7 open-decked *bergantines* with between 1,700 and 2,400 men, some of whom were infected with smallpox. When Narváez arrived at Cozumel, he found around 80 Spaniards from the Alonso de Parada expedition who had been shipwrecked and were stranded on the island. Taking some of De Parada's men aboard, he left others together with some of his own men to organize a small outpost on the island before Narváez sailed away to catch up with Cortés. This was the first Spanish "settlement" on Cozumel, but did not last long before the outpost was closed down. However, the settlement's effect on Cozumel was long-lasting; the smallpox virus that the soldiers brought with them from Cuba soon spread among the island's inhabitants and the de-population of Cozumel began. When Narváez got to Veracruz, his crew continued to spread the disease among the native population, who had no natural resistance.

Cristóbal de Olid

In 1524, Hernán Cortéz sent Cristóbal de Olid to Honduras with orders to claim the area around the present-day town of Tela in Cortéz' name and make a settlement there. Having been to Cozumel earlier, Olid surely must have stopped at the island on his way by, but there are no records of such a visit. When he arrived at the designated spot in Honduras, Olid claimed the new territory for himself, naming it Triunfo de la Cruz. Although some of his men went along with this betrayal of Cortéz' confidence, around sixty others did not. Later, when Olid led a contingent of his faithful followers to subdue a neighboring Indian village, these sixty men (led by a man named Valenzuela) revolted and ransacked the settlement before trying to sail back to Cortéz. On their voyage back, they shipwrecked on Cozumel. Although they were at first graciously received by the Maya on the island, the men soon began to wear out their welcome, demanding that the islanders support them in a lavish style they felt they deserved. When word of these shipwreck survivors reached Cortéz, he sent his cousin, Juan de Avalos, to rescue them and take them back to Cuba, along with some wounded soldiers he also wanted to send back home convalesce in Cuba. Avalos picked up the shipwreck survivors on Cozumel, much to the relief of the islanders, but wrecked his vessel within sight of Cuba. Most of the men aboard the ship drowned, including Avalos, but 15 made it to shore and survived to tell the tale.

Francisco de Montejo

Francisco de Montejo had been along on both the Juan de Grijalva expedition of 1518 and the Hernán Cortéz expedition of 1519, though he was only with Cortéz until the end of that year before he was sent back to Spain to oversee the delivery of the plunder from the Aztec capital that the conquistador was sending back to the King. After delivering the booty, Montejo stayed at court, where he pulled strings and called in favors, until on December 8, 1526, King Carlos V granted him the hereditary title of *Adelantado.* Montejo was also read a royal decree which granted him the power as *"Capitán General y Alquacil Mayor de Yucatán y Cozumel"* to raise an army, conquer, and colonize the Yucatán Peninsula.

Montejo's fleet of three ships and 400 men sailed from Sevilla, Spain in 1527, to Santo Domingo, where horses and more provisions were loaded aboard. One of the vessels stayed behind in Santo Domingo, while its captain tried to round up more supplies as Montejo and the other two ships sailed on to Cozumel. The two vessels arrived on the island at the end of September, 1527. Montejo had no interpreter with him, and though communication with the islanders was difficult at best, he still found the Maya of Cozumel to be as peaceful and welcoming as had all the previous Spaniards who called on the island before him. He gave the Maya town of Xamancab the new name of San Miguel, after the saint whose feast day it happened to be on the day he landed on the island. Naum Pat, the *Halach Uinik* of Xamancab, helped the Spaniards to replenish their water barrels and then bade them farewell after only a few days, as Montejo was eager to get on with the business of claiming land for himself and the Crown.

Montejo's ships crossed over the channel to Xala (Xel Há), which soldier Blas Hernández says the Maya called Solíman. This statement must be taken with a large grain of salt, as Hernández had been on the earlier 1517 Córdoba expedition and was the person responsible for the erroneous report to the Governor of Cuba that the Mayan name for the peninsula was "Yucatán," an error which nevertheless resulted in this name being used to describe the peninsula from that point onwards. After reading a document aloud to the puzzled Maya of Xala informing them that they were now vassals of the King of Spain, the Spaniards built a small settlement on a headland a mile south of the Maya village and named it Salamanca de Xala, after Montejo's home town of Salamanca in Castilla y Leon, Spain. Today we call this site of Montejo's camp, Punta Solíman, most likely due to the Maya's mispronunciation of Salamanca, which sounded like "Solíman" to them.

The original name of the Maya village Xala (which appeared on Spanish maps as Xala, Cela, or Sela through the 1800s) was replaced by the new name of Xel Há by the Yucatecan historian Juan Pío Pérez Bermón in the mid-1800s. It was a name he invented out of two Mayan words; *Xel*, part or piece, and *Há*, water. He most likely made this substitution because he could not find any other meaning of the term Xala in the Mayan language, and sought to find a similar sounding word or words. This line of reasoning seems faulty, when one considers there are often names of towns and villages all over the world today that have names that will probably lose their original meanings in the centuries to come. It would be like some future historian trying to change the name of Chicago to Chicken Go, because he did not know the word we use today for the windy city is a corruption of the Myaamia Indian word for wild onions; *Shikaakwa*, and recorded as "Checagou" by French explorer René-Robert Cavelier, Sieur de La Salle in 1679.

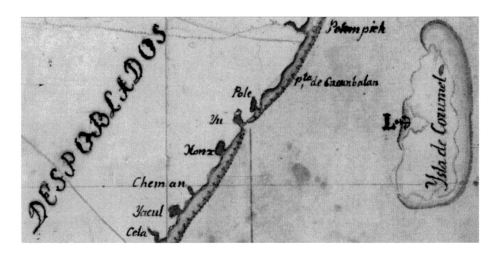

Above: Early map showing Xelha (near the bottom of map) as Cela.

The provisions Montejo's expedition brought from Santo Domingo quickly ran out and after bullying the local Maya into turning over their own foodstuffs to the Spaniards, things began to deteriorate. The Maya deserted their villages in order to avoid dealing with the demanding foreigners and the Spaniards began to go hungry. Within two months, 50 of Montejo's men were dead from disease and starvation and the remainder began to mutiny. To prohibit the disgruntled soldiers from deserting and sailing back to Spain, Montejo scuttled the two ships, just like Hernán Cortés did eight years earlier. He then left 40 of the crew at Xel Há under the command of Alonso Dávila and another 20 at nearby Polé (Xcaret) while he marched 125 others on a reconnaissance of the northeastern coast. Dávila had also been along for the ride on the Grijalva and Cortés expeditions with Montejo, but when he had been sent back to Spain with gold for the King, his ship was captured by the French and he spent a good while in a French jail before making his way back to Spain.

As Montejo marched his hungry troops northward toward Córdoba's "El Gran Cairo" (the Maya village near Cabo Cotoche on the northeast tip of the Yucatán peninsula) he had the good luck to run into Naum Pat, the *Halach Uinik* of Cozumel who was in route to a kinsman's wedding on the mainland. Pat helped the Spaniards with food and supplies and introduced him as a friend to the local Maya leaders at Xamanhá (Playa del Carmen) and he was treated accordingly. Montejo then renamed the Maya town Salamanca de Xamanhá. After regaining their strength, the Spaniards marched northward, meeting various Maya leaders and informing them that they were now Spanish vassals. None of the Maya had any problems with this new situation, which they just chose to ignore as long as the Spaniards kept on marching and away from their particular area of influence. Eventually, Montejo and his men reached "El Gran Cairo," the Maya city the Córdoba expedition had visited in 1517. There, they were ambushed by some Maya who took offense to the idea of being annexed by the Spanish King. After a bloody battle, the Spaniards had to make a hurried retreat, marching back to Xel Há.

When Montejo got back from his march, he had only 60 men left with him of the 125 troops he had taken with him on this recon trip. In addition to those losses, all 20 of the soldiers he had stationed at Polé had been killed and only 12 of the 40 he left at Salamanca de Xala (Xel Há) were still alive. When the ship Montejo had left behind earlier at Santo Domingo finally arrived with fresh provisions, Montejo sent Dávila and 50 of the men (13 of them on horseback) on a march south towards the Bay of Chetumal, and later he and all but 20 of his troops, who he left to man the garrison at Xel Há, sailed south to meet up with them.

Montejo arrived at Chetumal Bay first, where it is said he found out that the shipwrecked Spaniard, Gonzalo Guerrero, was living in nearby Ichpaatún. He supposedly sent a letter to the renegade Spaniard, again offering him a chance to rejoin his fellow countrymen, but the now thoroughly "Mayanized" Spaniard refused the offer. The messenger who brought Gonzalo's refusal back to Montejo also informed the Spaniards that Dávila and all his troops had been killed. Montejo believed the lie, while unbeknownst to him, Dávila, who was actually alive and nearby, was being told the same fate had overcome Montejo and his men. Dávila fell for the ruse and returned to Xel Há. Gathering up the men he had left there earlier, he moved the garrison north to Xamanhá (Playa del Carmen).

Meanwhile, after deciding to abandon his attempt to take Ichpaatún, Montejo sailed father south to Honduras. Before long, he abandoned that effort as well and returned to the garrison at Xel Há, which he found abandoned. Dejected, Montejo sailed over to Cozumel, where Naum Pat informed him that the message telling of Dávila's death was a lie, and that Dávila and his men were still alive and living in Xamanhá (Playa del Carmen). Montejo sailed back across the channel, where he finally reunited with Dávila and the rest of his troops. After catching up on events, Montejo and Dávila planned a new assault on Ichpaatún: Montejo would sail to Veracruz to pick up more supplies and reinforcements for the endeavor while Dávila held the fort at Xamanhá (Playa del Carmen).

Once Montejo arrived in Veracruz, he changed his mind about returning to fight the Maya of Ichpaatún and sent ships back to Playa del Carmen to pick up Dávila so they could join him and renew their efforts to conquer Yucatán; this time from the Spanish town of Santa María de la Victoria in Tabasco, a Spanish outpost that had been abandoned earlier. After that, Cozumel was left on its own until Montejo "El Sobrino" returned to the island in 1540.

CHAPTER 6

Colonial period in Cozumel

After working together with Francisco de Montejo for several years, bringing more and more of Yucatán under the *Adelantado's* control, Alonso Dávila was sent back to Ichpaatún in 1531 to try once more to establish a foothold there. After marching with 50 of his troops across the Yucatán peninsula to the Bay of Chetumal, Dávila setup camp near Bacalar Lagoon and named the place "La Villa Real de Chetumal." After several months of planning, Dávila again attempted to subdue the Maya of Ichpaatún, but was soundly defeated. He beat a hasty retreat to Honduras, where he and the other 23 survivors managed to flag down a passing Spanish vessel and hitch a ride back to Montejo's camp in Tabasco.

In 1540, the *Adelantado's* named his son, Francisco de Montejo "El Mozo," as Lieutenant Governor and ordered him to subdue the Maya of Yucatán once and for all. "El Mozo" worked hand in hand with his cousin, Francisco de Montejo "El Sobrino," in carrying out his father's orders. In 1541, "El Mozo" set up his headquarters in Campeche and started out on his campaign of conquest. He took Tihó (today's Mérida) then Techoh and Dzilam. One by one the Maya towns and villages fell to the Montejo clan. In 1543, "El Sobrino" established a new town first called Villa de Valladolid at the Maya town of Chohuac-há (Valladolid was later re-located to its present location) then charged on through Ecab to Polé and Xala (Xel Há) which both surrendered to him and his band of thirty soldiers peacefully. When he crossed the channel to Cozumel, the island also pledged its allegiance to him without any fight.

In 1544, Montejo "El Mozo," sent Gaspar Pacheco, his son Melchor Pacheco, and nephew Alonso Pacheco to confront the Maya living along the coast of Quintana Roo south of Xel Há. The Spanish priest Bienvenida described them as the cruelest men he had ever known and wrote of how the Spanish troops decimated the towns and villages they found in their path, reducing settlements of 500 to 1,000 homes to hamlets of less than 50. Disease was also spread by the Spaniards and the depopulation of the coast began. Yucatán was soon after divided by the Spanish into four provinces; Campeche in the west, Mérida in the north, Valladolid in the northeast, and Salamanca de Bacalar in the southeast. The old *kuchkabal* of Ekab was divided into six *encomiendas* (tribute-paying dependencies), which now fell under the jurisdiction of the Province of Valladolid. Montejo "El Adelantado" granted the *encomienda* of Cozumel to his friend and fellow conquistador, Juan Nuñez, although this grant had not been approved by the King.

In 1547 the Maya rose in revolt and fought hard for a full year, but in 1548 the revolt was crushed. The subjugation of the Maya was almost complete. Many Maya towns were by then abandoned or nearly so. A census taken at Polé in 1549 showed there was only 76 adults left living at the village by then.

In 1549, Franciscan priest Luis de Villalpando visited Cozumel for a short three days. At this time Cozumel was still the *encomienda* of Juan Nuñez, who was a resident of San Francisco de Campeche, Yucatán. A list of tributaries dated 1549 stated that the 220 married Indian males of Cozumel must send their tribute to Nuñez at his residence in San Francisco de Campeche and some of them must work for him a certain number of days as part of the tribute. It also stated that these Maya would receive religious instruction while they were working in San Francisco de Campeche. Apparently, there was no priest to give these lessons in Cozumel, nor was there a church. In 1552, Cozumel changed hands and became the encomienda of Juan de Contreras. Soon after, Contreras erected two *visitas*, or churches on Cozumel that could be used by visiting clergy; one at San Miguel de Xamancab and another at Santa María, near Cedral.

In his 1991 article, *Rural Chapels and Churches of Early Colonial Yucatán and Belize*, archaeologist Anthony Andrews states: *"In the ramada, the townspeople gather to hear the sermon and mass, which is celebrated in a large chapel placed at the beginning of this same ramada: it is celebrated by the Indians from the chorus, located at one side of the chapel, where also the font is usually found, while the sacristy is on the opposite side. This is the way it is in every village of this province, there where a convent is found as well as there where there is no convent; this is necessary for the excessive heat of the place, though in a few villages they have the baptistery in the chapel itself, and in others, they have it in a private room and hall."*

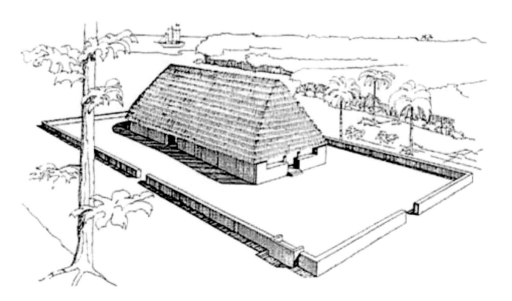

Above: A reconstruction of a 16ᵗʰ century ramada *chapel, much like the one in Cozumel would have appeared, by Anthony P. Andrews*

In 1563, the bishop of Yucatán, Francisco de Toral, made a three week visit to Cozumel and wrote a letter to the King of Spain about it in 1564. The text read, in part: *"Pasé a la isla de Cuçamil o Cozumel que estaba tan necesitada de doctrina que nunca ha pasado a ella religioso, sino que fraile Luis de Villalpando, ahora quince años, y estuvo alli sólo tres días. Yo estuve allí tres semanas, y asi con lo que allí trabajé, como por haber yo enviado delante quíen les prepararse se hizo fruto por la bondad del Señor y quedaron todos bautizados, casados, y confirmados. Es muy buena gente, sincera, sin malicia ni maldad. No tienen más de una mujer y muerta aquélla, toman otra. Saben la doctrina y dejéles allí, en su lengua, cierta instrucción para su buen vivir. Derroquéles todos sus templos antiguos, que era como Roma o Jerusalén entre nosotros aquella isla entre éstos... Convendrá que Vuestra Magestad tome para sí aquella pieza y mande dar otro tanto como renta a Juan de Contreras en esta tierra y no se le hará agravio y podrá se hacer fácilmente pues se encomiendan indios dándoles los primeros que vacaren tanto por tanto y aquella isla quédese para Vuestra Magestad. La renta de ella se podrá dar a un ministro que esté allí para el bien de aquellos naturales y descrgo de Vuestra Magestad y nuestro y no hay otro medío como aquello se ponga en la Real Corona y haya doctrina."* (I went to the island of Cuzamil or Czumel that was so in need of the teaching of doctrine which had not happened before except fifteen years ago, when Friar Luis de Villpando was there for only three days. I was there three weeks and with the work I did there I have prepared it for future missions, as by the goodness of the Lord they were all baptized, married, and confirmed. They are very good people, sincere, without malice or wickedness. They do not have more than one wife and if she dies, they take another. They know the doctrine and I left it there, in their language, some instructions for good living. I tore down all its ancient temples, which was to that island like Rome or Jerusalem is to us…. It would better suit your Majesty to take that encomienda for himself and give another with the same income to Juan de Contreras it will not aggrieve him and it may be easily done by transferring the tribute of the Indians little by little so therefore the island will revert to your Majesty. The income from it may pay a Minister that works for your Majesty and us and there is no other way than that to promote the holy doctrine for the Royal Crown.)

On March 4, 1564, the King ordered the Governor of Yucatán to send two priests to Cozumel, but the order was not carried out. Nobody in Yucatán felt that the place was worth the effort to develop and the Spanish authorities left the island to fend for itself. As long as it sent its tribute payments to Contreras, Cozumel was rarely visited by Spanish government officials. However, it did have other visitors occasionally. Ships stopped by once in a while for provisions; sometimes paying for them and sometimes not. Twice, the islanders were victims of extortion by these visitors. Once, a Portuguese ship captain named Juan Gonzales conned the townfolk into believing he was a priest come to set up in the church and perform weddings and baptisms. He demanded a pre-payment for his services, which the Maya dutifully provided, then they watched in dismay as the ship sailed away with their money and goods.

Another time, a Spanish ship visited the island for a whole week. This visit was uneventful until one of the crew wandered into the woods near town and found a Maya shrine that was still being kept up and used for idolatry, contrary to orders from the clergy and the Spanish government. He blackmailed the islanders into paying him 60 *tostones* in return for not turning them in to authorities.

Toral's suggestion to return the *encomienda* of Cozumel back to the King and use the tribute from it to support a priest and the churches on the island was approved in 1565. However, Luis Cespedes de Oviedo, the Governor of Yucatán, refused to make the change until the clergy supplied him with a priest who could speak Mayan. Bishop Toral could not find any bilingual clergy, but he later sent Padre Cristóbal de Asencio to Cozumel to make a recon of the island, celebrate Mass, and give some religious training to the islanders while he was there, since it had been, in Toral's words: *"pues ha veinte años que* [Contreras] *goceis de los indios y no habéis tenido sacerdote ni menos habeis dado ornamento ni lo necesario para el culto divino."* (as it has been twenty years that [Contrereas] has had the use of the Indians [of Cozumel] and they have had no priest nor even less had any ornaments or acoutrements for divine service.)

On May 20, 1564, Diego de Quijada, The Alcalde Mayor de Yucatán, wrote to the King saying that *"un clerigo va de seis a seis meses y esta dos o tres dias alli y no vuelve otra vez hasta que pasan seis meses."* (A cleric goes every six months and stays there two or three days and does not return again until six months have passed.) In the margin of this letter, a scribe had written: *"Carta al gobernador con relacion de esto para que provea como vayan a esta isla dos religiosos que residan en ella y administren a los indios y hagan iglesia conforme a lo acordado que les envie."* (Letter to the Governor, in relation to this in order to show how two priests go to this island and minister to the Indians there and lead worship in accordance with the decree sending them there.) It appears that either Quijada or Toral was lying about the clergy visiting Cozumel in the years previous to Toral's visit in 1563.

Padre Asencio went to Cozumel in 1570, but after five months on the island giving religious instruction, a letter arrived on Cozumel from

Contreras instructing the *Batab* of San Miguel de Xamancab to cease cooperating with the priest and that the Cozumeleños should no longer listen to, or obey him. The *Batab* took the order seriously and from that point on no one attended Mass or religious instruction classes. A month later Father Asencio left the island. In the report he made of his trip to the island, Father Asencio mentions the two churches in Cozumel, saying *"… y asi pase mis doctrinas y escuelas en cada pueblo* [San Miguel de Xamancab and Santa María]*, reformandose las iglesias que estan como cosa de prestado."* Padre Asencio also wrote of the poor condition of the church at San Miguel de Xamancab, stating: *"Un lunes dicha la misa de las ánimas ante el altar dije Batabe Francisco Pat: Hijo, yo no puedo decir misa en este altar, es necesario alzarlo y esta pared también, para que esté santo crucifijo esta bien…"* (One Monday I said the Mass for the souls in Purgatory in front of the altar, I told the *Batab* Francisco Pat: Son, I cannot say Mass at this altar, it is necessary to reconstruct it and this wall as well, for the Holy Crucifix to be safe.)

This letter makes it quite clear that the *visita* church at Xamancab was not only a "temporary" structure, but was begining to fall apart in 1570. In his report, Father Asencio included a census of all the adults living on the western coast of Cozumel (the renegade Maya in the interior and east coast of the island were not counted) and the total came to 159 in San Miguel and 202 in Santa María de Oycib (Cedral).

In 1571, a group of French corsairs in a ship named *L'Espérance* and captained by Pierre Chuetot began preying on the coastal towns of Yucatán. In Ecab, on the mainland just north of Cancun, they holed up in the local church where, according to later testimony, *"escribían letreros en francés y en español y el capitán de ellos era pintor y pintaba personajes todo lo cual después los españoles les hacían raer a los indios."* (they painted signs in French and Spanish and their captain was the painter and he painted caricatures which afterwards the Spaniards made the Indians scrape off the walls.) The Frenchmen also set fire to the priest's home there and burned all the church's books before reboarding their vessel and heading southward along the Quintana Roo coast.

Above: The Boca Igesia church, as photographed by Gregory Mason during the Mason-Spinden Expedition of 1926.

Arriving in Polé (Xcaret), they stole the tapestry over the altar of the church there, tearing it into strips to use as wicks for their *arcabuses,* or matchlock long-guns. From Polé they crossed over the channel to Cozumel and at first were treated well by the inhabitants. But, they eventually took up residence in the church at San Miguel de Xamancab and for the next 22 days terrorized the island. Later testimony described the scene inside the church: *"estaba junto al altar un gran fuego que tenían para calentar y a una parte y otra, camas en que dormian y en el altar habia petates en que habían dormido y todo muy sucio y en la sacristia habia mal olor de orines porque se orinaban en ella y todas las paredes de la dicha iglesia pintadas de cosas profanas como a ellos se les antojaban, que era navios y personajes."* (Next to the altar they had a big fire that they made to warm up and on both sides they had beds and on the altar they had mats where they slept and everything was very dirty and in the sacristy there was a bad smell of urine because they urinated in it and all the walls of the said church they painted whatever profane things they liked, that were ships and characters.)

Above: Xcaret as it looked in 1926. Photo by Gregory Mason.

The Spanish government forces had been pursuing the pirates and sent troops to Cozumel to apprehend them. When the troops got to the island, they confronted the band of Frenchmen, killing eight, mortally wounding two, and capturing ten. Captain Pierre Chuetot and one of the other badly wounded pirates were turned over to the islanders, who dragged them off and hanged them. The others were taken to Mexico City, where four were sentenced to death; Etienne Gilbert, Isaac Dorven, Jean Luayzell, and Claude Ivilin. The others were sentenced to life as galley slaves, rowing the King's ships for the rest of their lives. These included Jacques Montier, Pierre Sanfroy, Marin Carnu, Guillaume Coquerelle, Guillaume de Siles, and Guillermo Poitiers. All were under twenty-eight years of age, the youngest being only seventeen. More like a street gang than what we typically think of as a boat load of your classic *"yo-ho-ho"* pirates.

For some reason or other, the legend that surrounds this event holds that Pierre Sanfroy was the pirates' captain. This is not true. Sanfroy was only a member of the crew. The captain, Pierre Chuetot, was killed by the Cozufmeleños. It was also the captain, and not Sanfroy, who painted grafiti on the church walls in Ecab and Cozumel.

In October of 1573, the governor, Diego de Santillián, sent two Spanish priests to Cozumel to build a monastery in Santa María de Oycib: Father Gregorio de Fuente Ovejuna and Father Hernando Sopuerta. They were accompanied by an interpreter, Agustín Ytza, who was to explain to the islanders that the two priests were there to take possesion of the site where the monastery was to be built, and that the deed be done "with a procession and a wooden cross." Money was set aside for the construction of the monastery, but the two priests decided it was not worth the effort, as there were only 139 adult Maya living in San Miguel de Xamancab and 301 in Santa María. Many more unconquered Maya were living along the east coast of the island, but they were unaffiliated with the towns of San Miguel de Xamancab and Santa María, paid no tribute to Contreras, and were considered unreachable by the Spanish government. After only 50 days on the island, the two priests went back to the mainland and the idea of a monastery on Cozumel was abandoned.

When Juan de Contreras died in 1572, he passed the *encomienda* of Cozumel down to his son, Diego de Contreras Duran. In 1579, Diego complained in a letter that: *"suelen acudir a la dicha isla franceses, y puede haber un año, o poco más o menos, que los franceses robaron la dicha isla, llevandoles gran cantidad de maíz, gallinas y mantas de mi tributo, y la canpana de la iglesia."* (The French went to the said island, and it was about a year ago more or less that the French raided the said island, carrying away a great quantity of corn, chickens and blankets from my tribute, and the bell of the church.)

In 1580, Gregorio de Montalvo, the Bishop of Yucatán, sent Father Pedro Maldonado to Cozumel. Although the priest made it to the island, two of his assistants did not, having been drowned in the crossing, allegedly by their own Maya canoe-paddlers because they had ridiculed them about the pagan ceremonies they had celebrated prior to their crossing of the channel. Dean Pedro Sánchez de Aguilar, in his 1613 report *Informe contra idolorum cultores del obispado de Yucatán*, also states that Maya canoe paddlers drowned the priest "Francisco" de Aguirre; a misnaming of the priest Diego López de Aguirre) on his trip to cozumel around 1580.

In 1582, the Franciscan order turned the religious training of the Indians of Cozumel over to the secular clergy and Bishop Montalvo sent another priest to Cozumel. It can only be assumed that he eventually managed to either repair and re-establish the old temporary church building that the previous priests had made do with up until that time, or he built an entirely new one, because the remains of the church described in later testimonies by visitors to the island in the early 1800s certainly sound more like it was a substantial building and not a temporary *visita,* like the one Father Asencio complained about in 1570.

Diego de Contreras kept the *encomienda* of Cozumel until July 15, 1583, when he exchanged it and two other *encomiendas* of his for the *encomienda* of Yuxkukul. The new *encomendero* of Cozumel was Miguel de Arroyo. Also in 1583, the *oidor,* García de Palacio, commissioned several laymen to seek out and destroy the Maya idols. One of the men charged with the task was Alonso de Arévalo, who went to Cozumel that year with the *juez* Martín Güemez and *escribano* Juan Romero in search of these outlawed pagan statues. Arévalo later claimed in his report to have collected and destroyed over 5,000 statues belonging to the islanders.

In 1590, Father Baltasar de Herrera and Vicar Hernando de Salinas went to Cozumel and surprised the Maya living there as they were worshiping their old idols. A formal complaint was sent up the chain of command, and the Lieutenant Governor of Yucatán sent troops to help support the priests in their effort to punish the pagans. Over forty Maya from Santa María (today's Cedral) and Polé (today's Xcaret), were arrested including *cacique* Juan Pat, *el maestro de capilla* Gaspar Chuc, Antonio Cumux, Juan Cumux and Pedro Cumux, who were given forty lashes each and ordered to pay the expenses of the trial and fined ten reals each, for *"haber idolatrado con ritos y ceremonias y haber reincidido cada uno dos veces sin esta en el dicho pecado."* (having worshiped idols in rites and ceremonies and each one having relapsed two times not counting this time in this sin.)

On December 3, 1590, Father Herrera preached against idolatry in the San Miguel Church, but the Maya in attendance rose up against him. If it had not been for the armed Spaniards accompanying him, he probably would have been killed. As it was, the Maya *cacique,* *regidores, alcaldes,* and a few of the mob's leaders were arrested, tried, and punished.

By 1600, the resident priest on Cozumel was Padre Francisco Ruiz Saluago, who was provided with an annual stipend derived from the tribute of the island. In 1613, Dean Pedro Sánchez de Aguilar wrote a report to the King stating: *"Los indios desta isla de Cozumel son grandes idólatras el día de oy... y usan un baile de su gentilidad, y flechan bailando el perro que han de sacrificar; y cuando han de pasar al pueblo de Ppole, que es tierra firme, usan muchas supersticiones antes de embarcarse..."* (the Indians from this island of Cozumel are big idolaters to this day... they use a pagan dance, where they shoot an arrow into a dog they have to sacrifice; and when they pass to the village of Ppole, which is on the mainland, they use many superstitions before embarking...) Sánchez de Aguilar added that he thought it would be a very good idea to remove all the Indians from the island and transfer them to the mainland; one would guess where they could be monitored much better.

In 1619, Bishop Gonzalo de Salazar decided the priest on Cozumel was not being strict enough, so he replaced him with Father Nicolás de Tapia. Accompanied by the *encomiendero* Arroyo, Father Tapia went to Cozumel on November 20, 1619 and at the *capilla* de San Miguel, he officially took over the reins of the island's churches. He headed an *Auto de Fe* (religious trial) in San Miguel, had the usual suspects hauled in and punished, and then destroyed a considerable number of idols. Father Tapia also reported that many Maya from the mainland were still making pilgrimages to Cozumel in order to make sacrifices. He crossed over the channel to Tulum in 1620 and held another *Auto de Fe* there, reporting that the Maya priests in Tulum were still using codices with hieroglyphic texts in their pursuit of their pagan religion. He burned what codices he found and destroyed many more idols, before returning to Cozumel in 1622.

Back in Cozumel, he found the island was into idolatry once more and he reported destroying more than one thousand idols made of clay or wood, but he complained that as soon as he destroyed them, the Maya made more. In 1625 he went back to Tulum, held another *Auto de Fe*, then another in San Miguel in 1625, then another in Polé in 1626. After seven years of trying to stamp out pagan practices on Cozumel, Father Tapia threw in the towel and requested a transfer. He left Cozumel in 1626.

By 1643 the adult population on Cozumel had grown to 498. In the subsequent years, the legends say, the constant harassment of Cozumel and Polé by marauding French and British buccaneers took its toll on the island and its mainland port. Cogolludo states that because of these raids, the population was relocated to Xcan Boloná on the mainland in 1655 and then Cozumel became a *visita* of Boloná. Becoming a *visita* meant that Cozumel no longer had a resident priest, and it is probable that the island's two church buildings were begining their decline at this time. Cogolludo states that the patron saint of the church at San Miguel was Archangel Michael, and that of the church at Cedral was Mary of the Holy Assumption.

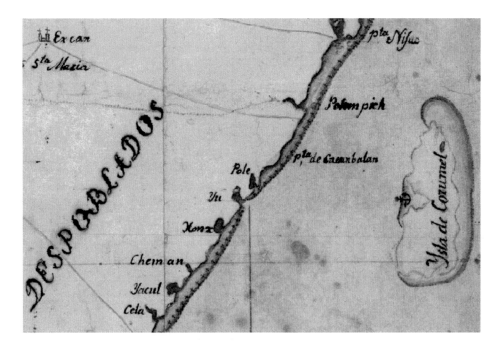

Above: Ex Can Boloná, located at the top left on this 18th century map.

However, we know that not all the island's population left in 1655, because we have documents that show there were still two functioning towns on Cozumel in 1673, 18 years after the population was supposedly moved. In that year, the *Batab* of San Miguel de Xamancab was Martín Cuzamil, the *alcalde* was Pedro Oxté, the *regidor* Gaspar Chablé, and the *escribano* Mateo Chan. In Santa María de Oycib that same year, Sebastian Poot was governor, Antonio Cab the *alcalde*, Diego Couch and Francisco Tzamá the *regidores*, and Francisco Cumux the *escribano*. All of these men signed the documents in 1673, so obviously, not everyone was evacuated in 1655.

After the Spanish government turned their back on Cozumel, the Maya there began a long tradition of fending for themselves and ignoring any Spanish laws that they found inconvenient. Although it was expressly forbidden to trade with the English, whom the Spanish labeled *piratas* (meaning people dealing in contraband), documents and sworn testimony show English logwood woodcutters were in Cozumel as early as 1670. A letter from Jamaican Governor Thomas Modyford dated October 31, 1670, addressed to British Secretary Lord Arlington, shows English woodcutters were in Cozumel at that time. The letter states: *"They go to these places either inhabited by Indians or void, and trespass not at all upon the Spaniards."* In a letter dated April 20, 1671, Fernando Francisco de Escobedo, the Governor and *Capitán General* of Yucatán, wrote to the King of Spain that: *"the English woodcutters... on the Island of Cozumel... have set up settlements and have warehouses just like in their own lands and they trade with Jamaica."* He went on to write: *"at this time they have fearlessly encamped in the Laguna de Términos, Isla de Santa Ana, Cozumel, Isla Mujeres y Zacathán, where they make a huge business of the cutting and exporting of logwood in a volume that is larger that made by ports occupied by the Spanish Government."* Logwood, dyewood, or *palo de tinte*, as the Spanish called it, was a hot commodity at the time. The wood was used to make fabric dye and commanded a steep price in Europe.

In another document, a sworn testimony dated November 3, 1672, the ship captains Philip Osborne, John Mitchell, James Smith, William Coxon, and John Coxon stated they: *"...had been engaged in the* [logwood] *trade for two and a half years between Boca Conil and Cape Catoche and from there down to Cozumel where, they said, the English had always had huts and houses and people to the number of 100 or 200 there resident. They had met with no interruptions to the trade from Spaniards or Indians."*

Above: The heartwood of the Haematoxylon campechianum tree (also known as dyewood, logwood, or palo de tinte) provides a fabric dye that was very popular and costly in the 17th century, before the creation of synthetic dyes.

If the two Maya towns on Cozumel (San Miguel de Xamancab and Santa María) had enough organization to put together reports detailing their municipal governments officials in 1673, and English court testimony states English *palo de tinte* cutters were living and working on the island in 1670, 1671 and 1672, obviously there must have been some kind of understanding, some kind of "live-and-let-live" agreement between the two groups that allowed them to coexist peacefully on the island.

Eighty years later, the English were still on Cozumel. In a Spanish document dated September 20, 1751, (entitled *"Descripción y noticias del río Balis, río Nuevo, Isla Cozumel, la de Mujeres, Vontoy y Blanquitta..."*) it was stated that the English were still cutting *"palo de Campeche y Brazielette"* on Cozumel, as well as other places on the Yucatán mainland. This situation was formalized in the *Trato de Febrero 10, 1763* in which the Spanish King granted England, in return for dismantling British forts in Honduras, the right for English woodcutters *"to work without impediment and to occupy without interruption their houses and warehouses"* in the *"Bay of Honduras and other locations in the Spanish Territory in that part of the world."*

In 1766, Spanish *Visitor-General* José de Gálvez wrote a report about Yucatán that included the statement: *"se celará que los extranjeros no nos roben el ébano, así en estas costas como en la isla de Cozumel, a donde principalmente han ido a cortarlo a su arbitrio..."* (it is prudent to keep our guard up so that foreigners do not steal our ebony, from these shores as well as on the island of Cozumel, where they mainly have gone to cut it at their discretion...) That same year, Martín de Mayorga, the Governor of Guatemala, wrote that the Spanish had not visited Cozumel for years and *"por cuio motivo lo executaban muy a salvo las de la Brittanica, unos con Negros a cortar Hevano, otros a Pesca del carey."* (for that reason the British work there in total safety, some with blacks to cut Ebony, others to catch turtles.)

In 1783, the 1763 treaty was replaced by the Treaty of Versailles in which England received not only formal recognition of their possessions in Belize, but also the right to *"fish in the adjacent coasts and islands and to build houses and warehouses."*

The English logwood cutters and turtle fishermen living on the island were commonly called *"piratas"* by the Spanish at the time because they paid no tax to the Spanish Crown. This unfortunate nomenclature was made formal on June 22, 1672, when the Spanish Crown issued an edict declaring all foreigners who were trading in Spanish overseas ports without a license to be *"piratas."* This word conjures up a vision of a swash-buckling buccaneer, cutlass in hand, a patch over one eye, and a parrot on his shoulder, but in reality it merely meant a *"contrabandista;"* a person who earned his living dealing in contraband, or merchandise upon which he had paid no tax. That misinterpretation of the word *"pirata"* is what led to the commonly-believed myth that asserts Cozumel was a "pirates' lair" in the 1600s and 1700s. This legend is far from the truth. There is absolutely no evidence that any buccaneers ever used Cozumel as a base of operations, regardless of the lore and legends. There were a few incidents in the late 1500s and early 1600s when some second and third tier French and English corsairs raided or looted the villages on Cozumel, such as the band of French buccaneers led by Pierre Chultot in 1571. However, none of these minor league rogues ever used the island as a base of operations, and none of the better known buccaneers ever bothered to stop at Cozumel. The persistent myth that Jean and Pierre Lafitte, Henry Morgan, Francis Drake, Laurent de Graff, (*Lorencillo*), Cornelio Hol (*Pata de Palo*), Abraham Diego (*El Mulato*), *Cara Cortada*, and Juan Cruyés *(Capitán Bigotes)* all called Cozumel home at one point, is as absurd as the claim made in the 1994 edition of *Baedeker's* that asserts Long John Silver, a fictitious character in the novel <u>Treasure Island</u> by Robert Louis Stevenson, also used Cozumel as his base of operations!

CHAPTER 7

The Real Story of the Dread Pirates of Cozumel

There is a persistent myth that Cozumel was once a pirate stronghold during the 16th and 17th centuries. Although absolutely no evidence exists to support this claim, it is oft repeated and reprinted in countless websites and articles about the island and is even included in several otherwise serious books on Yucatecan history. One source of this myth is the 1958, volume 15 edition of the magazine *Vision*, in an article entitled *"Cozumel se Acapulquiza,"* which states Jean and Pierre Lafitte were based in Cozumel. This same article says Henry Morgan used Cozumel as his base of operations; another fairytale with no basis in fact. Over the years, countless authors have added to this list of buccaneers that were supposed to have used Cozumel as their headquarters.

Although none of this is true, a few minor pirates did, in fact, briefly visit Cozumel during the 16th and 17th centuries. One such visitor was Pierre Sanfroy, who is often reported to have been a blood-thirsty pirate captain who used San Miguel's church as his base in the 1570s. The truth is he was only a 27-year-old crewmember aboard the Chuetot expedition that spent 22 days on Cozumel in 1571. The story of this expedition is well documented in over 300 pages of court testimony taken between 1572 and 1574 during trials that took place in Mérida and Mexico City.

The real story about Pierre Sanfroy begins on May 19, 1570, when a group of 40 young French Huguenots and lapsed Catholics banded together and set sail from La Rochelle, France in the French-flagged vessel *L'Espérance*, on an expedition they hoped would make them rich. The men aboard the ship were:

Pierre Chuetot, ship's captain, a Catholic from Rouen
Nicolas de Siles, a Huguenot, and master of the ship
Bouvier, the first mate

Martin Cornu, the ship's barber-surgeon, age 24
Etienne Gilbert, pilot
Roger Grifel, merchant
Pierre Sanfroy, crewmember, age 27
Guillaume Siles, crewmember, age 19
Guillaume Coquerelle, crewmember, age 19
Guillaume Poitiers, crewmember
Robin Poitiers, crewmember
Guillaume Montier, crewmember
Jaques Montier, crewmember, age 27
Jean de Luayzell, crewmember
Mairiac, crewmember
Isaac Dorven, crewmember
Claude Ivilin, crewmember
Jean Hoscorno, crewmember
Robert Hoscorno, crewmember
Broutouneau, crewmember
"La Pombrea," crewmember and ex-fraile
"El Gitano," crewmember
Marco Vilu, crewmember
Plus 15 more crewmembers and 2 cabin boys, for a total of 40 souls aboard

They first headed to Honfleur, France, then south to the Canary Islands where they took on water and food stores. From there they sailed south to Cape Verde Island, where they purchased cow hides. Near Madeira they captured a small Portuguese *galeota*, killing her crew and taking the small vessel along with them. From Madeira they sailed to Sierra Leone (on the coast of Africa) where they purchased ivory, which they planned to sell along with the hides in the Dominican Republic. Heading back north, the two vessels sailed to Guinea to acquire a few black slaves to add to the cargo. When they got ready to leave, a couple of the crew decided to quit the voyage and stay in Guinea. This turned out to be a good decision on their part, because soon after the *L'Espérance* and the *galeota* left port, they were chased into a storm by the Portuguese Navy where the larger of the two vessels sank. Thirty of Chuetot's crew managed to survive by shifting over to the small *galeota* and under these cramped circumstances sailed onward to Margarita Island, off the coast of Venezuela. There they captured a *caravela* owned by Melchior de Rivas with fourteen or fifteen people aboard, including two women, a sick Franciscan priest, a lay cleric, and the ship's Genovese pilot, Bernardo de Burdeos. The pirates' next stop was Nombre de Dios, Panamá, where the band captured a small Cuban vessel loaded with wine and owned by a Sr. Parada. They took the wine aboard and then killed the captured ship's crew as well as the captives they had taken earlier, save Bernardo, the pilot. Shortly after, the Frenchmen captured another Spanish merchant ship, loaded with fine ceramics, hardware, linen, tiles, and religious books.

Chuetot's band then sailed to Cozumel, where they captured another ship anchored off San Miguel de Xamancab. It was owned by Hernando Díaz and Gaspar de Chinchilla of Puerto Caballos, Honduras and under the command of Cristóbal de Hernández. The ship had recently left Trujillo, Honduras, with a load of merchandise to Rio Lagartos, Yucatán. After unloading at Rio Lagartos, it had come to Cozumel and taken aboard 4,000 cotton *mantas,* 200 *arrobas* of beeswax, 200 *botijas* of honey, and a few other commodities including lard. Opting not to land on the island, the Frenchmen took Hernández' ship along with them and sailed north to Boca de Conil, the opening to the bay between Holbox and the mainland, where they again took a prize; the *Nuestra Señora del Rosario*, owned by Pedro de la Mazuca, who was unfortunate enough to be aboard at the time. Vicente Estévez, the pilot of the *Nuestra Señora del Rosario,* was also captured and forced to guide Chuetot's ship through the reefs and flats of northern Yucatán. Mazuca was later to report how the French corsairs cut off his pilot's leg with an ax for sport, before stabbing Mazuca himself four times in the arm.

The pirates transferred all their booty from the ship they had captured in Cozumel to *Nuestra Señora del Rosario*, and since the ship they had captured off Cozumel was old and in bad shape, they burned her and let her sink. The Frenchmen then rounded the north coast of Yucatán and landed at Sisal on the western shore of the peninsula. From there, they marched inland to Hunucmá, Yucatán (a small settlement 15 miles south east of Sisal), where they robbed the village, desecrated the church, and took two *caciques* as prisoner. With the priest's robes and altar cloths they had taken from the church, one of the crewmembers fashioned caps, underwear, and stockings.

News of this raid reached the government in Mérida and a 40-man posse was marshaled to speed to Hunucmá and capture the pirates. Arriving to find the culprits already gone, the posse headed on to Sisal, but got there just in time to see the last of the pirates boarding their two ships, as they hurled insults at the Spaniards ashore. One of the survivors of the pirate raid at Sisal told Francisco Tamayo, the captain of the posse, that he had overheard the Frenchmen say they were going to Telchac to ransom their two captive *caciques,* so Tamayo sent word to Campeche asking for a ship to try to head them off.

Meanwhile, the Frenchmen sailed back to Dzilam, where the two captive *caciques* managed to escape. From Dzilam, the pirates sailed to the village of Ecab and proceeded to sack the town and church. At Ecab, the crewman known as "El Gitano" burned the parsonage and the church's books and then the rest of the crew defiled the church. Chuetot himself drew graffiti on the interior walls of the church, graffiti reported later by Rodrigo de Tapia, to consist of *"...entre otras cosas- un rótulo en castellano que decía que el rey de Castilla no valía nada, y que ellos bastaban solos a darle guerra; y que también pintaron navíos y hombres y mujeres que se abrazaban y besaban y otras suciedades y naturas de hombres."* ("...among other things, a sign in Spanish that said the King of Castile was worthless and they were only good for making war; and that they also painted ships and men and women that were embracing and kissing and other dirty things and penises.")

Other witnesses reported seeing graffiti of *"... sailing vessels...and the Virgin Mary together with a seven-headed monster."* Alonso de Villanueva testified that *"among other things, they wrote 'Viva el Rey de Francia!' on the walls of the church."*

When news of the pirates' raid reached Valladolid, Juan Gutiérrez Coronel, the town's *Alcalde*, organized another posse to try and overtake them. Arriving at Ecab, the posse confronted the pirates, but only managed to kill a few before the pirate band split into two groups: One group boarding the *Nuestra Señora del Rosario* and sailing back to

France; the other group of twenty escaping in the small *galeota* and sailing down the coast.

Above: The Church at Ecab, now known as Boca Iglesias.

This second group eventually reached Polé (Xcaret) and robbed the church there and made wicks for their matchlock guns from the altar cloth. From Polé, the pirate band crossed the channel to Cozumel, where the islanders at first gave them a friendly reception. Soon, however, the Frenchmen demanded more than the islanders were willing to give, and they began harassing the Cozumeleños, calling for more food and drink, whipping the ones who refused their requests and generally running amok. The band took up residence in the church at San Miguel de Xamancab for the next 22 days, drawing graffiti on the walls, urinating and defecating inside the building, and making the altar at times a bed and at other times a table where they took their meals. In front of the church, the Frenchmen built a set of stocks, where they would lock-up any islander who gave them problems. Pedro de la Mazuca later testified *"...en San Miguel, en Cozumel, escribían letras por las paredes y pintaban personajes, que no debiera ser cosa buena; sobre un altar tenían trapos viejos y andrajos."* ("...in San Miguel, in Cozumel, they wrote letters on the walls and painted caricatures, which was not a good thing; over an altar they had old clothes and rags.")

But the pirates' reign on Cozumel came to an end when their prisoner, Pedro de la Mazuca, escaped and sailed the pirates' *galeota* back to Polé, where he reported the events of Cozumel to a third Spanish posse that had just arrived from Valladolid. The posse then crossed over the channel and surprised the French sentries, who had been stationed on the beach. The sentries abandoned their posts and ran to the church, alerting their comrades. Sneaking out the back under the cover of nightfall, the French fled to Santa María de Oycib (Cedral), where they barricaded themselves in a corral and awaited the Spanish to attack. In the morning, after a brief fire-fight, the pirates ran out of gunpowder and surrendered. The Spanish posse had managed to kill eight of the Frenchmen and wound two more (including Captain Chueltot), whom the islanders carried back to San Miguel de Xamancab and summarily hung. The rest were taken by ship to Telchac, then overland to Mérida.

In Mérida, the ten remaining Frenchmen were tried and found guilty of piracy. Pilot Etienne Gilbert and crewmember Isaac Dorven were hung on July 17, 1571. Jean Hoscorno and Claude Ivilin were hung the following day. Pierre Sanfroy, Guillaume Siles, Guillaume Coquerelle, Martin Cornu, Jacques Montier, and Guillaume Poitiers were made slaves in the service of various Mérida households.

But they did not remain slaves for very long. On September 13, 1571, Pierre Sanfroy and his five crewmates were ordered to stand before a new trial at the offices of the Holy Inquisition in Mexico City. Between March and August, 1572, the six Frenchmen were sent one at a time to Mexico City to be tried not for being pirates, but instead, for being Lutheran heretics. However, only five made it to Mexico City: Guillaume Poitiers managed to escape en route and was never heard from again.

On June 7, 1572, Sanfroy, Siles, Cornu, Montier, and Coquerelle were accused of the crimes of *"being Lutheran, for uttering injurious words against the Pope, for uttering injurious words against the King of Spain, for eating meat on Friday, for reading aloud the psalm of David, for robbing the church at Hunucmá, for mocking the holy Mass and the sacraments, for profaning churches, and for robbing villages in Yucatán."* Jaques Montier never lived to see his trial. He died in detention in Mexico City on December 24, 1572.

Testifying against the French pirates were the *batab* of San Miguel Xamancab (Francisco Pat) and the two *batabs* of Santa María de Oycib (Pedro Pot y Juan Mah), all of Cozumel. Pablo Pat of Ecab also testified for the prosecution, as did Juan Ye, Juan Pat, and Diego Niho of Polé. The captured ship-owner, Pedro de la Mazuca, testified as well, along with Alonso de Villanueva and Rodrigo de Tapia.

On the morning of December 11, 1573, Sanfroy was ordered to be interrogated under torture on *el potro* (the rack) and submitted to *"toca hechar agua"* (similar to waterboarding) *"in caput propio et alienum,"* (until he confesses to his own crimes and those of others he witnessed). He was taken from the court room and led to the torture chamber where he was stripped down to his underwear. For four hours he was tortured on the rack and water-boarded until 12:45, when he confessed to eating meat on Fridays and of sympathizing with the Lutherans. At that, he was untied and allowed to dress.

Pierre Sanfroy was a 27-year-old French seaman from Saint-Vigor, on the coast of Normandy. He was described as *"white, good-looking, with a red face and a thick, reddish-blonde beard and a scar close to his left eye, just above his beard."* Pierre's father was a French gentleman, Charles Sanfroy, who was a Catholic. Charles had Pierre baptized as a child and raised him as a Catholic.

Pierre Sanfroy's first experience in warfare was when he had fought for nine months with the Catholic captain Forian against the Protestants in France. Later, he fought against the Anglicans at Le Havre. Still later, he fought against the Calvinists under Captain Villers, before joining Captain Pierre Chuetot on his expedition. When he was incarcerated in Mérida, Sanfroy had only nine *reales* on him, which were confiscated and applied to the cost of his prison meals.

Above: The Rack

Above: **"Toca hechar agua."**

On January 12, 1574, Sanfroy received his final sentencing: he was to be paraded through the streets of Mexico City while given being 200 lashes *de vehementi.* After that, he was to serve as a galley slave, rowing the King's ships without pay for six years.

On the 28 of February, 1574, Sanfroy was removed from his cell and taken to the courtroom to make a formal statement repenting his sins. The next day, he was dressed in a yellow *sambenito*, or penitent's robe with the cross of Saint Andrew on the front, given a lit *cirio penitencial*, or green candle to carry, and paraded through the city to the steps of the main church. There he was stripped from the waist up and given his 200 hard lashes. A few days later he was shipped off to begin his sentence as a galley slave, and was never heard from again.

Above: The robes of the sambenito, *ranging from the robe assigned to the least offensive heretic, (on the left) to the most offensive (on the right). Sanfroy was forced to wear the style third from the left.*

Guillaume Siles, Sanfroy's 24-year-old crewmate, escaped by digging under the wall of his cell, along with four other prisoners being held with him. The arrest warrant issued after his escape on March 9, 1573 described him as *"Guillermo de Silice, Frenchman, about 24 years old, short, fair complected, scant blond beard, small blue eyes, dressed in doublet and pants of coarse cloth."* He was soon recaptured and sentenced to 200 lashes and 4 years rowing the King's galleys.

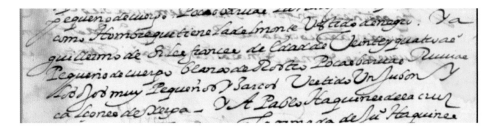

Above: Portion of arrest warrant issued for escape Guillaume Siles.

Guillaume Coquerelle, a 23-year-old crewmember, was sentenced to 200 lashes and 6 years rowing. Martin Cornu, age 29, was garroted, his body burned, and his ashes strewn in the gutter. Guillaume Poitiers, who had escaped while being taken to Mexico City, was judged guilty *in absencia*, excommunicated and burned in effigy.

Above: A penitent carrying a lit cirio penitencial, *or green candle.*

Miguel Molas; he was a "pirata," not a buccaneer!

Another "pirate" who did stay on Cozumel at one time was Miguel Molas, a Catalan from Barcelona who immigrated to México. In 1810, he moved into the old Spanish fort of El Cuyo, near Rio Lagartos, Yucatán. The fort had been abandoned since the late 1600s, but Molas had been employed by the Yucatán government as a military commander to preside over a newly formed watch-guard there assigned to enforce the laws concerning unlawful trade with foreign vessels bringing contraband goods into Yucatán. In 1814, Molas quit his job at El Cuyo, after finding he could make more money helping the smugglers than he could on a government salary. Molas had made many contacts in the illegal trade over the past four years, so he began cruising the coast of Quintana Roo, guiding the *contrabandistas* and eventually writing a book in 1817 detailing the reefs, shoals, and ports of that coast, entitled *Derrotero de la Península de Yucatán desde todas las costas e islas, bajos, puertos, y arrecifes, trabajado por la práctica, y cumplido conocimiento de Don Miguel Molas, en el año 1817*. It was in this book by Molas that Punta Molas in Cozumel was first christened. Contrary to local legend, Molas never actually lived on the point; he just named it after himself when he drew the map in 1817.

The ex-government employee was soon branded a *"pirata"* by the government, who used the same word, *pirata*, to describe both dealers in contraband as well as marauding buccaneers, similar to the way we used the word pirate to describe the act of counterfeiting videos and CDs. He was never actually what today we would consider a buccaneer. When the Yucatán government wanted to open the new port of Nueva Malaga on the north coast, Molas managed to sweet talk his way back into their good graces and in 1821 he was re-hired by the government to collect taxes there. Nueva Malaga was renamed Yalahau in 1823.

In 1821, the year México finally gained its independence from Spain, Molas led his men in a fight at Cancun and Isla Mujeres with Pierre Lafitte, the brother of Jean Lafitte; both pirates (and true buccaneers!) of world renown. Pierre died of his wounds shortly thereafter. That affair was not enough to redeem Molas in the eyes of the law though, when a warrant was made out for the *contabandista's* arrest, along with his side-kick, Buenaventura Leon, for trafficking in slaves in 1823. Back in custody again, the fast-talking Molas did his best to persuade the government that they would be better off by pardoning him and letting him help them ward off the coastal interlopers. In 1824, the government did just that. However, Molas couldn't resist temptation and soon he was up to his old tricks. Before long there was another order issued for his arrest and in 1828 he was once more captured and sent to Mérida, where he was sentenced to death by hanging.

Molas somehow managed to escape the gallows (some say he bribed his way out with the government's own money) and fled to Cozumel with his wife and two children. Once on the island, the fugitive built a farm where the town now stands and named it Rancho San Miguel, using the name that Montejo had given the place 300 years earlier. During his two-year residence on the island, he built a sloop, which he used to abandon the island in 1830. Moving farther south to present-day Belize, he sold his sloop and then sold his Rancho San Miguel to another *contrabandista* who had moved to México from Cataluña, Vicente Alvino Cammaño. After selling off his ranch and sloop, Molas moved to Tankah and put down roots.

Still believing he was a wanted man, Molas stayed in hiding, unknowing that with the change in government, he was no longer considered a fugitive. After a few years, he became ill and walked to Chemax to get medicine, but died on the road back to Tankah. A Maya who had accompanied him on the walk back buried the old rascal and went on to the ranch to tell his family. Two young men were sent out to dig up the body and bring it home for a family burial, but after carting the putrid corpse for miles, then loading it unto a sailing canoe to get back to Tankah, they said the body slipped overboard in a storm. More likely they just couldn't take the smell anymore and dumped it!

Chapter 8

When Cozumel was for sale

George Fisher, the man who almost bought Cozumel

Djordje Shagic was born in Hungary to Serbian parents in 1795. During his studies to be a priest he found he was adept at languages, and by the time he was 17 he had mastered over a dozen languages, including Latin, Greek, English, German, French, Portuguese, Italian, Spanish, Magyar, Serbian, Russian, Polish, Bohemian, Moravian, Slovenian, Croatian, Dalmatian and Montenegrin. However, adventure called and he left school to join and fight with the Serbian revolutionary forces against the Ottoman Turks during the first Serbian Revolution. After the revolution failed, he fled Austria and worked his way across Europe to Amsterdam and sailed as a stow-a-way to Philadelphia. In 1814, he assumed the name of George Fisher for the first time. In 1817 he moved to Port Gibson, Mississippi and married Elizabeth Davis there in 1818, becoming an American citizen. That same year he was initiated into the Masons and in 1823 became a Royal Arch Mason. Nine years after moving to Mississippi, Fisher moved to Mexico City while his wife stayed in Mississippi and raised their five children. Working as an editor for the *Correo del Atlántico* newspaper in Mexico City, Fisher met and was befriended by Joel Roberts Poinsett, the US Minister to México after whom the Poinsettia Christmas flower is named, and together they founded the first York Rite Masonic Lodge of that city. Fisher became a Mexican citizen in 1829, and in 1830 was given a land grant (formerly called the Haden grant) by the Mexican government where he was to settle 500 families in the Mexican territory of Texas.

Once the families had settled in, Fisher moved to Galveston, Texas and became the island's customs officer. Removed by General Manuel de Mier y Terán after only a few months, Fisher moved to San Felipe in 1830 and was hired by Stephen F. Austin to be the secretary of the *Ayuntamiento* there. Shortly thereafter, Fisher was fired as a suspected Mexican spy, but was immediately reinstated in his old job as customs officer for Galveston in 1831. His enforcement of the requirement that all ships coming to Texas pay customs duty at Anahuac regardless of their port of entry caused a fierce reaction against the Mexican government and the ensuing "Anahuac Disturbance" (led by James Walker Fannin, who later became the commander of the Texian forces at the Alamo) was one of the first preludes to the war for Texas independence. In 1832, he was fired once again from his Galveston post and he moved to Matamoros, where he first worked as a customs collector, then as the Commissary General of War, for the Eastern Internal States of México, (composed of Tamaulipas, Nuevo Leon, Coahuila, and Texas). After a dispute with District Judge Luis Gonzaga Martínez, he was again removed from service. In 1834, he became an auctioneer, worked as an official interpreter, founded a stationary store, began a job-printing business, and founded the *Mercurio Del Puerto de Matamoros* newspaper. In 1835, the year before Texas was to win its independence from México, his newspaper's editorials were deemed offensive to General López de Santa Anna and Fisher was given six days by Mexican authorities to leave Matamoros, losing all his printing equipment and personal belongings to the judge who signed the warrant. Fisher then moved to New Orleans and joined together with the Mexican Brigadier General José Antonio Mexía to help organize a revolt against General Santa Anna's centralist government. During his participation in the "Tampico Expedition" (as a Lt. Colonel serving as both Expedition Secretary and Commissary General), he befriended two other expedition members; Colonel Martín Peraza, the exiled former *Comandante del Batallon del Pueblo Viejo*, as well as Mr. George Robertson, the American Consul of Tampico, two men who would later play a part in his first attempt to buy Cozumel.

When the Texian forces defeated Santa Anna's troops at San Jacinto in 1836 and Texas declared its independence from México, Fisher took out Texas citizenship, first becoming a commission agent in Houston and then a Justice of the Peace. He moved back to Galveston in 1838 and assisted, in conjunction with Generals Sam Houston and Thomas J. Rusk, in forming several Masonic Lodges and Grand Lodges. One of the lodges he was instrumental in establishing (Harmony Lodge No.6 A.F. & A.M. of Galveston, Texas) counted Texan Navy Captain James P. Boylan as a founding member as well. A year earlier, Captain Boylan was ordered to take his schooner of war, *Brutus*, and accompany Commander Henry Livingston Thompson, of the Texan schooner of war *Invincible*, on a putative expedition along the coast of Yucatán in retaliation for Mexican attacks on Texan ships and the blockading of Texas ports.

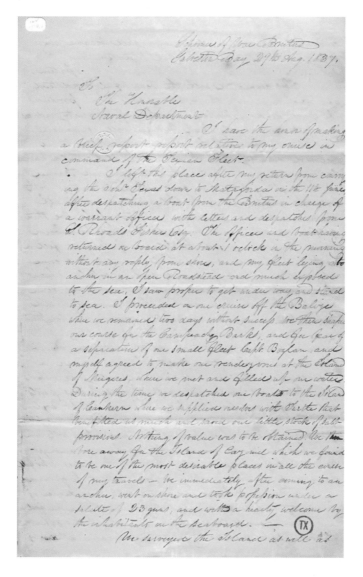

Above: Commander Thompson's report, stating how they planted the Texas Flag on Cozumel, claiming it for the Republic of Texas in 1837.

On July 13, 1837, the two ships reached Cozumel and on August 29, 1837 Commander Thompson sent a dispatch to his headquarters in Galveston regarding this foray, containing the following lines: *"We then bore away for the Island of Cazomel which we found to be one of the most desirable places in all the circle of my travels. We immediately after coming to an ancher went on shore and took possession under a salute of 23 guns and with a hearty welcome by the inhabitants on the seaboard. We surveyed the Island as well as circumstances would admit and still became more infatuated with its delightful situation and the salubrious trade wind which blows without cessation. This connected with the beautiful roadstead and anchorage and the richest of soils which produces the finest kind of timber and that of a variety induces me to think, not only think but am well convinced that it will be one of the greatest acquisitions to our beloved country that the Admiral aloft could have bestowed on us. I hoisted the Star spangled Banner at the height of forty five feet with acclamations both from the inhabitants of the Island and our small patriotic band, the crews of our two vessels. We then filled our water and made sail on our homeward bound passage, passed the Island of Mujeres."*

Captain Boylan wrote a report as well, which reads in part: *"Report of the cruise & transactions of the Texian Schooner of War* Brutus. *Saturday June 10th 1837 pursuant to orders received I got under weigh & stood out to sea in company with the* Invincible. *After having conveyed the Texian Schr. [Schooner]* Texas *to Matagorda bar, returned again to Galveston Bar. Sent a boat on shore which returned at midnight. We immediately got under weigh & stood to the East. Cruising near the mouth of the Mississippi in hopes to fall in with some of the Mexican vessels but not succeeding stood for the coast of Mexico, on the 1st July parted company with the* Invincible *having previously agreed to rendezvous at the Island of Mugeres. Cruised some days near Cape Antonio on the coast of Cuba but nothing appearing run for the Isle of Mugeres. On the 7th made the Island of Cantey & Mugeres on the 8th anchored in company with the* Invincible *in a few days completed & watering the vessels made several excursions to the neighboring Islands & main land found abundance of Turtle in pens & help ourselves caught some small perogues of but little account destroyed some liberated all the prisoners. On the 12th stood out to sea again & run down to the Island of Cozamel. On the 13th anchored the vessels on the S. W. point of the Island. Landed with our boats. Planted the single Star Banner of our Country in the soil of this delightful Island. The Inhabitants were but few but expressed their good feelings for us at the same time swearing allegiance to our cause. We made such surveys and remarks as our limited time would admit of. The anchorage are indeed safe & commodious for any number of vessels. The soil is delightfull. The climate salubrious. The forest abound in the finest Kinds of Timber, [?], mahogany, & Spanish Cedar and abundance of fruits of various kinds. There is also [an] abundance of water. On the whole I think it is amost desirable acquisition to our Government and I would respectfully recommend it to the consideration of our Congress. On the 16th of July started again for the Mexican Coast. On the 17th anchored on the west side of the Island of Cantey. Found domestic animals but no inhabitants although there were recent marks of people having been in the houses. Found many pens full of turtles. Took a fresh supply on board. Sent our boats on an expedition to a Town said to be near Cape Catoche. Next day they returned unable to find the place. Brought a canoe with them having on board nearly or perhaps all the saints in the Calendar with some female toggery & a whole host of Virgins alas they were all composed of [?] 19th sailed again for the coast of Yucatán. 21st landed at Silar but did not find any thing of consequence. From thence stood down to Leuckwe? I sent Lieut Wright on shore to take the town. This he soon accomplished. The Alcalda making a formal surrender of the town to the Texian Government. 22d Captured Schooner* Union of Sisal *loaded with log wood. Chased several vessels but they were all neutral. Captured a number of Perogues some having valuable property on board. On the 24th anchored off the Town of Chiblona."*

However, when the two Texan ships returned to Galveston on August 26, 1837, their spontaneous and unauthorized "annexation" of Cozumel was annulled by the President of Texas. That was not the end of Texas' meddling with Cozumel, though. Captain Boylan was a Mason in the same Galveston Masonic lodge as George Fisher and as it becomes clear later, Boylan must have praised the fine qualities of Cozumel to his lodge brother. Fisher was soon to try his hand at grabbing the island as well.

In 1838, a cotton plantation was established on the island of Cozumel by the Governor of Yucatán, the first *Alcalde* of Mérida, and Colonel Martin Peraza. They took around 30 debtors and criminals from the prison in Mérida and sent them to the island to use as forced labor. Vicente Alvino Cammaño, the Spanish-born *contrabandista* who ran a smuggling route from Belize to Sisal, had been living on the island since 1830 on the rancho originally settled by another *contrabandista,* Miguel Molas, where he farmed a little cotton with Maya labor. The Governor, *Alcalde,* and Colonel placed Alvino in charge of the plantation and gave him a share of the profits. In 1840, Alvino's conscripted workers revolted, and he had to flee the island with only his clothes on his back.

Meanwhile, back in Texas, Fisher obtained a divorce (granted by special act of the Texas congress) in 1839 from his wife Elizabeth, who had refused to leave Mississippi to be with him during all his travels. He promptly remarried after the divorce. Later, Fisher was admitted to the Bar and elected to the City Council of Houston in 1840. In October the same year he was served with three lawsuits for bad debts. During this rough spot in his life, he wrote to his friend, Texas Governor Henry Smith, asking for an appointment to some sort of position, saying *"I need excitement under my present oppressed state of mind, which can only be had by traveling, and I wish to do so, with honor to myself and profit for my country. The compensation is no object to me. I must have a diversion."* The energetic man of the world was casting about for new opportunities and, using his many contacts within the Texan and Yucatecan governments, Fisher put together a plan to buy the island his friend Captain Boylan was so enamored by and establish a plantation and logging operation there.

The British Consul in Galveston, William Kennedy, maintained a network of spies and he would periodically send reports back to the Earl of Aberdeen in London, regarding the movements of the Texan Navy and plans of the Texan government. In one such dispatch, Kennedy outlined the evolution of a plan by George Fisher, Mr. George R. Robinson (the former US Consul at Tampico), Texan Navy Commodore Moore, and several others to buy Cozumel for the sum of $100,000. The original plan fell through, but in 1841, Fisher made a second attempt, this time with the help of Col. Peraza who was returning to Austin via New Orleans as a special envoy from Yucatán to meet with the Texan Government. In another diplomatic dispatch, Kennedy wrote that he had in his possession a letter from Col. Peraza sent to an unnamed recipient, stating the colonel would do *"all that he could"* to help Fisher.

Kennedy states in the dispatch that on October 14, 1841, a company was formed in Galveston by three partners (and five others who had an option to purchase shares in the partnership later) to take advantage of new legislation enacted by the new governor of Yucatán, Miguel Barbachano. This new law, passed on April 5, 1841, allowed unoccupied land in Yucatán to be sold by the government. Now, Fisher's company was angling to buy the island under the provisions of the new law.

Fisher was sent by the other partners to Mérida with a down payment and authorization to buy two square leagues of the island. Included with the down payment was a map of the island with the first, second, and third sections of the land to be purchased marked on the map. After arriving in Sisal, Yucatán in 1841 aboard the Texan schooner of war *San Antonio*, Fisher made his way to Mérida where he met with one of his partner's, Ex-consul Robinson, who arrived previously via the US ship *Lucinda*. Fisher got permission from the government to survey and set apart <u>six</u> square leagues of the island, which he did by setting crosses as boundary markers. Fisher then sent a letter back to his partners, stating that *"from time to time, [we could] acquire the whole island gradually, but not at once, in order to avoid suspicion."*

During their trip to Yucatán In 1841, John Lloyd Stephens and Frederic Catherwood visited Mérida, where they ran into Fisher. The Serb/American/Mexican/Texan showed the two around town and helped them make contacts for their trip to the Quintana Roo coast, even introducing them to Vicente Alvino Cammaño, the last man to occupy Miguel Molas' old rancho at San Miguel, Cozumel. Later that year, when Stephens and Catherwood visited Cozumel (and sketched a drawing of the buildings of the San Miguel ranch for the book *Incidents of Travel in the Yucatán*), Vicente had just re-visited the old rancho to retrieve some of his goods that he had left there when he fled from his irate workers. In the book, Stephens tells of Fisher's recent purchase of 18 miles of coastline in Cozumel and how he had sent up crosses along the beach to mark the boundaries of his land.

Above: Djordje Shagic, (also known as George Fisher), as he appeared when he was a major in the Texas Army in 1843.

Unfortunately, the remainder of the funds Fisher needed to complete the transaction never arrived in Mérida (due to a bank failure in New Orleans) and Fisher had to return to Galveston in July, 1842 with only the confirmed contract to purchase, and not a signed deed. For whatever reason, the partnership fell apart, and the effort to buy Cozumel was abandoned.

In 1843 Fisher became a Major in the Army of the Republic of Texas. From 1846 to 1848 he was translator and keeper of the Spanish records of the General Land Office of Texas, having been previously paid to interpret the Convention that framed the State Constitution and to act as interpreter and translator to the Senate of the Republic. Fisher later moved to Panamá in 1850, where he worked as an interpreter for a while. In 1851 he sailed to California, where he served on various city boards and councils. He was elected in 1860 to the office of Justice of the Peace of San Francisco, and became one of the judges of the County Court, an office he held for several years. Soon after retiring from that office he was appointed by the King of Greece as Consul for that nation, an office he held to the time of his death in 1873.

Texas Navy seamen try to homestead on Cozumel

Texas Navy Lieutenant James S. O'Shaunessey, who had been to Cozumel with the *Brutus* and *Invincible* in 1837, became obsessed with the memory of the island and convinced his crewmates that if they mutinied and sailed to Cozumel, the Yucatán government would award them land and they could retire, happy ever-after in a tropical paradise. While aboard the Texas Navy vessel *San Jacinto* and anchored off Veracruz in October of 1840, O'Shaunessey gathered his men and they sailed the vessel without orders towards Cozumel and their dream. The only thing that stood in their way was the Arcas Islands, which they ran into during a storm and grounded the ship. The waves generated by the storm broke the vessel apart during the night. The crew was rescued on January 2, 1841, but O'Shaunessey soon deserted and was never prosecuted for his unauthorized cruise.

This was not the last time Texas Navy seamen tried to stake a claim on the island. In 1843, the Texas Navy was protecting the coast of Yucatán from a possible invasion by Mexican President Santa Anna in return for $8,000.00 USD a month in gold. Word had reached them that the Yucatecan government would reward their service by allowing them to stake out homesteads on *"terrenos baldías,"* or vacant government land. They decided to choose spots in Cozumel in which to settle. However, on August 23, 1843, William Kennedy, the British Consul in Galveston, got wind of the plan and sent a secret dispatch to London. In the dispatch, Kennedy states: *"Information has been brought by the Texan War Vessels lately employed in aiding Yucatán, that the Government of that State had granted the American officers and Seamen, in their Service, the privilege of settling a certain portion of Vacant public land, and that the said officers and Seamen were making preparations, - when the Texan Vessels left Campeche – "to visit the island of Cozumel and locate their Claims upon it."* Apparently nothing ever became of the officers' and seamens' plan, as no more word is ever mentioned of it again.

Belgium wants the island

In 1842, Belgium decided it would be advantageous to acquire a foothold in the Caribbean, so they put out feelers to see if any country there would be interested in selling them some territory. México responded with a solid "maybe," so an expedition was sent to check out likely spots, one of which was the island of Cozumel. The *Louise-Marie* cruised the Caribbean and Gulf of Honduras for a few months, but for one reason or another, failed to actually land on Cozumel. In the expedition's official report, only hearsay was recorded about the island, one piece of data being that there was a plantation there run by a European, referring to the property being purchased by George Fisher.

The idea of Belgium gaining a colony in México did not sit well with England, and they mounted a serious effort to undermine the project. Richard Pakenham, the British minister to México pulled out all the stops and was able to derail the project and it was eventually dropped by the Belgians.

However, other folks were still interested getting their hands on Cozumel, by either buying it or stealing it. In May, 1842, the President of the Republic of Texas, Sam Houston, had an odd conversation with the French chargé d'affaires Alphonse Dubois de Saligny, which Saligny dutifully recorded in his dispatch to Paris. Houston had been trying on behalf of the Texan government to get a loan of several million dollars from France, but so far he had been unable to get his hands on the funds. During a visit Saligny made to see President Houston at the port of Galveston, Houston had said to the Frenchman *"France has need of new colonies. Why does she not look for some close to us? It would be very easy to find something among the Mexican possessions to suit her taste."* Saligny reported to his superiors that he had told President Houston that France had *"renounced all idea of aggrandizement or conquest, and he did not see what right, under what pretext, or by what means she could seize some part of Mexican territory."* To which President Houston was supposed to have replied *"If that is all that is troubling you, nothing would be easier to arrange. We would take care of that. If Texas were to seize a portion of Mexican territory by force of arms, and, after holding it for a time, then chose to cede it to France, I, for my part do not see who could stand in the way."* Houston was unable to complete the conversation due to the departure of the steamer he was boarding in Galveston, and didn't have time to reveal that the "portion of Mexican territory" that could be seized by Texas and ceded to France was none other than the island of Cozumel. It wasn't until later, in February 1843, during a coach ride with Texas Secretary of War George Washington Hockley, that Saligny was told by the Secretary that the island of Cozumel was the looming target of a Texas land grab.

Yucatán offered free to any nation that can help

In 1841 Yucatán declared its independence from México, but in 1847 the internal conflict now known as the War of the Castes had broken out on the peninsula and the Maya Cruzoob rebels were winning. As a last-ditch effort, on May 25, 1848, Yucatán's Governor Santiago Méndez sent identical letters to Spain, Great Britain and the United States offering up the sovereignty over Yucatán to whichever nation could save them from the Maya rebels' wrath. US President Polk rejected the offer, but then invoked the Monroe Doctrine, warning all European nations to stay out of the conflict. Shortly after that, Governor Méndez resigned and Miguel Barbachano became the new governor. Barbachano reissued the offer and included an additional letter to Cuba as well, but the threat of retaliation by the US for becoming involved kept any nation from accepting. In late 1848, Yucatán rejoined the Republic of Mexico in return for its military help in fighting the rebels.

Abraham Lincoln tries to buy Cozumel

Most Americans were brought up to believe Abraham Lincoln was one of our greatest Presidents. As schoolchildren, we were told his belief in the equality of man led him to free the black slaves through his Emancipation Proclamation in 1862. However, reviewing the transcripts of his public speeches, the memoirs of those he worked with, and the public records, a very different Abe Lincoln comes to life. It would seem that the main reason he wanted to free the nation's slaves was to be able to then deport them, preferably back to Africa.

Above: Freed black slaves being shipped back to Africa.

Since the 1840s, Lincoln had been a member of the American Colonization Society, a group that was instrumental in setting up colonies along the shore of Sierra Leone in 1820 with the help of the US government for the express purposed of receiving deported black freedmen. The colonies were managed by a hodge-podge of missionaries, functionaries appointed by the American government, and black entrepreneurs. The colonies were not very successful until most of them banded together in 1838, renaming their capital Monrovia and their new, unified colony Liberia. In 1847 they declared their independence, drawing the wrath of the US government, who refused to recognize the new nation. The ships bringing deportees stopped coming.

Above: The American Colonization Society's territory on the west coast of Africa in 1829. It would later become Liberia.

Above: Lincoln's letter donating $200 to the American Colonization Society's efforts to rid the US of black ex-slaves.

On August 21, 1858, in his first debate with Stephen A. Douglas in Ottawa, Illinois, Lincoln said: *"My first impulse would be to free all the slaves, and send them to Liberia,—to their own native land. But a moment's reflection would convince me that whatever of high hope (as I think there is) there may be in this, in the long run, its sudden execution is impossible. If they were all landed there in a day, they would all perish in the next ten days; and there are not surplus shipping and surplus money enough in the world to carry them there in many times ten days."*

Above: A political brochure of the 1800s promoted shipping freed black slaves back to Africa, an idea Lincoln strongly encouraged.

Later, on September 18, 1858, in his fourth debate with Stephen A. Douglas at Charleston, Illinois, Lincoln stated: *"I will say then that I am not, nor ever have been in favor of bringing about in any way the social and political equality of the white and black races - that I am not nor ever have been in favor of making voters or jurors of negroes, nor of qualifying them to hold office, nor to intermarry with white people; and I will say in addition to this that there is a physical difference between the white and black races which I believe will forever forbid the two races living together on terms of social and political equality. And inasmuch as they cannot so live, while they do remain together there must be the position of superior and inferior, and I as much as any other man am in favor of having the superior position assigned to the white race."*

Since Mexican President Benito Juárez was on good terms with Lincoln, the US President felt that perhaps México might be able to provide a place for the US to send its freed black slaves. Word was passed down the chain-of-command to send out feelers. In 1861, Montgomery Blair, the Postmaster General and a personal friend of Matias Romero, the Mexican *charge d'affaires* in Washington at the time, met several times to discuss the matter. Romero reported to his superiors that Blair had told him *"Cozumel is a deserted island which in no way serves the Mexicans, and the white race could not possibly acclimatize itself on Cozumel or Yucatán, which is inhabited by Indians. These regions are destined to be populated by Negroes. We need to rid ourselves of them, and we could not encounter another place more appropriate to send them than that island."*

Romero later sent a dispatch to México stating: *"Today I met with Montgomery Blair. He related to me that Edward Dunbar and Domingo de Goicuria had visited him to propose the sale of the island of Cozumel to the United States government. This project pleased him because he believed Cozumel would be a very apt place to send the Southern Negroes. He inquired if Goicuria had the authorization of the supreme government to negotiate an arrangement of this kind with the United States. According to my understanding, I replied, he did not, since his current commission was solely for the purpose of obtaining money in New York. Moreover, I did not believe it would be possible to celebrate a convention in that form, I told Blair, because the government and the people of Mexico were firmly decided against alienating another inch of national territory. If the United States, I said, wishes to transport to that island some or all of the Southern Negroes, it can conclude an arrangement with Mexico. I do not doubt that my government will be favorably disposed toward such an arrangement. Consequently, the colonization will be done in the form the United States desires, provided, however, Mexico does not lose sovereignty over the island."*

After Romero's meeting with Blair, Secretary of State William Henry Seward (who was later to purchase the Russian Territory of Alaska for the US in 1867) also met with the *chargé d'affaires* to talk further about the possibility of purchasing the island of Cozumel for this purpose.

Romero informed him that the purchase would be next to impossible, but they would be amenable to taking certain, selected, freed-slaves in as immigrants.

Unaware that the Cozumel purchase was doomed to failure, Senator James Rand Doolittle, head of the Senate's State Foreign Relations Committee, introduced a bill to allow the President to go through with a purchase of foreign territory. Doolittle hoped the area chosen would be Cozumel and was instrumental in getting the bill passed, which it did, breezing through the Senate vote. Blair also wanted to see the deal work. He said he wanted to place the black freedmen of the United States *"...in the hot lands of Southern Mexico where they could do the agricultural labor for which they were deemed suitable."* However, as Romero had predicted, the sale of the island to the US was a non-starter, and Lincoln abandoned the Cozumel project.

On May 20, 1862, the American Consul-General in Cuba, Robert Wilson Shufeldt, presented Manuel Doblado, Benito Juárez' Minister of Foreign Relations, another plan by President Lincoln to send freed, black, American slaves to México. This time the intended colony would be the Isthmus of Tehuantepec, a strip of land that the US had been trying to buy from México since the 1840s in order to build a road and railway across it to join the Atlantic and Pacific. This plan to send the freed blacks to Tehuantepec was rejected by México as well.

On August 4, 1862, Lincoln gave an address at the White House, expressing his hope that a foreign territory could be purchased by the US to relocate freed, black slaves. In the address, Lincoln said, *"You [blacks] and we [whites] are of different races. We have between us a broader difference than exists between almost any other two races. Whether it is right or wrong I need not discuss, but this physical difference is a great disadvantage to us both, as I think your race suffers very greatly, many of them by living among us, while ours suffer from your presence. In a word we suffer on each side. If this is admitted, it affords a reason at least why we should be separated. Your race is suffering, in my opinion, one of the most grievous injustices inflicted on any people. But even when you cease to be slaves, you are yet far removed from being placed on an equality with the white race. You are cut off from many of the advantages which the other race enjoy. The aspiration of men is to enjoy equality with the best when free, but on this broad continent, not a single man of your race is made the equal of a single man of ours. Go where you are treated the best, and the ban is still upon you."*

"It is better for us both, therefore, to be separated. I know that there are free men among you, who even if they could better their condition are not as much inclined to go out of the country as those, who being slaves could obtain their freedom on this condition. I suppose one of the principal difficulties in the way of colonization is that the free colored man cannot see that his comfort would be advanced by it. You may believe you can live in Washington or elsewhere in the United States the remainder of your life as easily, perhaps more so than you can in any foreign country, and hence you may come to the conclusion that you have nothing to do with the idea of going to a foreign country. This is (I speak in no unkind sense) an extremely selfish view of the case."

In September 1862, Lincoln's next effort to send black freedmen to a foreign territory began with attempt to ship off 50,000 of them to colonize land owned by Ambrose W. Thompson in the Chiriquí Province of Panamá. Due to the vocal complaints of neighboring countries, the plan was abandoned. That same September, a fourth attempt was made, this time to set up a black colony in *Ille a Vache* off the coast of Haiti. 500 black freedmen were sent as a first wave, but the project was a miserable failure and the starving colonists had to be rescued by the US military a year later. After that, Lincoln gave up all hope of acquiring a foreign territory for the black freedmen, and refocused his attention on the Civil War.

CHAPTER 9

The "True Blue" Tale
of Cozumel's *Repobladores de 1848*

In 1836, the Mexican territory of Texas achieved its independence from México at the Battle of San Jacinto, a town adjacent to present day Houston, Texas. The Mexican general who lost the battle, war, and province was Antonio de Padua María Severino López de Santa Anna y Pérez de Lebrón. He was captured at San Jacinto and capitulated, signing the Treaty of Velasco with the newly independent Republic of Texas stating the Rio Grande River was the southern border of Texas and the northern border of México. He reneged on the pact as soon as he was released from custody. Santa Anna first tried to blockade the new republic's ports, but the plan backfired and the Texans captured and sank many of the Mexican Navy's vessels. The fight simmered off and on for years, but México made no progress on regaining the old province. On December 29, 1845, the Republic of Texas joined the United States as the 28th state of the union.

On April 26, 1846, Mexican cavalry elements attacked a US military force that had taken a position just north of the Rio Grande, the river Santa Anna's treaty had defined as the southern limit of Texas. The US retaliated and declared war on México on May 13, 1846. The US calls this war the Mexican-American War. México calls it the *La Intervención Estadounidense en México*.

The loss of the breakaway province of Texas and the war with the US weren't the only problems México was facing at the time. In October, 1841, Yucatán (at the time, an area comprising today's Campeche, Yucatán, and Quintana Roo) declared its independence from México as well. However, regardless of their new status as an independent nation, the Yucatecans were up to their own elbows in alligators, as the Maya living on the peninsula had rebelled in 1847 and were quickly gaining the upper hand in the revolt, a conflict that came to be called the War of the Castes.

The Maya rebels were known as the *Cruzoob*, or "people of the cross," because of their belief in a mystic talking-cross that told them it was time to rid the peninsula of all non-Maya. To this end, the *Cruzoob* were steadily hacking their way northward up the peninsula towards the capital city of Mérida, cutting to pieces every non-Maya they found along the way. In January of 1848 the rebels reached Valladolid and surrounded the city, causing panic within. On March 14, 1848, the frightened populace abandoned the city in a wild melee. A column of around 10,000 men, women, and children raced away from Valladolid with only what they could carry on their backs, fleeing from the Maya horde that was decimating their rear ranks. One group of about 600 refugees began making their way northward towards the coastal village of Dzilam, under the protection of a small company of Yucatecan soldiers led by Captain Sebastián Molas Virgilio, a nephew of the *contrabandista* Miguel Molas. Once the group got to Dzilam, there was nowhere else to go, so they hunkered together, hungry, unprotected and their backs to the sea. The Maya were just a few miles behind, and catching up fast. All must have seemed lost.

The US signed the Treaty of Guadalupe Hidalgo, ending its war with México on February 2. Although it had been waging war against México, it had maintained good relations with México's break-away province of Yucatán and had kept a US consular presence in the new country during the war. So, when word reached the American Consul in Campeche that Valladolid was being abandoned and much of the populace was racing towards Dzilam, he began a series of dispatches to the Commodore of the US Home Fleet, which was now moored at Laguna Terminos. The Consul, John F. McGregor, told Commodore Matthew Calbraith Perry (who was to later sail to Japan in 1852 and open that reclusive country to US trade for the first time) about the plight of the refugees. McGregor stressed that some kind of rescue mission must be attempted quickly, or the civilians would be killed by the machete-wielding *Cruzoob*. On March 22, 1848, McGregor wrote to Commodore Perry:

"My dear sir:
If you can possibly spare me a steamer, you will be doing a great act of charity. There are now thousands of men, women and children on the

beach, suffering and in want. I cannot go; had I the Falcon *or a steamer, I could relieve, in a great part, the suffering of these refugees."*

Commodore Perry responded on the 28th by sending the *USS Falcon*, a US Schooner of War, to Dzilam with orders to assist in the evacuation. On April 2, 1848, the captain of the *Falcon*, John J. Glasson, wrote the following dispatch to Commodore Perry, after the *Falcon* had finished its rescue mission and was back in Campeche:

"In conformity of your orders of 28th ultimo, I proceeded to the windward to give such succor to the people from the cruelty of the Indians along the coast of Yucatán as was pointed out in it. The nearest point was Selam [Dzilam], about 120 miles to the eastward of Campeachy [Campeche], at which I anchored. Proceeding to the shore, I **boarded a small vessel with English colors, at anchor, named the "True Blue," James Smith, master, bound to the island of Cosumel, crowded with persons, who, according to the statement of the master, preferred the Island of Cosumel as an asylum as there was an English settlement.** *I landed at the town of Selam and found a number of persons there from the city of Valladolid, who had fled at the capture of it by the Indians and anxious to proceed with me to Campeachy. I took on board 121 persons. Many of the inhabitants had arrived and left for Sisal with the hope of reaching Campeachy. It was said that the Indians were within seven or nine miles."*

The US Congress later acknowledged Captain Glasson's humanitarian act, noting that he: *"extended protection, food, and shelter to fleeing white inhabitants in their destitution and despair, and those thus aided were a portion of the people of a country with whom we were at war."* The *Falcon* carried the 121 refugees it loaded aboard at Dzilam onwards to Campeche. The English-flagged vessel *True Blue* carried its load of refugees to Cozumel, and some Spanish-flagged vessels (Spain was neutral during the Mexican-American War) carried other refugees to Havana.

Many US newspapers ran accounts of the panicked exodus to Dzilam, such as the one printed in the Lafayette Courier on May 12, 1848. The article stated that: *"some thousands have taken shelter in the islands of*

Cosmel, of Mageres, and of Contoy. The coast between Boca de Cotnil and Sisal is flocked with men, women, and children from the interior of the country, laid waste, who are wending their way to Sisal, and embarking as opportunities offer, to Campeachy.... They are in a starved, miserable, and helpless condition.... The wealthy families are reduced to poverty and many have nothing but the clothing on their backs." The Geneva Courier ran the same story on April 13, adding: *"the most urgent steps were being taken to press every bungo and canoe to the immediate relief of the people along the coast, in order to embark them without delay, as the latest information represented the Indians from seven to nine leagues of the coast about Silan."*

All of this is well documented, but the facts don't fit well with the local myth of the arrival of the *"Repobladores de 1848"* to Cozumel. The oral history of these 20 or so "founding families" never mentions the *True Blue*, Captain James Smith, the *USS Falcon*, the route from Dzilam, or any of the above events. The question that begs to be asked is: Why?

The *True Blue* was described in the 1829 edition of the <u>Honduras Almanack</u> as a 23-ton sloop, owned by Nicholas Campbell of Belize. She carried a crew of six and was a "coaster," or coastal trading vessel and she specialized in contraband. According to a Belizean shipwright who had performed some repairs on her sometime prior to 1850, she was a fine ship *"and her framing, which was also of Mahogany, was in perfect condition after being up more than 17 years."*

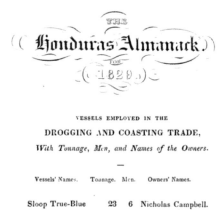

Above: A page from the 1829 Honduras Almanack.

Looking into the earlier history of the *True Blue*, it turns out that the British-flagged ship, its master, and its cargo were seized by Yucatecan authorities on October 20, 1840, when its Belizean captain and Yucatecan crew was surprised *in flagrante* unloading contraband cargo on a beach near the port of Telchac on the north coast of Yucatán. The cargo belonged to Francisco Camoyano, a merchant/agent/resident of Belize, and was consigned to Ignacio and José Antonio Medina, both residents of Motul and well known *contrabandistas*. The *administrador de aduana* of Sisal, Manuel Arcadio Quijano and the *comandante de celadores*, Pedro Cámara, arrested the Belizean captain and placed the cargo and ship up for auction. However, before the ship was sold, Belize sent the British corvette *Comus* to Sisal to demand the ship be returned as well as a recompense for the auctioned cargo. The town was given 48 hours to turn over the *True Blue* plus damages of $8,193.00 dollars or Sisal would be bombarded by the cannons of the *Comus*. Within hours, the Sisal authorities capitulated and the *True Blue* and its captain were freed. On January 2, 1841 the Yucatán government approved the payment to Camoyano.

In 1845, the *True Blue* was once again caught unloading contraband cargo, this time in Honduras. Records show the Honduran authorities caught the *True Blue* unloading "*26 barriles de harina, 19 barriles de carne de cerdo, 2 barriles de galleta de soda, una carga de cadenas, ejes para carretas de bueyes y otros implementos.*" All of this shipment was destined to the Belizean woodcutter Robert Wardlaw for his illegal woodcutting camp on the Limón River in Honduras.

A pattern, perhaps? It is clear that the Belizean vessel *True Blue* was a frequent visitor to the waters between Honduras and Sisal between 1840 and 1848, delivering contraband products from Belize to English camps and other interests up and down the coast. The captain must have known every port between Sisal and Trujillo very well. The fact that he was taking the refugees to Cozumel in 1848 seems to underline the argument that it was a place he knew they would be well received, not just an empty, deserted island in which to dump them. But what was this mysterious "English settlement" that the refugees said they knew to be on Cozumel? It was the English logwood-cutters who had been making Cozumel their base of operations since 1670.

When the two Texas Navy vessels, *Brutus* and *Invincible,* landed on Cozumel near Laguna Colombia on August 29, 1837, they were met by some of these inhabitants of the island. Commander Thompson of the *Invincible* later sent a dispatch to his headquarters in Galveston regarding this foray, stating they had *"a hearty welcome by the inhabitants on the seaboard,"* and that the symbolic act of raising the Texas flag and laying claim to the Island of Cozumel was met *"with acclamations both from the inhabitants of the Island and our small patriotic band, the crews of our two vessels."* Captain Boylan's report of the 1837 landing also mentioned the people living on Cozumel: *"The Inhabitants were but few but expressed their good feelings for us at the same time swearing allegiance to our cause."* These two documents show that, unlike what the oral tradition leads us to believe, Cozumel was indeed inhabited (by people apparently happy to become Texans), prior to the arrival of the *Repobladores de 1848.*

In August 23, 1843, the British Consul in Galveston, William Kennedy, sent a secret dispatch to Lord Aberdeen in London touching on the possibility that Texas might be trying to acquire Cozumel. In the letter, Kennedy wrote that Cozumel has *"two excellent harbours, Brutus Cove and Port Thompson. Easy to be defended and offering many advantages for shipping, Cozumel is said to be well adapted for the establishment of a Commercial Nation; possessing local facilities for supplying Southern Mexico, the Bay of Honduras and Colombia."* This description does not square with the image of a useless, deserted island.

An interesting article by Martín Francisco Peraza appeared in the 1846 edition of volume III of the *Registro Yucateco.* In the article, the author states: *"Los bosques de la isla* [Cozumel] *abundan en hermosos cedros, zapotes, jabines, guayacanes, y ébanos, aunque estos últimos casi los han agotado los cortadores de madera de los establecimientos británicos de Honduras."* (The forests of the island [Cozumel] abound in beautiful cedar, *zapotes, jabines, guayacanes* and ebonies, although the latter have been almost exhausted by the British wood-cutting establishments of Honduras.) This complaint was nothing new. In the report entitled *Apuntaciones para la estadistica de la provincia de*

Yucatán que formaban de orden superior en 20 marzo de 1814, it was stated that Cozumel *"produces ebony, logwood, and cedar"* and that *"the English of Walix* [Belize] *are settled there, and they are stealing our fish, turtles, caray, and amber that washes up on the beach."*

It was always a problem visualizing the mythical version of the arrival of the *Repobladores* to Cozumel. Imagining dozens of families comprised of landholders, artisans, businessmen, their wives, servants, and children arriving on the empty beach of an abandoned island and setting up a new life from scratch was just too difficult to picture. Where did they all sleep the first night? Where did they get food and water? Why would they opt for a deserted island rather than the safety of towns like Mérida, Sisal, or Campeche? All they had with them when they landed on Cozumel was what they could carry; no pigs, cows, seeds, farm implements, tools, or the other items necessary for building a new colony. All they must have had was the gold and currency they brought with them as they were running for their lives in the panicked rout from Valladolid to Dzilam, just hours ahead of the machete-wielding *Cruzoob*. What good would gold and currency do them on a deserted island?

It never made sense until now. If there was already an English woodcutting camp on Cozumel where the captain of the *True Blue* regularly dropped off supplies and other ships came to pick up cargoes of logwood, then that means the refugees didn't land on an empty beach. Huts, wells, kitchens, and a supply-line to Belize were already in place. Offer these Belizean woodcutters/turtle fishermen some of your gold in exchange for their huts and supplies and surely they would gladly hang their hammocks under a new, temporary lean-to and help you to settle into their old abode. It would be much easier for the Belizean workers to earn a salary as a helper for one of these refugee families than it was cutting wood or fishing for turtles for a living.

So who, exactly, were the English inhabitants of Cozumel who welcomed the *"Repobladores de 1848"* to the island and what kind of buildings were already in place? We can get a good idea of the kind of bstructures waiting for them from a drawing made of San Miguel's beachfront that was drawn in 1842, six years prior to their arrival. It appears in John Lloyd Stephen's account of the journey he took through the Yucatán Peninsula along with Fredrick Catherwood during the years of 1841 and 1842. The book is entitled <u>Incidents of Travel in Yucatán</u> and was first published as a two volume set in 1843 in the United States. On page 246 of volume II of the first edition of the book, there is a copper plate engraving that Joseph Napoleon Gimbrede made from Catherwood's original drawing, entitled *"San Miguel, Isla de Cozumel"* and listed in the book's contents page as plate XLIII. Gimbrede's etching of Catherwood's drawing depicts the rancho of the *contrabandista* Vicente Alvino Cammaño.

Above: An etching made by Joseph Napoleon Gimbrede from Frederick Catherwood's 1842 drawing of San Miguel de Cozumel.

Alvino had acquired Rancho San Miguel from fellow *contrabandista* and Catalan immigrant Miguel Molas when Molas moved away from the island permanently in 1830 after living there for two years while on the run from the law. For the next few years, Alvino used Cozumel as his base of smuggling operations and even began to grow cotton in a field near the rancho.

Alvino had a regular smuggling route that stretched from Sisal to Belize and he got along well with most of those he dealt with on the route. He also had a much better relationship with the Yucatecan government officials than did Molas. The relationship was so much better, in fact, that in 1838 the Governor of Yucatán made him a deal: In return for a lion's share of the profits, a new partnership made up of the Governor, the First Alcalde of Mérida, and Coronel Martín Francisco Peraza would send Alvino thirty prisoners to use as slave labor on the San Miguel cotton plantation. The deal also guaranteed Alvino that the government would turn a blind eye to his other illegal endeavors. For a while, the partnership flourished. Cotton was harvested and shipped to the United States, where it was judged to be an excellent quality and fetched a good price. It seemed everybody was happy, except for the slave laborers.

In 1840, Darío Galera became the new *Alcalde* of Mérida. Although he is known to have bought and sold logwood harvested from Cozumel previously, it was most likely during this period he became even more familiar with the island through his close personal friendship with Colonel Martín Peraza, one of the partners in Alvino's plantation. It is also likely that it was during this period Galera staked his claim to the parcel of land on Cozumel he sold later in the mid-1850s to the *Repoblador* Juan Bautista Anduze. This was the hacienda that Anduze re-named Hacienda Colombia de Todos Santos.

Later in 1841, Col. Peraza traveled to Austin, Texas with a box containing 8,000 dollars in gold, the first of several monthly payments to Texas to insure the Texas Navy would patrol and protect the Yucatán coast from attack by Mexican President Santa Anna. During his visit, Col. Peraza offered his political pull to Captain Boylan's Masonic brother, George Fisher, the Serbian-born Texan who, together with Texan President Sam Houston and other partners, was to try to buy most of Cozumel from the Yucatecan government in 1841. Towards this end, the group filed documents in Galveston, Texas on October 14 of 1841 establishing their partnership. The other partners included Commander in Chief of Texan Naval Forces Commodore Edwin W. Moore, George Washington Wheelwright (a Captain of one of the Texan schooners of war and a close friend of Houston's), George Fisher, and four others who had the option of joining the partnership at a later date.

Coronel Peraza's influence worked, and Fisher subsequently made a trip to Mérida (where he ran into Stephens and Catherwood) and arranged a contract to purchase about one-third of the island with the Yucatán government. This purchase was planned to be the first of several subsequent purchases, after which the island would be entirely owned by the Texas company. After Fisher made a down payment on the purchase price, he had the island surveyed and erected crosses to mark the boundaries of certain parcels. Unfortunately, his deal to buy the island fell through when the bank in New Orleans that was holding the balance of the funds that were needed to pay off the purchase went bankrupt. Alvino's cotton plantation also went bust in 1842, when the prisoners rebelled and chased Alvino away. Then, shortly before Stephens and Catherwood landed on Cozumel, the prisoners also fled the plantation.

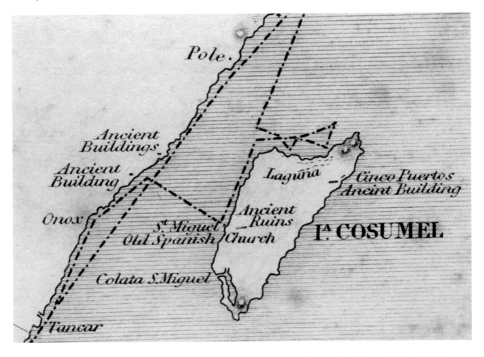

Above: The route Stephens and Catherwood took aboard the Sol *to Cozumel. San Miguel and Caleta are shown too far south on this map.*

In Stephens' account of his visit to Cozumel in 1842, he stated that the island was unpopulated at that time. This description has been used often as proof that the *Repobladores de 1848* were the first to resettle Cozumel. However, Stephens and Catherwood were on Cozumel for only two and a half days; hardly enough time to see much of the island by foot. The route they took aboard their sailboat, the *Sol*, was recorded in the first edition of Incidents of Travel in Yucatán and shows that they visited Isla de la Pasión and Rancho San Miguel, but did not pass anywhere near Cedral or Laguna Colombia (although they placed San Miguel a little too far south on their map in error). There could have been several hundreds of people living on the southern end of Cozumel and the two adventurers would have never known.

Besides the buildings at Rancho San Miguel, there must have been some kind of settlement near Darío Galera's property at Colombia Lagoon. He was actively selling logwood obtained in Cozumel to the United States throughout the 1840s and 1850s, like the load he sent aboard the US brig *Henry Leeds* in July of 1844. Was Galera's logwood-harvesting endeavor on Cozumel operated by Belizean woodcutters? Was this the English settlement the *"Repobladores"* spoke of as being on the island?

Above: Cozumel on a map dated 1848. Shown are: Caleta San Miguel, Rancho Sta. María, Cinco Puertas Maya ruins, and three aguadas.

On May 12, 1848, just a few short weeks after the evacuation of the *Repobladores de 1848* at Dzilam, a report was filed by Juan Bautista Topete y Carballo in Havana, from aboard the Spanish schooner *Cristina*. Topete had returned to Cuba from a visit to Cozumel only a few days earlier. In his report, he mentioned that when he left Cozumel, there were *"around 400 individuals of all sexes and ages that had made their houses on the western part of the island, in the form of bohios* [huts] *of chit* [palm thatch]." Four-hundred individuals is a lot more that the *True Blue* carried over in April of 1848. Most likely this figure included the Belizeans who were already living on the island when the *Repobladores de 1848* arrived.

Once the *Repobladores* were established, most of the woodcutters would have returned to Belize to their families, richer for the experience. These Belizeans likely had never planned on making Cozumel their permanent home; most were just itinerant workers moving from camp to camp in search of tortoise-shell, mahogany, and logwood. Besides, their presence on the island was only tolerated by the Mexican government because it didn't have the manpower to enforce their eviction. It was never intended to be a recognized settlement like Belize. The refugees, on the other hand, chose to stay on the island and use it as a base for a new enterprise; within the year they were earning their livelihood by selling captured Maya *Cruzoob* rebels to the Cubans to work in the their sugarcane fields of that island nation.

The *"Repobladores"* also dealt in valuables that were looted during the chaos on the mainland. On July 17, 1848, Pedro José Garma testified to the alcalde of Motul, Antonio Cervera, that: *"...in Cozumel there is José Alcocer, brother-in-law of the deceased Juan Vázquez, who sold in Belice a considerable number of silver pieces taken from the churches in Valladolid. Pacheco, the brother of Bonifacio Novelo, is the ringleader of these barbarians and other criminals."*

The *Repobladores* may have started a few farming and ranching operations on Cozumel soon after they landed on the island, but any such endeavor would have taken many months, even years, before it would begin to pay off. The new Yucatecan residents of Cozumel needed to get established quickly. They did not have time to fell trees, clear fields, sow crops, build pens, and wait for livestock to begin reproducing in quantities sufficient for market. They needed income in a hurry. Selling captured Maya *Cruzoob* to Cuban slave traders filled that bill nicely.

The *Repobladores* did not waste any time getting started. The *Cristina's* visit wasn't an anomaly; ships were stopping by Cozumel on a regular basis. The Maya *Cruzoob* prisoners of war were typically sent by sea to Cozumel from Rio Lagartos or Sisal and there seems to have been a large number of small vessels plying the waters between Cozumel and the northern Yucatán coast back then. In early 1849, just a short eight months after the chaotic evacuation of Dzilam and the arrival of the *Repobladores* in San Miguel de Cozumel, the *Alcalde* of Cozumel submitted a report to the Yucatecan government detailing the number of vessels arriving to the island, along with their cargos and the names of their masters. For the month of January of 1849, the report tallied 10 vessels: 1 American, 1 British, 5 Belizean, and 3 Mexican. Were these the only vessels that called on the new port? Definitely not. Most of the voyages, like those of the *True Blue*, were clandestine and went unrecorded. A few of these contraband and/or slaving ships, however, did leave behind a record of their passing. For example, on December 21, 1850, it was recorded that the Cuban vessel *Alerta,* captained by Francisco Martínez, arrived in Cozumel with an empty hold. This vessel was one of the many that belonged to the Cuban slave-trader Francisco Martí y Torrens, also known in Cuba as Pancho Martí. Pancho Martí held a special concession to fish in Yucatán waters, granted to him by the Yucatecan government, which he used to disguise his slave-trading enterprise that operated in Cuba, Yucatán, the American Gulf Coast, and Africa. It is a pretty safe bet that when Pancho Martí's boat left Cozumel for the trip back to Cuba, its hold was no longer empty, but full of Maya slaves destined for the Cuban sugarcane fields.

Often the facts of a slaver's voyage were recorded only because of some unforeseen event, as in the case of the 35-foot-long sailing vessel *Sol,* captained by Feliciano Peraza. It was the same boat that had carried John Lloyd Stephens and Frederic Catherwood to Cozumel 11 years earlier. The *Sol* sank on May 10, 1852, with a cargo of 9 slaves (described as "servants" in the report of the wrecking event made by Enrique Angulo, the second *Alcalde* of Cozumel) belonging to Juan Bautista Anduze. Two of the slaves drowned, but seven made it safely to the shore and freedom. Peraza managed to raise the *Sol* and he had repaired the vessel by that June, when he returned to Rio Lagartos to pick up more "servants" for Sr. Anduze. After rounding up another group of Maya and securing them aboard, the *Sol* anchored at Punta Francés in Holbox for the night. The captured Maya took advantage of the stop-over, breaking their bonds, killing Peraza and severely wounding his two deckhands, Pantaléon Rosado and José Carrillo. Rosado was able to sail the boat to Isla Mujeres, where a posse was assembled and sent out to recapture the escaped "servants."

In June, 1852, another boat lost four "servants" who had escaped when that boat also stopped overnight at Holbox on the way to Cozumel. This same month, the *Petrona*, captained by Guadalupe Pech, carried 13 Maya to Cozumel consigned to Colonel José Dolores Cetina. A few days later, Manuel Gascas' *Joaquina* out of Telchac struck a reef off Cozumel and sank with an unspecified number of "servants" aboard consigned to Tómas Mendiburu, the owner of a rancho on Cozumel. Before the month was out, the *Segunda Antonia*, captained by Casiano Cosgaya and out of Sisal, docked at Cozumel with a cargo of 17 Maya who Pilar Canto had shipped to the island from Mérida.

What percentage of the slave trade these few reports represent is unknown, but it is most likely a very small one. The route was well established. The Maya rebels captured in Yucatán were taken first overland to Rio Lagartos and then to Cozumel and Isla Mujeres by sail. There, the slaves would be held while the islands' slave-traders awaited Cuban "fishing" boats to come to the islands and purchase them. The slaves would then be taken to Cuba inside the fishing boats' *viveros* or "live pens" and sold to sugarcane plantation owners.

Not all of Cozumel's slave traders got away clean. Juan Bautista Anduze was eventually arrested in Belize by British authorities and was sentenced to four years in prison for shanghaiing Maya rebels near Bahía Asunción. Belizean court records show that in 1853, a *"John Baptiste Anduze, resident of St. Thomas with a British passport,"* hired an English-flagged ship, the *Jenny Lind,* to sail from the port of Belize to Bahía Asunción with a cargo of clothing, lead shot, and supplies which was sold for $2,500 pesos to the insurgent Maya. Once the goods and money changed hands, 36 of the Maya were offered a ride up the coast, ostensibly to take them closer to their homes, but they were not to arrive. Instead, the Maya were kidnapped and taken to Isla Mujeres, where they were transferred to a Cuban vessel owned by the Cuban slave-trader, Francisco Martí y Torrens, and shipped off to work in the Cuban sugarcane fields.

One of the *Jenny Lind's* crewmembers, a creole from Belize, reported the incident to the Belizean authorities and an order was issued for John Baptiste Anduze's arrest. When Anduze was caught by Belizean authorities, he still had with him the letter from slave dealer Pancho Martí y Torrens with the prices he was willing to pay for captured Maya: 25 dollars for each adult male, 17 dollars for adult females and adolescent males, and eight dollars each for boys under 12 and girls under 16.

For the crime of *"fitting out a vessel in order to deal in persons intended to be dealt with as slaves,"* Anduze was sentenced in Belize to four years hard labor, his cohort Carlos Carrillo to three years, and Martí y Torrens was ordered to return the Maya to Yucatán and reimburse them for their trouble. Pancho Martí shipped 27 back on the *Alerta,* the same ship he had been using to bring Maya slaves to Cuba in years past.

Juan Bautista Anduze apparently did not serve his entire four-year sentence. Records show that he was back in Cozumel when he paid $1,069 pesos on August 31, 1855 to the wealthy Darío Galera. Later, in 1856, a land tax was collected from all the landholders in Cozumel. Of the 73 taxpayers, the one that paid the third highest tax ($120 pesos) was Juan Bautista Anduze.

On August 18, 1856, Juan Bautista Anduze was once again in hot water for engaging in the slave trade. In a letter to the Foreign Office in London, the English Consul in Havana reported that he had opened an investigation based on a tip from the British Vice-Consul Pedro de Regil y Peon in Mérida that Anduze was holding 82 captured Maya rebels on

Cozumel and was about to ship them aboard his schooner *Ramona* to Havana for his old partner-in-crime, Pancho Martí. Anduze had named his schooner after his first wife, Ramona Pinto, whom he had married on Cozumel sometime between 1848 and 1856.

Anduze was not the only person that we know about who dealt with Martí y Torrens. Luis Luján, former resident of Isla Mujeres and manager of Rancho Santa María in Cedral, had a large stable of "servants" working his rancho and also owned the vessel *Josefa*, which he used in several dealings with the Cuban slave trader.

Juan Bautista Anduze

Just who was Juan Bautista Anduze? In January 1850, the census taken in Cozumel shows *"Juan Bautista Anduce,"* age 22, a white male, arriving from Philadelphia. Although Anduze may have landed on Cozumel on a ship arriving from Philadelphia, he was, in fact, a native of St. Thomas, Virgin Islands. Years later, two entries in the Civil Register of Cozumel that record his children with his second wife list *"Santo Tomas"* as his birthplace. This *"Repoblador"* is the eldest son of Jean Baptist Anduze, the senior partner in J. B. Anduze & Fils. He most likely came to Cozumel because of the new business opportunity that the capturing and selling Maya *Cruzoob* rebels presented. The Anduze family business certainly had plenty of experience in the slave trade.

The surname Anduze originally designated someone from the town of Anduze, France. The ancient village is located south of Ales, in the Gard department of Languedoc-Roussillon. The surname Anduze is not uncommon in the area. The given name "Jean Baptiste" is a popular one in the region and can be alternately spelled "Juan Bautista" in Spanish. The last name of Anduze is also subject to variations in spelling, alternately appearing as Anduze, Anduz, Andueza, Anduse, and Anduce. It is not unusual to run across members of the Anduze clan in the Caribbean today; there are branches of this family in Puerto Rico, Virgin Islands, Venezuela, Trinidad and Tobago, and in Yucatán and Quintana Roo, México.

The father of the first Anduzes to come to the Caribbean was Antoine Anduze. He was born in Saint-Michel-de-Lanés, Aude, Languedoc-Roussillon, France in 1732. He married Claire Safforis and together they had a son, Jean-Pierre Anduze, also born in Saint-Michel-de-Lanés. On July 2, 1782 the couple had another son in Saint-Michel-de-Lanés, Jean-Baptiste Anduze.

The oral history of the Venezuelan branch of the Anduze family says that around the end of the 1700s, the two brothers, Jean-Pierre and Jean Baptiste first moved from France to Haiti, then a French colony. However, the Haitian revolution that raged between 1791 and 1804 may have been what caused the white Anduzes to abandon their new home there and move to St. Thomas, Virgin Islands (at the time, a Danish possession) sometime prior to 1801. Although the route they took from Southern France to St. Thomas may be conjecture, what is a fact is that in 1801, one of the partners in the St. Thomas, Virgin Islands' business of Labadie & Anduze was the older of the two brothers, Jean-Pierre Anduze. This fact is supported by testimony in a Puerto Rican court proceeding in June, 1801, regarding the Labadie & Anduze company. In the court testimony, the description of Jean-Pierre Anduze reads: "Negociante en San Tomas y con legitimo pasaporte." (Businessman in St. Thomas with valid passport.) The company was operating at that time in St. Thomas as well as in Puerto Rico.

In 1796, in the town of Charlotte Amalie in St. Thomas, a small group of French Sephardic Jews founded the *Beracha Veshalom Vegmiluth Hasidim* synagogue, today the oldest synagogue in continuous use in the United States and the second oldest in the western hemisphere. We know that the Anduze Company worked intimately with the Jewish companies in St. Thomas and it was because of these close relationships that they were soon involved with the other Jewish houses of commerce in St. Thomas and other parts of the Caribbean in the illegal slave trade.

In 1812, Jean-Pierre Anduze purchased part of the island of Lovango that lies between St. Thomas and St. John for 1,000 Spanish dollars from Abraham Helm. In August, 1813, he purchased the rest of the island from Helm. Sometime between 1813 and 1815, Jean-Pierre Anduze left

St. Thomas and in 1815, his younger brother, Jean Baptiste Anduze, began operating the company under the name J. B. Anduze & Gil in partnership with the Spaniard, Manuel Gil.

In April of 1825, Jean Baptiste Anduze was implicated in a complicated plot involving falsifying ships' manifests, unlawfully changing a ship's name, and altering customs reports in order to hide the fact that a ship that the company represented was carrying black slaves from Africa to St. Thomas, St. Eustache, and Mayaguez in Puerto Rico. The ship in question was captained by Luis Guïon, the same captain who sailed the ship *l'Aurore* to Paramaribo in 1821 where he had unloaded 143 black slaves. In 1822, the same vessel, this time under the command of Captain L'Oiseau, delivered another load of black African slaves consigned to a Jewish company in Paramaribo headed by Solomon de la Para. In 1825, the partnership of Anduze & Gil also received one-half ownership in the Cano de los Jueyes plantation in Aguas Príetas, Puerto Rico, worth 33,628 pesos, as repayment of the loan they made to Joaquín Vargas, the owner of the plantation.

The company of Anduze & Gil remained in business under the same name until Gil's death in 1836. The firm then took on new partners and continued as Anduze, Yverne, & Company, with Adolph Gremon as a junior partner and José Yverne and Jean Baptiste Anduze as senior partners.

On October 8, 1838, Jean Baptiste Anduze, the senior partner in the new Anduze, Yverne, & Company, was summoned to testify against charges claiming his company was involved in the irregular customs clearance submitted on February 11 of that year for the Spanish vessel *Con La Boca*, captained by a Sr. Ferreira. *Con la Boca* was supposedly empty when it arrived in St. Thomas from Sierra Leone. When the ship left on its way to Havana the next morning, the documents submitted by Anduze's company indicated that it also left empty. However, a black man from Sierra Leone, who had been aboard the ship and managed to escape while it was in port for this one night, later reported his story to the authorities that refuted this statement. He testified that *Con La Boca* was a slave ship, carrying a load of black slaves who were purchased in Sierra Leone. The trial testimony shows that the firm of Anduze, Yverne, & Company was certainly involved, but the charges against them were dropped. Anduze, Yverne, & Company had three clerks at that time: Pierre Constance Peché, Victor Mancilla, and Jules Anduze, Jean Baptiste's second-eldest son, who would later marry Jeanne Giovanetti.

By the 1840s, the Anduze business had expanded and had many new holdings and interests, among them factoring, coffee trading, acting as ships' agents, and operating the Commercial Hotel & Coffee House (today's Grand Hotel, a Virgin Island National Monument in St. Thomas), which J.B. Anduze purchased on January 31, 1843. The Anduze family held the hotel property until 1914.

On November 14, 1844, Jean Baptiste Anduze arrived in the port of New Orleans aboard the schooner *L. L. Sturges* via Turks Island. Whether the father or the son made this trip is unclear, but in either case, it was most certainly in regard to the company's slave-trading business, since New Orleans was one of the main centers for slave auctions in the US at that time. In 1849, Anduze's company changed its name to J. B. Anduze & Fils, indicating that at least one of his sons was then included as a partner in the business, most likely Jules, who had been a clerk for the company earlier.

Above: The old Anduze office building is now a museum in Saint Thomas, Virgen Islands.

Jean Baptiste Anduze, the younger of the two French brothers who immigrated together to St. Thomas prior to 1801 and the father of the *Repoblador* Juan Bautista Anduze, died on June 24, 1856. His company, Anduze & Fils, continued to operate under the leadership of one of his other sons, Pablo Anduze. Today, the old office building of Anduze & Fils at the foot Government Hill in St. Thomas houses the St. Thomas Historical Trust Museum. In the museum, the Anduze family four-poster bed is on display.

Far from being simple, non-violent refugees fleeing the War of the Castes, Cozumel's forefathers were a group of well-connected, street-savvy opportunists who were clearly well-versed in both the contraband and slave trades. The island's early economy was based solidly upon these twin illegal enterprises, contrary to the old myth of the peace-loving *Repobladores de 1848.* There has been far too much reliance on oral histories and traditional beliefs regarding the founding of the island. Most of these stories were crafted by the participants themselves and passed down as family histories; they tended to paint the actions of the *Repobladores* in a much better light than the early documents show was the case. A re-examination of the documentary evidence is well warranted.

The origin of the statue of Saint Michael in the downtown Cozumel Catholic church

There have been many garbled and fictitious stories published about the statue of the Archangel Michael in the church at Juárez and 5 Avenue in downtown San Miguel, Cozumel over the years. Most of the stories have at least a few of the following points in common:

1. The statue is about 500 years old.

2. It was found by farmers digging in a field north of town (sometimes it is construction workers) over 100 years ago.

3. It was originally brought to Cozumel by Juan de Grijalva in 1518.

4. *Since the find came on Sept. 29, the saint's feast day, they decided to name Cozumel's main urban area San Miguel in honor of the saint.*

5. *Juan de Grijalva introduced Christianity to the island and placed the statue in a Catholic church that was located in the town's central plaza.*

6. *The original statue was made of ivory (sometimes the story says gold) but when it was sent to Mérida for restoration, the restorers kept the original and sent back another statue in its place.*

In fact, although these statements have been printed and reprinted in many guides, books, and web pages over the years, not a single one of these statements is true. If you want to know about the statue and the early history of Cozumel, here are the facts:

Juan de Grijalva was sent to the Yucatán from Santiago, Cuba by the Governor to explore the mainland of México as a follow up to Francisco Hernández de Córdoba's expedition of 1517. Grijalva first landed on the north-eastern shore of Cozumel Island on May 3, 1518, the day the Spanish celebrated as the day of the Holy Cross, so he named the island Santa Cruz. Grijalva's ships then rounded the southern tip of the island and landed on the south-western shore, where they found Maya buildings and named the place "San Felipe y Santiago." Saint Philip and Saint James were two apostles whose holy days are celebrated together, on May 3 as well. Later, on May 6, they reached the Maya village of Xamancab (the site of today's San Miguel de Cozumel) and named it San Juan Ante Portam Latinam, or "Saint John before the Latin Gate," after the Apostle Saint John, whose holy day it was. The Portam Latinam portion of the name is a reference to a gateway in Rome where the apostle was thrown into a pot of boiling oil. Grijalva then had a Mass said on the steps of one of the Maya temples at the Maya village. The Spaniards' stay in Cozumel is documented in reports written by two of the expedition members. One of the reports was entitled *Itinerario de la armada del rey católico a la isla de Yucatán, en la India, en el año 1518, en la que fue por comandante y capitán general Juan de Grijalva, escrito para Su Alteza por el capellán mayor de la dicha armada,* and was written by Juan Díaz Núñez, the expedition's chaplain.

We now only have an abstract of a translated and edited version of this report, but it says <u>absolutely nothing</u> about a statue being given to the Maya of Cozumel, something one would assume would be of great interest to a chaplain. Bernal Díaz del Castillo also wrote about being on Cozumel with Grijalva, but he says nothing about a statue being given to the islanders either.

A later expedition to Cozumel led by Hernán Cortés was also well documented by two of his expedition members, and it was recorded <u>in both accounts</u> that Cortés left an image of the Virgin Mary with the Maya when he left. It seems likely that this account of Cortés leaving a religious icon on the island somehow became confused and superimposed over Grijalva's visit by folks later retelling the story.

On September 29, 1527, Francisco Montejo "el Adelantado" landed on Cozumel and gave the village there the name San Miguel de Xamancab, after the Mayan name of the place, Xamancab, meaning "Northland," and for the saint whose day was celebrated on September 29, the Archangel Saint Michael *(Archangel San Miguel)*. This is the first time the name San Miguel is associated with the village.

In 1846, Yucatán declared itself independent from México. The same year the United States and México declared war with one another. In 1847, the Maya revolted against their white and mestizo oppressors and the conflict known as the War of the Castes began in Yucatán. As the war in Yucatán progressed, the Maya gained the upper-hand. In 1848, the townsfolk of Valladolid began fleeing the city, just minutes ahead of the invading Maya. One group of refugees, numbering about 600, began making their way towards Rio Lagartos, under the protection of a small group of Yucatecan soldiers under the command of Captain Sebastián Molas. Some of these refugees were able to board the American warship *Falcon* and were carried away to Campeche. Others boarded a Spanish ship and went to Havana. The rest of the refugees were picked up off the beach by the Belizean ship *True Blue* captained by James Smith and taken to Cozumel. The priest Doroteo Rejón was included with this group of refugees, and it was he who brought the statue of Saint Michael the Archangel to the island.

The group of refugees the *True Blue* brought to Cozumel eventually settled in the old rancho of San Miguel. Another group, made up mainly of Maya farmers who wanted no part of the war, took up residence in the old Maya town of Oycib, re-naming it Cedral. On November 21, 1849, the government of Yucatán officially recognized the town founded by the group of refugees who had settled on Molas' old rancho as the "Pueblo de San Miguel de Cozumel" and linked it to the municipal government of Tizimín. San Miguel was also granted a four-year moratorium on any taxes and the adult men living there were granted an exemption from military conscription by the Yucatecan government in order to assist the fledgling settlement. In 1850, a census showed San Miguel's population had grown to 341 adults and an unspecified number of children. Only 6 of the adults were over the age of 50. It was also noted that in this year, the town had two streets and a square.

From November 1876 until June 1877, Alice and Augustus LePlongeon visited Cozumel during their tour of Maya sites in the Yucatán. At this time, Padre Rejón was still San Miguel's resident priest. The LePlongeon's described the town as *"a scattered village of 500 souls."* Alice wrote that there was no hotel or guest house on the island, so they were offered *"a dirty thatch-roofed room at the southeast corner of the immense grassy square that was the town plaza."* Padre Rejón took the two under his wing and showed them around Cozumel, including many of the ruins and cenotes. While viewing the cenote that is now a park on Avenida 65, Agustus fell and cut himself seriously, but was still able to remove a Spanish olive jar and a Maya water jar from the cenote.

Padre Rejon also let the Leplongeons in on a secret: he believed that he had the "evil-eye." He added that his congregation also believed that he had the ability to fix his gaze on something, or someone, and cause them harm. The old priest went on to tell them that he believed that the house they occupied was haunted.

Above: Photograph taken by Augustus LePlongeon in 1876 of his wife (in white skirt and dark top, on left) walking on Calle 1 about to cross 5ª Avenida. The house where they were staying in is the one behind her; the grass to the right in the fore of the photograph is the plaza.

The Catholic church that now stands on the corner of Calle 10 and Avenida Juárez was not the one used by Padre Rejón, but a new one built by the Maryknoll Missionaries during the years 1945 and 1946. The statue of Saint Michael the Archangel that is in the church today is the same one that came to Cozumel with Padre Doroteo Rejón in 1848. It was placed in the church when the first mass was said in the new building by the Maryknoll missionary, Jorge Hogan, on May 26, 1946 and has been there ever since, except every September 21, when it is carried in a procession down to the municipal pier and placed in a boat for a short ride.

Above: The San Miguel Church shortly after its completion in 1946. Later, Avenida 10ª was widened paved, and the church garden paved over.

Notice in the picture above, the marble plaque that erroneously states that the first Catholic Mass was said on this spot had not been erected yet. The plaque also states, erroneously, that the first mass in Mexico was said near this site. The Catholic clergy of Cozumel have been granted a small tract of land near Playa Casitas (near the statue of Ix Chel and the ersatz Maya ruin) where they hope to erect a chapel commemorating this "first mass." One would imagine they will then claim that the new chapel marks the original spot.

Above: The statue of the Archangel Michael (which is made of wood, not ivory or gold) in the San Miguel Church.

CHAPTER 10

Hacienda Colombia

Darío Manuel Galera Encalada was born in 1811 to Manuel José Galera Quijano and María Crisanta Encalada Aguilar. At an early age, Darío found he was adept at business and politics and entered both with relish. He became a trader of logwood (*Haematoxylon campechianum*, also known as dyewood or *palo de tinte*) and using his political connections, amassed a huge fortune prior to the War of the Castes in 1847. Much of this fortune he invested in properties around the peninsula, including some on Cozumel.

In 1840, Darío Galera became the new *Alcalde* of Mérida. Although he is known to have bought and sold logwood harvested from Cozumel before that time, it was most likely during this period he became even more familiar with the island through his close personal friendship with Colonel Martín Peraza, one of the partners in Vicente Albino Cammaño's cotton plantation on the island. It is also likely that it was during this period Galera laid claim to the parcel of land on the southern end of Cozumel that later became known as Hacienda Colombia. Later in 1840, Col. Peraza offered his political pull to George Fisher, the Serbian-born Texan who, together with Texan President Sam Houston and other partners, was to try to buy most of Cozumel from the Yucatecan government in 1841.

In 1841 Galera was named Lieutenant Colonel of Mérida's artillery brigade and in charge of accompanying Andrés Quintana Roo, who was sent to Mérida by Mexican President López de Santa Anna to negotiate with the Yucatán government on behalf of the Mexican Republic. In October of the same year, Galera traveled to Havana to procure 2,000 muskets with which the new Republic of Yucatán could use to defend itself from Mexican President Santa Anna. Not finding them available in Cuba, Galera then sailed to New York, where he was finally successful in buying the arms. He returned to Sisal with the muskets in November of 1841, and delivered them to the Yucatán government, making a handsome profit on the transaction.

On July 10, 1844, Galera shipped a load of logwood from Cozumel to the US via the US Brig *Henry Leeds*, of which Henry A. Holmes was the captain. It was just one of many loads that Galera would harvest from the island.

In 1845, Galera purchased the building on the Plaza Central of Mérida next to the Casa de Montejo (owned by Juliana de Solís Barbosa, a direct descendant of Montejo el Mozo), a property that had been in the Montejo family since the conquest. Galera refurbished the building and made it his home. By this time, he also owned parts of Isla Mujeres. In 1846 he became a *suplente diputado* in Mérida.

In June, 1852, Darío Galera shipped 251 tons of logwood and 4 tons of Guayacán from Cozumel aboard the US ship *Nacogdoches*. In June 1855, Galera lost a court battle with the Ayuntamiento of Mérida, forcing him to liquidate some of his real estate holdings to come up with quick cash. A receipt for 1,069 pesos dated August 31, 1855 showing funds received by Galera from Juan Bautista Anduze, of Cozumel, may have been for Anduze's purchase of Hacienda de Colombia; regardless, Anduze was then the owner of Hacienda Colombia until the day he died. Galera also owned the paddle boat *Mérida*, which often called on Cozumel in the 1860s. When the Empress Carlota came to visit Mérida in 1865, it was in Galera's home on the plaza that she stayed during her visit.

Juan Bautista Anduze married Ramona Pinto and together they had three daughters; Ana, born in 1859; Emilia born in 1860, and; Engracia, born in 1864. Ana was to later marry an American mining engineer from Whitehall, New York, named James Wallace Caldwell.

When James Wallace Caldwell signed the Cozumel civil register at the time of his marriage banns to Ana Anduze Pinto on March 11, 1878, he spelled his last name with an "a." Shortly before the birth of his son Oscar, James left Cozumel and never returned. When Oscar's birth was recorded in the civil register by Ana's new husband, Primo Aguilar, Primo misspelled *Caldwell* as *Coldwell*, and the spelling with the "o" has stuck ever since.

Above: The page in the Cozumel civil register signed by James Wallace Caldwell and Ana Anduze Pinto.

On October 6, 1865, Juan Bautista Anduze married his second wife, María Concepción Urcelay Peniche in Mérida, Yucatán. His first wife, Ramona, may have died in childbirth prior to this second marriage. On September 12, 1869, Juan Bautista Anduze and María Concepción had a son in Mérida and named him Juan Bautista Anduze, after his father and grandfather.

On December 31, 1873, the birth of another daughter to Juan B. Anduze was recorded in the Cozumel civil register. The entry lists Anduze's birthplace as *"Saint Thomas"* and that of his second wife, María Concepción Urcelay, as *"Mérida."* The daughter born at that time was named Concepción, after her mother.

On November 2, 1877, Concepción Urcelay de Anduze recorded the birth of a second daughter, Olivia. In this entry, Juan Bautista's birthplace is also listed as *"San Tomas."* Before dying in 1880, Concepción Urcelay de Anduze had one more daughter with Juan Bautista Anduze and named her Dagmar Anduze Urcelay. Dagmar later married Serapio Baqueiro Barrera (the son of historian Serapio Baqueiro Prevé) and that couple had three children, the last one a son, writer Oswaldo Baqueiro Anduze.

When Alice LePlongeon and her husband Augustus visited Cozumel in November 1876 through June 1877, she wrote about her experiences on the island in her book Here and There in the Yucatán. In the book, published in 1889, she described visiting Hacienda Colombia: *"Tobacco* grown in Cozumel is quite equal to the weed produced in Cuba, and many cigars sold as 'Havanas' are from Cozumel, whence they are sent boxed ready for the market. The principal planter there, Mr. J. Anduze, took us through his plantation, fifteen miles from St. Miguel, and gave us a little useful information. The principal occupation of the islanders is tobacco growing and cigar making."

Above: Alice Dixon LePlongeon in Yucatán at 22 years of age.

Writing of her departure from Cozumel, Alice again brings up the subject of contraband cigars: *"Having waited long for an opportunity to leave Cozumel Island for British Honduras, we decided to go on the* Triunfo *notwithstanding its uninviting appearance. It was a twelve-ton schooner, badly in need of paint; as for order, the limited space made that impossible. The captain, called Antonio, was as unclean a specimen of the Spanish sailor as we have ever had the misfortune to see. The mate was 'Antonio the Second,' to distinguish him from his superior; black 'Jim' was cook and general assistant; a man named Trejo serving as pilot. There was no compass on board. Such a thing can rarely be found on those coasting vessels. There were four passengers besides ourselves, all of us having plenty of luggage. Add to this twenty-five enormous turtles; some on deck, some below; a large party of hens; two big cages full of doves; another of canaries; a spoiled lapdog; cat and kittens; two goats; and a colony of cockroaches of the largest species. There was not a square inch to spare. We more than suspected that there was a considerable amount of "contraband" on board; were also well aware that the coast-guard was cruising about on the look-out for just such vessels as the Triunfo; consequently the grim face of the captain did not often relax into a smile. He betrayed his anxiety by asking for the loan of our field-glasses very frequently, rather to our annoyance, for there was much that interested us to be seen on the coast. On the third day out we reached the Island of Ambergris, and stopped at San Pedro, a picturesque fishing village, surrounded by groves of cocoanut palms. Here, our suspicions of there being contraband on board were verified, for at dusk about 20,000 cigars were slyly put into a small dory, and taken ashore with many precautions, to be afterwards conveyed to Belize on fishermen's boats."*

In 1885, the US Fisheries Department at Woods Hole sent a research vessel to Cozumel. The expedition photographer, N. B. Miller, was met by Juan Bautista Anduze and carried back to Hacienda Colombia for an overnight visit. Miller reported: *"I left the ship on the 24 of January, with Mr. J. B. Anduze, in the steam launch for a trip to his plantation, located on the southern end of the island, about 12 miles distant. When we reached the landing the surf was so heavy that we were landed from the boat on the backs of natives. The plantation being about three miles in the interior, we were compelled to make the rest of our journey on small ponies that are used in all tropical countries.*

The road, or rather a narrow bridle-path, led through a dense forest of twisted knotty trees whose trunks and limbs were covered with creeping vines, so that it was almost impossible to distinguish the leaves of the trees from those of the vine. Many of the vines bore some remarkably beautiful flowers which made a very pretty scene; the foliage meeting overhead completely shut out the rays of the sun, and the total absence of buzzing insects made the ride a very pleasant one. I saw a large number of birds both large and small, some of which were very beautiful, also butterflies of every color imaginable.

We reached the plantation at 5 o'clock in the evening, too late to take photographs. This plantation consists of a farm of a half league square, around which is a high stone wall, the fields being divided off by rail fences. There were large fields of bananas, and plantain trees, pineapples, corn, and ginger, with immense groves of orange and lemon trees, but all seemed neglected entirely or very poorly cultivated. Farming implements of the crudest kind, no modern appliances being used, may account for the appearance of the fields. The houses were five large thatched structures arranged in a square. These are used for the servants to live in and also to store the products of the plantation as they are gathered. In the center of the square is a large stone building with a thatched roof, which is the residence of Mr. Anduze.

This must have been a beautiful place once, but now it is sadly out of repair. While waiting for supper we went to an Indian village which was located on the plantation. Here, I found a collection of about fifty houses occupied by thirty families."

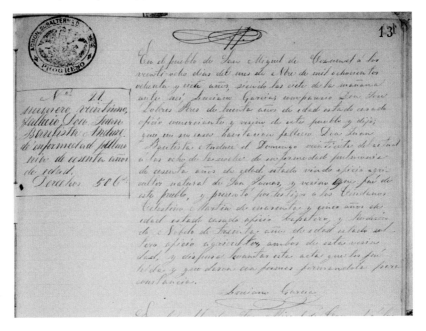

Above: Juan Bautista Anduze's death act in the Cozumel civil register.

The Cozumel Civil Register records that on April 27, 1887, Juan Bautista Anduze died of pneumonia. His will left the Hacienda de Colombia (440 *hectáreas*) to his daughter, Engracia F. Anduce. Oscar Coldwell Anduce, the son of Juan Bautista's eldest daughter, Ana, became owner of Rancho Cinco Puertas (47 *hectáreas*) and Rancho Santo Domingo (18 *hectáreas*).

By the late 1880s, Hacienda Colombia was also producing henequen for export as well as tobacco, coconuts, pineapples, oranges, mamey, bananas, watermelons, cashews, and key limes, and henequen, but in 1903 a hurricane destroyed the hacienda's pier and workers' housing. Once the installations and housing were rebuilt, the hacienda began shipping once more.

In 1914, the US Bureau of Foreign and Domestic Commerce reported that on Cozumel *"Coconuts are grown for export, the largest plantation being owned by Mrs. Engracia F. Anduze, while Coldwell & Bonastre have a four-year-old coconut plantation containing 25,000 trees. The former also has 618 acres in henequen, the plantation being equipped with the most modern machinery for extracting the fiber."*

Above: Engracia Anduce and her workers in Laguna Colombia in 1909.

Above: The henequen drying racks, Decauville tracks and storage builds at Hacienda Colombia in 1909.

Above: A Decauville locomotive, like the one used on Hacienda Colombia by Engracia Anduce.

In 1918, the archaeologist/spy Sylvanus Morley wrote in his report to the US Office of Military Intelligence that 100 people lived on Hacienda

Colombia. One of those living and working at the hacienda was Nicanor Canto, who ran the henequen processing machine Engracia hired Juan San Germán to install earlier.

Above: A henequen field at Haciend Colombia in 1909.

By the 1920s, Hacienda Colombia's products were sent mostly to the US ports of Mobile and New Orleans aboard the *Jupiter, Lucia,* and *Rosita,* but some shipments entered at Tampa and Key West aboard the *John Francis.* In addition, a smaller amount of fruit was shipped to Belize and Progreso, Yucatán aboard the *Alberto.* Coconuts were shipped to Havana on the *Norman.*

In 1921, after the wartime demand for sisal fell, only 7 men and 5 women were living at Colombia. At the same time, 6 men and 12 women were living at the Celarain lighthouse. As a point of reference, there were only 1,340 people in the whole island then. By the 1930s, Rancho Colombia had passed into the hands of Engracia's nephew, Oscar Coldwell Anduce. By the 1950s, the rancho had been abandoned, except for use as a cattle grazing area. Today, a portion of the old Hacienda forms a part of the Parque Ecoturistíco Punta Sur. The old hacienda cemetery and the rusted hulk of the Decauville locomotive that hauled the henequen to Laguna Colombia from the hacienda are hidden deep in the bush on private property nearby.

Above: The plans for the new lighthouse that was built at Punta Celarain near Laguna Colombia in 1909, to take the place of the old lighthouse, the steps of which are still visible nearby. Later, the taller masonry lighthouse was built and that one still stands today.

CHAPTER 11

The War of the Castes and other conflicts

Cult of the talking cross

In July of 1847, Maya rebels declared war on the non-Maya landowners in Yucatán and began attacking haciendas in and around Tepich and Tihosuco. The Yucatecan government launched a counter attack and slowly began to drive the Maya back south. By 1850, it had begun to look like the government troops might be able to turn the tide of the war. The Maya rebels were demoralized and in retreat, but a small contingent of the insurgents found renewed faith in their cause on October 15, 1850, when they stumbled upon a Yucatán army deserter named José María Barrera and his Maya ventriloquist friend, Manuel Nahuat, living in the woods near Kampocolché. Barrera had carved three crosses into the bark of a tree near a cenote there, and by throwing his voice, Nahuat tricked the rebels into believing the crosses could speak. The words they spoke, Barrera assured the rebels, were the word of God and the message God had for them was that the rebels were his chosen people and their job was to exterminate all non-Maya.

The rebels rallied round these two charlatans and the the Cult of the Talking Cross (el Culto de la Cruz Parlante) was born. The members of this cult were called the Cruzoob, the Spanish word for "cross" pluralized by the Mayan suffix oob. A new town was established around the cross, Xbalam Na Kampocolche Chan Santa Cruz. A new theocracy sprang up within the rebel cross-worshipers as well, headed by the priests who interpreted the messages of the ventriloquist. The Maya were true to their roots; they still believed the gods spoke through idols and that only the priests could interpret the idols' words.

In 1851 Manuel Nahuat was killed by Yucatecan troops, but the rebels soon replaced him with a high priest, who presented God's wishes to the Cruzoob in written form. Barrera died in 1852, but soon, other centers of Cruz Parlante worship sprang up, in villages like Muyil,

Xpalma, Chumpón, San Antonio Muyil (near Caleta Chacalal), and Tulum. Although the War of the Casts ended around 1918, the Cult of the Talking Cross survived. To this very day, in the center of Tulum Pueblo, *Cruzoob* honor guards still take shifts to protect the talking crosses housed in the *Centro Ceremonial Maya* located in the block bounded by the streets of Acuario Sur, Sol Poniente, Mercurio Poniente, and Júpiter Sur.

Cozumel profits from the conflict on the mainland

Even though slavery had been abolished in México in 1829, once the War of the Castes got underway the *"Repobladores de 1848"* in Cozumel lost no time in establishing a slave-trading network that supplied kidnapped or captured Maya rebels to Cuban slavers. Bounty hunters and members of the Yucatán Army would take the captives to the northern Yucatán ports of Dzilam and Rio Lagartos, where small boats owned and crewed by Cozumeleños then took the Maya to Isla Mujeres or Cozumel. The rebels were incarcerated on these islands until they could be picked up by a boat sent from Cuba by one of several slave-traders, such as Francisco Martí y Torrens.

However, not all *Repobladores* were slave-traders. Some were gun-runners who supplied arms, lead shot, and ammunition to the Maya rebels. Cozumel's population apparently took full advantage of the war on the mainland and played it from both sides. Some Cozumeleños worked closely with the likes of Vitoriano (Vito) Pacheco, a Yucatán government turncoat, gun-runner, and smuggler who was also the brother-in-law of Maya rebel leader Bonifacio Novelo. Other *Repobladores* played both roles; like Juan Bautista Anduze who sold guns and ammunition to some of the rebels, but also kidnapped and sold other rebels to Cuban slavers. Still other *Repobladores*, like José Alcocer, made money from the sale of goods looted during the uprising, such as the silver accouterments stolen from the church in Valladolid that he later sold in Belize.

María Uicab, the high priestess of Tulum

For the next twenty years, the war on the mainland continued. Although the rebels were contained to the wilderness area later known as southern Quintana Roo, they were still a thorn in the side of the government and periodic raiding parties were sent out to harass them. These raids managed to kill or capture many of the insurgents, but the *Cruzoob* stubbornly held their ground. By 1870, the *Cruz Parlante's* high priestess (known as *La Santa Patrona*) was residing in Tulum. Her name was María Uicab, a charismatic and powerful woman who had left a string of husbands in her wake. María had converted Tulum into the center of the cult's operations, displacing Chan Santa Cruz as the most important rebel-held village in Yucatán. Sometime during her reign over the walled city, a Spanish missionary came by boat to call on the priestess. He was killed, the flesh removed from his skeleton and his bones set in cement in Tulum as a symbol of the power the *Cruz Parlante* had over the religion of the Spaniards. In 1978, I visited Tulum and took the photo below of what remained of the bones, which have since been removed.

Above: The bones of the priest set in concrete in Tulum.

On January 21, 1871, a thousand Yucatecan government troops led by Coronel Daniel Traconis attacked Tulum by surprise, capturing María's son and forcing the High Priestess to flee for her life. Regrouping her troops, María counter-attacked on July 3, 1872. This was answered by the Yucatecan government almost immediately and from that time on no word was ever heard from María, who was most likely killed in the battle.

Juan Bautista Vega and his evolution from kidnapped child to Cruzoob general

In the summer of 1897, a man reported to be a treasure hunter by the name of Dr. Juan Fábregas arrived on Cozumel with the intention of hiring a boat and crew to take him to Tulum. However, his request fell on deaf ears as the War of the Castes was still in full swing and no one on Cozumel wanted to risk their lives entering the mainland stronghold of the *Cruzoob* Maya rebels, or *Bravos* as they were called locally.

But money talks (in this case 13 pesos), and regardless of the danger, Fábregas eventually convinced Ruperto Loria to take him to Tulum. Loria picked out a mate, 22-year-old Ignacio Novelo, to help with the sailboat's rigging and at the last minute decided to take his 11-year-old stepson, Juan Bautista Vega, along for the ride. The trip across the channel was uneventful and the boat made landfall at Tulum beach safely. As the little group settled down for a quick lunch on the beach, they were approached by a group of Maya rebels from the pueblo of Tulum. One thing lead to another and soon Loria, Fábregas, and Novelo were all killed. Young Juan Bautista Vega was hauled off to the village of Tulum and tied to a tree. There he remained for several days, unable to communicate with his captors, as he spoke no Mayan and they spoke no Spanish. Eventually, the boy was marched through Muyil and Chunpom to Yokdzonot, where the *Cruzoob Gobernador*, Felipe Yama, ordered him to be executed. A black Belizean living with the rebels (known variously as Joe, José, Mr. Dyo, or Mr. Dio) pleaded for the boy's life, saying that the kid could be useful since he was able to read and write. Yama relented and Vega was allowed to live.

Vega stayed with Joe for the next several months while he learned Mayan, but was later turned over to the *Cruzoob* high priest of Chunpóm, Florentino Cituk, where he became the priest's secretary. The boy proved his worth, translating messages between the *Cruzoob* and the Yucatecan Army. He later married into Cituk's family and became thoroughly Maya, very similar to what happened to the shipwreck survivor known as Gonzalo Guerrero, almost 400 years earlier.

The *Cruzoob* rebels continued to fight engagements with the Yucatecan Army until a peace was negotiated in 1901. The treaty allowed the Maya to choose their own local government, but even so, many holdouts refused to honor the terms of the peace agreement and sporadic fighting continued to occur for nearly 20 more years. In 1915, after the death of Cituk, Vega was named High Priest of the *Cruzoob* and became their maximum leader, bearing the rank of General in the *Cruzoob* military. In 1918, the final peace agreement was worked out and the War of the Castes was over. Although he visited Cozumel in 1926 after being given a ride aboard the *Alberto* by Gregory Mason, he never returned to live on the island. Juan Bautista Vega died on July 28, 1969, still the highest ranking Maya rebel official.

Cozumel is invaded by rebelling Yucatecan army troops

In early 1915, Mérida's General Abel Ortiz Argumedo and his troops fomented a rebellion, so Mexican President Venustiano Carranza sent General Salvador Alvarado to snuff it out. Alvarado acted quickly and ruthlessly and by March Argumedo's men were fleeing in disarray. Fifty of these rebel troops under the command of Tomás Rodríguez decided they would seize Cozumel, so they began making preparations to cross the channel and surprise the poorly defended island. Word reached Cozumel before they could cross and the islanders were able to send their women and children to hide in the woods before the rebels arrived. At that time, the only loyal federal troops stationed on the island were a captain, a sergeant and five enlisted men. Not enough to hold off fifty well-armed rebels. When the rebel troops arrived, the small Cozumel garrison put up a brave fight, but after two of the enlisted men were killed the rest surrendered. The rebels occupied the town for three days, until word reached the island that a ship carrying federal troops was on its way to the island. Then, they packed up and re-crossed the channel, melting back into the jungle at Puerto Morelos.

Above: Downtown San Miguel in 1909.

Col. Zamarripa burns Cozumel's church

In 1915, General Salvador Alvarado ordered Coronel Isaias Zamarripa to go to Chan Santa Cruz and arrest the commandant there, General Arturo Garcilazo. Chan Santa Cruz was the capital of Quintana Roo at the time, but Zamarripa's orders were to move Quintana Roo's seat of government to Payo Obispo after General Garcilazo's arrest. Zamarripa stopped at Cozumel on April 21 of that year, on his way to Chan Santa Cruz with a large numbers of troops from Mérida,.

In a newspaper article appearing in the *Lehi Banner* in 1915, a visitor to Cozumel described San Miguel prior to Zamarripa's visit. He said the town of around 900 inhabitants was: *"quite a thriving, well-formed town. It has several wide, clean streets; a plaza, **a very presentable little church**, one large general store and several small ones, an inn, and municipal offices and a customs house; it also boasts a sort of esplanade running along the entire sea front, at one end of which is the lighthouse and at the other a landing jetty. Although most of the buildings are palm-thatched cottages, there are several strongly built stone houses and the main street has a two-story brick house and a modern bungalow."*

Above: Photo taken in 1909 before the clock tower was built, showing the lighthouse near the muelle (on the left), the plaza (a weed-filled field in the center), and the church on the corner of today's 5 Av. and Juárez (on the right in the photograph).

Zamarripa was a follower of the federal government's strong anti-clergy and anti-religious policies, and when he arrived in San Miguel he set about destroying the town's church, which was located on the corner of today's Juárez and Avenida 5. His men used the religious images in the church for target practice before he set fire to the building. While he did destroy the church's crucifix, some small statues of saints, and several religious paintings, the iconic statue of Saint Michael was saved by the townsfolk and hidden away for safekeeping. When Zamarripa departed for Bahía de la Ascensión a week later, he left a contingent of his troops stationed on Cozumel, where they used the burnt out church as a stable for their horses and the plaza as a corral. When Sweden's

Prince William visited Cozumel in 1920, he wrote that the town still had no church.

When Zamarripa reached Chan Santa Cruz in May, he arrested General Garcilazo and moved the seat of the Quintana Roo government (along with the electrical plant and the clockworks in the town's clock tower) to Payo Obispo. Chan Santa Cruz was later renamed Felipe Carrillo Puerto, Payo Obispo was renamed Chetumal, and General Garcilazo was executed by a firing squad.

San Miguel changes its name

The *Revolución Cristera* was a war waged by the Mexican federal government against Christian religious elements *(Los Cristeros)* all across México from 1926 to 1929 in which over 90,000 people were killed. During this war, churches were vandalized, priests were executed, and religious gatherings were outlawed. Cozumel's church had already been destroyed in 1915 by Coronel Isaías Zamarripa, so there was little that happened on the island during this conflict. The statue of Saint Michael Archangel that had earlier graced the church remained hidden during this period, not to reappear until after WWII. Once the *Revolución Cristera* was over, the government continued to suppress many aspects of religious freedom in México and on September 8, 1936, it went as far as changing the names of all towns that had religious connotations. San Miguel de Cozumel, named by Francisco de Montejo in 1527, had its association with its patron saint Archangel Michael broken and was renamed, simply, "Cozumel." Cozumel remains the official name of both the island and the island's largest town to this day, though in popular parlance, San Miguel remains the way the islanders refer to the town.

The same year the town's name was changed, the property where the old church building once stood on the plaza was appropriated by Goveror Rafael Melgar and the Benito Juárez School was built there.

Above: Benito Juárez School on the left, at the corner of 5ª Avenida and Juárez in 1939, on the northeast corner of the plaza, former site of the church. These buildings were later torn down and replaced with the shopping complex known as the "Plaza del Sol."

Above: A view of the old plaza.

Above: The streets were still unpaved by WWII.

Above: Some streets in Cozumel hardly every changed until the 1960s.

CHAPTER 12

Claude L. Goodrich and his American Colony

In 1874, a real estate huckster named Claude L. Goodrich self-published a 32-page booklet about Cozumel. The title was nearly as long as the book was: <u>Cozumel Island, the New Tropical Paradise; Its History, its Government, Character, Resources, Climate, Location, Soil, Products, Inhabitants, Etc., with the inducements offered immigrants to go there; free lands, perfect healthfulness and beauty of climate, splendid chance for homes and fortunes.</u> The booklet was a blatant attempt to convince unsuspecting investors to buy land and settle in Cozumel, touting the island as a veritable Garden of Eden. It was printed in St. Louis Missouri by the St. Louis job-printing company of Powell & Maynard, owned by Cuthbert Powell and Charles Maynard, with offices at 208 South Fourth Street, St. Louis, Missouri.

The first line of text on the front cover of Goodrich's booklet is the Spanish proverb *"quien no se aventura, no pasa la mar,"* meaning "he who is not willing to take a risk, will not cross the oceans." Goodrich had already shown he was a risk-taker and he further substantiated this fact by "crossing the sea" to Cozumel in 1873 and staying there for six months. He was captivated by the prospects he saw there and was determined to found a settlement of *"a few thousand"* American expatriates on Cozumel, whom he believed would bring to the island *"the influences of enlightenment."* He returned to St. Louis, Missouri and holed up at the Union Hotel on the corner of Fourth and Myrtle streets where he began to write. After finishing his booklet, he returned to the island to await the flood of American immigrants he hoped would join him.

On the opening page, Goodrich states *"The object* [of this booklet] *is simply to describe a country where the facilities for health, wealth and happiness are lying around vacant… waiting for people to come and pick them up."* He then outlines the reasons he believes many people would be interested in abandoning the US and moving to Cozumel:

1. To escape the fast-moving life of the 1870s; *"The American society is rapidly undergoing changes, which are too fast for some…"*

2. To escape poverty; *"The rich are growing richer and the poor are striving night and day to prevent growing poorer;"*

3. To escape Big Government; *"Popular government is becoming a mystery too metaphysical for ordinary brains;"*

4. To escape climate change and global warming (in 1874!); *"Even old Earth is becoming demoralized, and neither her storms or the intensity of her frigidity in the north any longer reliable;"*

5. To escape the illness and disease; *"Cozumel offers a sovereign remedy… for any disease which the doctors cannot cure;"*

6. Or, to escape one's past; *"[if] in whose house, politically or literally, there may be a may be a skeleton of any kind which they wish to get away from."*

Goodrich wrote: *"in these pages gather plain facts stripped of all romance,"* and *"there is no snare laid here to catch gudgeons – we do not offer to sell you any lands – our cure for consumption has no sequel with a long list of medicines at one dollar per box!"* He goes on to state: *"you are offered inducements so clearly superior all the western desert, colonization, and land-speculating railroad schemes…"* but then describes the island in the most unbelievable, fantastical superlatives: *"Under no sun was there a ever a fairer sky or a purer atmosphere; nowhere grow the flowers sweeter or more beautiful; never birds sang their songs more merrily nor in a more delightful and healthful locality, and in no land are the breezes more evenly tempered or more constant in their affections."* Goodrich calls Cozumel *"a tropical paradise, because of its everlasting freshness and beauty, its uniformity of climate, tempered by constant sea-breezes from either side, free from earthquakes, volcanoes and hurricanes [!!!], an eternal spring and summer, always painted and perfumed with flowers, possessed of birds of brilliant plumage and sweet voices; a garden of fruits, a land literally flowing with milk and honey; and indeed, blessed with direct providence from the Great Architect of the Universe for almost every want of mankind."*

And, it gets better: *"There are no sudden changes of weather; there are no miasmic swamps, no chills, no quinine, no doctors!... If there is a spot on earth free of Consumption it is Cozumel Island."* Goodrich wrote that the 800 residents of Cozumel *"are a mild, peaceable, inoffensive population, easily controlled by laws, well disposed toward each other and cautious to foreigners. There is little or no contention among them, crime is seldom committed, no inclination to be litigious exists, consequently there are no lawyers there. A community without lawyers or doctors ought to be a pleasant place to live!"*

Not only are there no lawyers on the island, wrote Goodrich, but *"the government of the Island is simple yet efficient; resident officers are appointed by the Governor of Yucatán, whom in his opinion are honest and capable. These officials receive no salaries, there is no premium upon them, no government stealings are heard of and no taxes are levied! There are no negroes on the Island, and they are not a necessity there... The lack of society will long be filled; several young men and a few families from Kentucky, Tennessee, Louisiana, and other Southern states are going... The natives want American enterprise to come and build up their island; they know their own lack of the arts and sciences... The Indian labor is very good and cheap: 37 ½ cents per day, the employer paying the debt, if any be due, to the former employer, for the full payment of which laborer is responsible, also for any debt contracted with employer afterward, and must perform reasonable daily tasks to entitle him to his regular wages. No cruelty is practiced toward these laborers, and general good feelings exist between master and servant."*

So, what kind of agricultural endeavors were available to pursue on Cozumel in 1874? Goodrich lists them in order of profitability: *"Cocoanuts... sell from $30 to $80 per M."* A man could start a coconut plantation of around 10,000 trees, wrote Goodrich, *"for $1,500 or $2,000"* and realize a profit of *"$54,000 per annum."*

The second most profitable crop, wrote Goodrich, was bananas, rendering a clear profit of $575 per year, per acre planted in banana trees. *"I put the prices in this estimate so low that the most unconscionable Dago or the most grasping Yankee would certainly not expect to ever go to the Island and purchase the fruit for less..."*

At $4 per thousand, Goodrich states that oranges are the next most profitable crop, while pineapples and mangoes would only be worth exporting if they were canned on Cozumel, but unfortunately there was no canning plant. Limes and lemons were also raised on the island, as was tobacco.

Goodrich wrote: *"The tobacco leaf has been a staple product with the natives [of Cozumel] for some years, and the article has a reputation in the Havana market almost equal to Cuba tobacco. President Grant smokes his genuine 'Havanas' (so called) everyday, the tobacco for which was grown upon Cozumel, but for the lack of American commerce it has to pass through Cuba. Of course, the value is increased several hundred percent, when it comes out from under the guns of Moro castle labeled with high-toned Spanish paper and bearing the name of some wily Cuban who perhaps bought it of our innocent Islander for 8 cents per pound! Cigars sell, on the island, at $10 per M, which are equal in quality to those you buy at retail at 15 cents each in the cities of New Orleans or Saint Louis. We make also the choice brands of Havana cigarettes, the labels being furnished by the Cuban buyers."*

Goodrich went on to write: *"Corn is raised in considerable quantities... Sugarcane grows vigorously, and there are two or three small sugar mills on the Island, enough being manufactured to barely supply home demand. Cotton grows splendidly... Heniquen grass is better, yet we export very little... Castor beans, arrow-root, sweet-potatoes, etc., are very prosperous... Tomatoes, melons, pumpkins, etc., are generally in supply. The turtle shell business includes an occasional catch of the most valuable kinds, the hawk's-bill (Chelonia imbricata) variety bringing as high as $25 each. There are several thousand head of cattle on the Island, beef selling at 6 ¼ cents. We also have horses, goats, donkeys, pigs and chickens...the horse is used for riding purposes only, as our natives have not yet arrived at so high a degree of enlightenment as to be possessed of wagons or other vehicles, or harness. A few rough carts drawn by bulls is as far as they have progressed in that direction."*

Goodrich notes that although México does have laws regarding duties on imported goods, he has some advice on how to avoid these duties. He explains that since there was no customs house in Cozumel, the new immigrant should avoid entering at the customs port of entry at Progreso and simply go directly to San Miguel with all their goods and outfits, where they should claim them as items *"for their own use."* Some of the items he suggests bringing to the island are *"saddles, wagons, harnesses, pianos, and other musical instruments, sewing machines, cooking stoves, tools, and household goods generally, saw mills, engines, presses, heavy machinery, and agricultural implements… axes, shovels. hoes… and bush cutters… a supply of shoes, hats, umbrellas… time-pieces, fine cutlery, silver forks and spoons, hardware, drugs, and most toilet articles… firearms and ammunition are not necessary, but as some Americans would consider them a wholesome precaution, it is suggested that they make as little display of them as possible."*

Goodrich's intention in printing his pamphlet was to cash in on the sale of lots on his land south of Caleta and the fees for his expertise that he hoped to charge the "new colonists," but only a few hardy souls from New Orleans and Key West ever came to the island to try to establish a foothold. Their stay was ephemeral. However, the US government took notice of the Goodrich endeavor and explored the possibility of establishing a US Consulate in San Miguel. Unfortunately, after they approached the Mexican government on March 24, 1874, their request was rejected the following January on the grounds that *"no such port of that stature existed in Cozumel."*

Although Goodrich managed to sell a few copies of his self-published book extolling Cozumel for fifty-cents a copy (postage included), it is clear that the colony was still not in operation in 1877 and that his opinion of the quality and cost of the native labor had changed. When Alice LePlongeon and her husband Augustus visited Cozumel in 1876-7, she reported her observations in her book, *Here and there in the Yucatán*. The book was published in 1889, though parts of it had been printed in the *New York Tribune* and other papers in 1885. Alice wrote of the Goodrich Colony: *"We then made up a boat party with some of our countrymen who were trying to form a colony there. The boat belonged to them; it was not more than fifteen feet long, but big enough to accommodate five people. After an hour's sail [south of San Miguel] we stopped to see where the American Colony was to be. It was a beautiful spot. The owner [Goodrich] complained bitterly that the native workmen did as little as possible and charged twice as much as they usually received from their own people. Further down the coast we stopped at a plantation belonging to Señor Angulo."* [The next day, the party sailed father south to Laguna Colombia].

So, what happened to his dreams of an American colony on Cozumel after Goodrich published his booklet? Not much. Although a few newspapers picked up the subject and printed an article or two on Goodrich's efforts, the influx of land-grabbing Americans he had envisioned never materialized. Below is an article that ran on Wednesday, December 8, 1875, in the *South Australian Register*:

A NEW AMERICAN COLONY.—It is mentioned by the *Philadelphia Times* that a colony has sprung up on an island in the Caribbean Sea. The name is Cozumel, and it belongs to Mexico. "The climate is delightful, being at an average temperature of 80 degrees, and the distance from New Orleans is four or five days' sail. The products of the island are sugar, tobacco, and all kinds of tropical fruits, while it also grows valuable timber, such as ebony, lignumvitæ, and logwood. To settlers the Mexican Government allows 2,471 acres of land in favourable locations on the payment of £25, which payment can run through several years. As this island is in the neighbourhood of the Channel of Yucatan it has a most favourable position in connection with the trade and commerce that must spring up with the[United States of Columbia and other parts of that vast region of South America. It will be a point of stoppage for all ships bound in that direction, and hence the importance of having it inhabited and its trade and commerce ruled by Americans.

Who was this Claude Goodrich, the island's promoter?

Claude Luther Goodrich was born in 1831 to Luther E. Goodrich and Clarisa Noble, in New York. The Goodrich family then moved to

Nottawa, St. Joseph County, Michigan, where siblings Dwight and Mary were born before Claude's mother died in 1850. In 1851, Claude's father married Mary A. Doughty and had four more children with her by 1858.

In November, 1853, Claude was hired as an apprentice at the Delphi Journal in Delphi Indiana. The same paper was to print his obituary in 1896.

In March, 1854, Goodrich moved to Oregon and arranged to buy the newspaper *The Oregon Spectator,* the first newspaper to appear on the West Coast, having been founded in 1844. In March 1855, just one year after he took over the paper, the presses were sold, the paper was closed, and Goodrich left town.

In 1857, Goodrich bought the *Alameda Gazette* newspaper of San Leandro, California just outside of Oakland. Two years later, in 1859, Goodrich sold the newspaper to William Van Voorhies and Isaac A. Amerman.

In 1867, Goodrich formed a short-lived partnership with H. C. Street and A. J. Boyakin, which contracted to buy the *Idaho Triweekly Statesman* from James S. Reynolds. A month later, Mr. Reynolds took the business back over from the Boyakin, Street & Goodrich partnership. In the summer of 1871, Goodrich founded the *Elk Falls Examiner*, a four-page weekly newspaper published in Elk Falls, Kansas. Along with the newspaper, he also did job-printing. His advertisement in the George P. Rowell's *American Newspaper Directory* showed his interest in real estate promotion:

Elk Falls Examiner,

PUBLISHED WEEKLY, AT ELK FALLS, KANSAS, · · · BY C. L. GOODRICH & CO.

OFFICIAL PAPER OF HOWARD COUNTY.

ADVERTISING RATES.—One column, 1 year, $80; fractional portions of column at same rate. ELK FALLS, a large, flourishing town, filling up very fast with farmers, stock raisers and manufacturers; its position is central, and easy of access from every quarter. Railroads must necessarily make this a point running east and west through the Wild Cat Valley; pronounced by engineers the best route within 50 miles. The chances for obtaining farms at low prices are, within a radius of 10 miles, the best to be found in the Western country. The soil is rich, deep and fertile, producing wheat, corn, oats, rye, barley, tobacco, &c., &c.

ELK FALLS Examiner; Saturdays; four pages; size 25x38; subscription $2; established 1871; C. L. Goodrich & Co., editors and publishers; circulation about 300; co-operative; *largest circulation in county or within radius of 35 miles; is the official paper of Howard county; independent; almost exclusively devoted to local affairs; situated in the best farming and stock-raising district in Kansas; has an extensive job office.*

In 1872, the following short article was published in the Wichita City Eagle, in Wichita, Kansas: *"The Examiner, published by C. L. Goodrich, at Elk Falls, comes out with a vignette of the falls and surrounding scenery at its head. We admire such enterprise. In some particulars, Goodrich is an odd genius, nevertheless a genius. The Examiner is one of the neatest papers in the state."*

Shortly after that, Goodrich closed the Elk Falls Examiner and moved to Fort Dodge, Iowa, where, together with a partner P. C. Hudson, they took over the *Iowa Real Estate Register* from its founder, Mr. E. C. Bayam. The paper was dedicated to real estate.

FORT DODGE, Iowa Real Estate Register; monthly; eight pages; size 28x42; subscription 50 cents; established 1871; Hudson, Goodrich & Co., editors and publishers; a real estate advertising sheet.

Iowa Real Estate Register.

HUDSON, GOODRICH & CO..................FORT DODGE, IOWA.

DEVOTED TO LAW AND REAL ESTATE.

Our circulation varies from **1,000** to **4,000.** We endeavor to reach every family in Webster County with each issue, and stipulate in our advertising contracts that the circulation **within the County** shall not be less than **1,000 per month.**

P. C. HUDSON, ATTORNEY AT LAW, EDITOR.

HUDSON, GOODRICH & CO., REAL ESTATE BROKERS, BUSINESS MANAGERS.

By 1874, Goodrich had found a new home in Cozumel and published his booklet extolling the island's virtues.

On January 30, 1877, 46-year-old Goodrich married 21-year-old Bonifacia Casanova on Cozumel. Considering he only claimed to be 36 the time, according to the Cozumel marriage registry, it looks like he was shaving years off his age to fool his much younger wife. Bonifacia was the daughter of Hermenegildo Casanova and Susana Sánchez. Bonifacia's older sister, Felipa, was born in Chemax in 1844 and came to Cozumel with her parents, but Bonifacia was born on Cozumel in 1856. On December 12, 1877, Víctor Guadalupe Goodrich Casanova was born to the Goodrich couple on Cozumel.

Goodrich's post-Cozumel life

In 1881, seven years after his booklet on Cozumel was published, Goodrich turned up in Belize where he began working as a printer with the *Belize Advertiser* at C. T. Hunter's Printing Office. In 1884, Claude's second son, Dwight Goodrich, was born. Dwight was later to move to Michigan and become a medical doctor.

In 1887, Goodrich began working with the *British Honduras Gazette (new series)*, published by George S. Banham. Shortly after, he became partners with Banham and formed Banham & Goodrich which then began publishing *The Independent*. The partnership ended in May, 1888, when Banham was forced out and Goodrich took over the operation.

Mr. George S. Banham has severed his connection with the Belize (British Honduras) *Independent*, which will in future be under the entire management and control of C. L. Goodrich.

In the October 1889 to September 1890 edition of *American Lithographer (Volume VII)*, a notice appeared, announcing Goodrich's acquisition of the *Belize Independent* newspaper. The announcement also contains a considerable amount of self promotion:

THE job printing rooms formerly belonging to Messrs. Banham & Goodrich, at Belize, British Honduras, have been merged with the Belize *Independent*, and Mr. C. L. Goodrich becomes sole proprietor. The establishment had just received the Happy New Year souvenir from Messrs. Golding & Co., announcing their success at Paris and congratulates that firm. The *Independent*, luckily, has one of the prize No. 7 jobbers at work and is therefore happy, as all its patrons and Messrs. Golding & Co. must know. Belize is full of "amateurs," but this press is intended to clear them out. The other day, one of your "as it is" fellows sent his press to an auctioneer, but when offered for sale got no bid. It lies there yet, a nameless, worthless "foot power," with no wheel, throw-off, or self-inking apparatus.

Shortly after that news item appeared, Goodrich was out trolling for a place in Chicago to send a "white boy" to be bound into apprenticeship for five or six years. Could this have been his 13-year-old son, Víctor?

C. L. GOODRICH, of Belize, British Honduras, writes as follows: "Can an opportunity be found in Chicago, to apprentice a smart boy (to be five or six years bound) from the tropics (white boy who speaks and reads English and Spanish) to learn job printing, lithographing, electrotyping, etc., where he would be properly instructed and well treated. If so, upon about what terms?" Parties desirous of obtaining further information should address as above.

In the pages of *The Inland Printer*, Volume 9, (1891-1892) the following notice appeared:

C. L. GOODRICH, editor and proprietor of the *Belize Independent*, Belize, British Honduras, being desirous of visiting the Worlds' Fair for several months in 1893, wishes to procure a trustworthy person to conduct the paper during his absence, or the newspaper plant and good will with the job and book department will be disposed of on good cash terms.

Not content with publishing, in 1892, Goodrich began to act as an agent selling a "new age" osteopathic book entitled *The New Science of Healing*. Below is the frontispiece of the book:

The
New Science of Healing
or the doctrine of the
Oneness of all Diseases
forming the basis of a
Uniform Method of Cure, without Medicines and without Operations.
An Instructor and Adviser for the Healthy and the Sick
by
Louis Kuhne.
Motto:
"He who seeks the truth must not count the suffrages."
Leibniz
Translated from the Third greatly augmented German Edition
By
Dr. TH. BAKER
Leipzig.
Published by Louis Kuhne.
Publishing Agents:
Williams & Norgate. London and Edinburgh. **Darter Bros. & Walton,** Cape Town
G. Robertson & Co., Melbourne, Adelaide and Sydney. **C. L. Goodrich,** Belize
The International News Co., New York. **J. Thomson,** Georgetown.
Tract & Book Depository, Mangalore. **Thacker, Spink & Co.,** Calcutta.
Kelly & Walsh Ld.. Shanghai. Hongkong Yokohama Singapore
Carstens & Co., Moulmein.

Louis Kuhne was a German naturopath primarily known for his cold-water friction sitz-bath which involved the patient sitting in a tub filled with cold water and rubbing their genitals with a rough linen cloth. The resulting stimulation was supposed to help eliminate toxins.

Claude Goodrich died in May, 1896. His obituary was run in the *Delphi Journal* where he first worked as an apprentice.

In 1897, the Goodrich Job Press was still in operation in Belize, being run by Claude's son, Víctor Guadalupe Goodrich. He later changed the name of the business to *V. Goodrich and Trumpet Press* through the 1930s. After Víctor's death, his own son, Eugene A. Goodrich, moved to Florida and married Vesta Mea Cheatham on June 20, 1953 in Ft. Lauderdale, Florida.

Claude Goodrich is Dead.

Mr. James B. Scott is in receipt of a letter announcing the death of Claude Goodrich which occurred at his home in British Honduras two weeks ago. He was the first apprentice in the Delphi JOURNAL office. Soon after Mr. Scott started the paper young Goodrich appeared and asked for a job. He was set to work in November and remained with the paper until spring when he left for Oregon. From there he drifted to British Honduras where he went into the newspaper business and was deservedly successful. A few older citizens remain who will remember him. His death resulted from heart disease.

Above: Claude L. Goodrich's obituary

CHAPTER 13

Eyewitness descriptions of post-1870 Cozumel

Several detailed descriptions of Cozumel from the 1870s to the early 20th century still survive. I have taken excerpts from a few of the more interesting ones and reprinted them below.

In 1873, Claude Luther Goodrich spent six months on Cozumel. When he returned to the US, he authored a small pamphlet with the purpose of enticing more Americans to immigrate to the island and (he hoped) hire him as their real estate agent and contractor.

The last chapter of Goodrich's pamphlet is his interesting description of the inhabitants of Cozumel. *"No lady promenades the streets in company with any gentleman, not even does a wife be seen walking out with her husband or brothers. Courtship may be carried on in presence of parents, though young people dance together, at home and abroad, and are not under very rigid surveillance, but no male escorts are apparently wanted in going or returning from church, festivals, balls, or any public assembly.... The inhabitants are up early in the morning, perhaps indulge in a bath, are sipping chocolate, or eating an orange, after which the morning hours are occupied with their usual avocations till 10 o'clock, the breakfast hour... Dinner takes place at 5 PM, and suppers are unknown... The poorer classes fare simply, upon tortillas, fish, game and vegetables, while the more affluent citizen dines upon a multiplicity of dishes, turtle, beef, kid, chicken, with eggs, milk, coffee, and the daintiest fruits and vegetables, well cooked and seasoned with rare spices and relishes. Foreigners can obtain first class boarding, with families, at $15 or $20 per month; there are no hotels or "boarding houses," but the ladies manage household affairs, and do not object to a boarder, especially if he have light hair and blue eyes —which they greatly admire... In domestic life, monogamy is adhered to and the marriage relation held sacred... The morals of the people average well; the youth are early taught good principals, virtue and happiness, and these are quite generally inculcated among the adult population. In no country have I ever observed the young ladies to be more prudent in* *their deportment, more modest or reserved, than the señoritas of Cozumel. There are no "girls of the period" there, no fast or precocious children, no corsets, no Grecian bends, kangaroo limps* or artificial hair! The ladies are handsome because they are natural."*

In the 1870s tight corsets and big bustles were all the rage. The posture forced upon women wearing these fashionable undergarments was called the "Grecian Bend." The "Kangaroo Limp" was another fashionable affectation of the 1870s that did not last very long. This little mention of these fashion fads in a newspaper article of the day seems to imply they would not be missed:

> "Dolly Varden," "Grecian Bend," "Kangaroo Limp," and other oddities and eccentricities of fashion have departed, and are being superceded by the "Straighten-up-Mary-Jane-and-show-your-breast-pin" attitude." The girls are delighted with it.

Below is an illustration of "The Grecian Bend." It is amazing what lengths some women went to in order to look "appealing back then!"

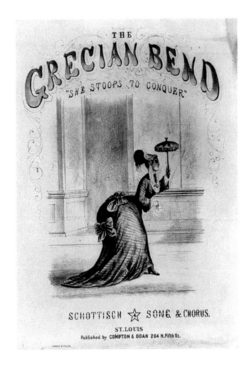

THE

GRECIAN BEND

"SHE STOOPS TO CONQUER"

SCHOTTISCH ☆ SONG & CHORUS.

ST. LOUIS

Published by COMPTON & DOAN 204 N.Fifth St.

Goodrich went on to write: *"Boys attend one school and girls another, to acquire the rudiments in Spanish, their native tongue, and after their earlier years are passed some of them are sent away to the capitol of the state to be better educated. All classes and ages are fond of music, dancing, gambling a little, feast-day sports, the recurrence of which are frequent, the innocent revelry of the Pastories, the parade and pomp of the Carnival. The guitar and violin, bugle and drums are most of the musical instruments, and all these are sadly out of repair! No piano or organ has ever yet been taken to the Island. Among the indulgences rum drinking is probably the greatest, yet it is very seldom that any drunk or disorderly persons are found... Almost everybody smokes cigarettes, even, sometimes, the babe on its mother's lap. Some families engage largely in their manufacture, also cigars... The dress of the natives is not an elaborate or extravagant one, and in some cases is extremely light, being arranged with more a view to comfort than to attract attention. The ladies dress with calicoes, cambrics, lawns, etc., with an occasional more valuable pattern, cut in plain robe styles, but they are unacquainted with polonaises, bustles, patent protuberances or other modern fashions of the enlightened world, and a 'love of a bonnet' has never been heard of among them. The hair of the ladies is worn in braids or flowing in profusion over the shoulders; while men cut theirs quite as short and trim as is customary in this country. Coats and pants are usually of linen or cotton goods; plain and straw hats are worn; shoes and sandals. Small children sometimes play in the streets arrayed in the outer cuticle. Everybody, large or small, sleeps in his or her own separate hammock, and very likely indulges in a short nap or siesta therein between breakfast and dinner. Hammocks are usually made of twine from the henequen grass, but strong wove cloth is preferable. And thus their simple lives go on from year to year, in indolence and harmless enjoyment, interspersed with a very small portion of work... The advent of Americans and a mixed nationality of race upon Cozumel Island will, of course, change the whole programme. Whether or not it will bring our natives any additional happiness is a question for the future to answer..."*

Augustus and Alice LePlongeon visited Cozumel from November 1876 until June 1877. Afterwards, Alice wrote several articles about the island for various newspapers and magazines, as well as a book, entitled <u>Here and there in Yucatan</u>.

"The center of the village of San Miguel is an immense grass-grown square, bounded on the west by the sea, and on the east by a thatched church, and on the north and south by thatched dwellings. The rest of the village is scattered along the beach and a little way back, not far, for there are only five hundred inhabitants. Having no tent to pitch, we emphatically insisted on a house, and were at last allowed to take possession of a one-room residence at the southeast corner of the square. It was gloomy, damp, dirty; the floor was thickly strewn with dry cocoa-nuts. It had two doors but no window,"

Of a trip Alice took along the coast of Cozumel, she had this to say: *"Our journey back to the village was a delightful contrast to the attempted trip to Buena Vista. We went on horseback, along the shore, through groves of palm-trees, passing now and then by plantations where luxuriant sugar-cane and other products showed the wonderful fertility of the soil... We then made up a boat party with some of our countrymen .... Further down the coast we stopped at a plantation belonging to Señor Angulo. We had an opportunity to see immense fields of garlic, ginger, sweet potatoes, and sago: from this last article excellent starch is made."*

Later, Alice attended and described an attempted murder, a wake, a baptism, and a funeral:

"When the storm abated, just as we were passing into dreamland, slumber was rudely dispelled by violent clanging of the church bells. A dozen peaceable citizens, disturbed from their rest, went to see what was the matter. They found an old woman pulling vigorously at the rope. She was quite demented and refused to stop her music. They drove her home, which so provoked her that in the morning she threw one of her grandchildren into a well, saying 'it must be killed.' The child's father being at hand, it was rescued uninjured, though much terrified.

In the villages throughout Yucatán, baptisms and funerals are great events, a wake being regarded as a mild entertainment. In Cozumel we had occasion to see one of those friendly gatherings. The patient was a

*young woman who had lived alone. Being suddenly stricken down in a
fit, from which she never recovered, a neighbor had taken her in. What
little property was found in her home — fifty dollars, some gold
ornaments, and clothes — was appropriated by the same kind neighbor
to defray expenses. The unconscious woman was placed on a camp-
bed, and preparations for the wake were at once begun. A demijohn of
strong liquor was bought with the money of the patient, also a lot of
cake, four pounds of chocolate, and plenty of black wax candles.*

*Soon the room was full of men and women, regaling themselves with
drinks and cigarettes. Young girls with flowers in their hair and powder
on their faces were seated around the room, in expectation of cake and
chocolate. On one table there were sundry small ornaments, and a
wooden crucifix before which burned wax candles. On another, a pitcher
of water, glasses, cigars, and beneath it, the demijohn of rum.*

*An old woman came in; the hostess offered her a cigar, which she
accepted, saying: 'Thank you, ma'am. Have you got her chickens?' 'Yes,'
replied the other; 'they are all in the coop. She will be dead presently,
and they will be killed for this good company.' 'Yes, yes,' rejoined the
dame, lighting her cigarette; 'woe to us! What are we in this world!'*

*The wake lasted two days and nights; by the time the woman really
expired, her money was all gone. A grave had been dug the day she fell
sick; now she was carried to it in a deal coffin. The priest was not called
to utter a prayer over the corpse, because, said they, there was no
money to pay him. That affair was a nine-days scandal, even among
those simple-minded people.*

*One Sunday evening we received a pressing invitation to the house of
Señior Mendiburu, the Alcalde, whose youngest child was to be
baptized. We found the parlor illuminated with three or four lamps,
several women seated on one side of the room, men on the other. Upon
a table there were goblets, and bottles of ale, more expensive there
than the best Spanish wine, hence preferred.*

The baby was brought from the bedroom to be taken to church by the sponsors and the male guests, the women remaining at home with the parents. On their return the infant was carried back to the bedroom, no one manifesting the least interest in it. Sponsors are expected to offer a gift according to their means. In the peninsula, well-to-do families scatter silver medios among those who follow the procession to the church. The guests are presented with pretty cards that have a silver or gold coin attached to them. On the card is printed the name of the child, the date of its birth, and a floral design or verses.

Having baptized the baby, Cura Rejon came to the house of its parents; then the bottles were opened, the host himself handing glasses of ale to the ladies, and inviting the gentlemen to help themselves. He expressed much regret at not having a band of music as intended — the musicians had been called to Island Mugeres — but hoped to do better next time. It was remarkable that hardly a word was uttered on this occasion — the silence was almost solemn; whereas at the wake there had been much animated conversation. Do they think death less to be regretted than birth? It is a fact that in those countries anciently, when a child was born, the first words addressed to it were 'Alas for thee! thou hast come to this world to suffer and weep.' Looking upon a corpse, they invariably say: 'At rest! To suffer and toil no more!' If the deceased is an infant, they wreathe it in garlands, exclaiming: 'Another little angel!'

Cura Rejon was called from the baptism party to a death-bed. Bidding us good night, he said: 'Ah yes! One after another I lay them to rest as they fall like autumn leaves around me, but there will be no one to minister the last sacrament to poor old Father Rejon when his time comes.'

At three o'clock on the following afternoon the funeral cortege started. The Cura, dressed in his robes, led the way. On his right walked an acolyte carrying a vessel of holy water; on his left, one with a prayer-book. They were followed by three or four amateur musicians; next, six men bearing the coffin, black, ornamented with white. It was open, the corpse, dressed in black, exposed. A man walked beside, with a table on his head. Men, women, and children, some mourners, others idlers, brought up the rear. The men were bareheaded, the women wore mantillas as at church. They looked sad, but the absence of a black hearse, and other funeral paraphernalia, seemed to rid death of half its horrors.

The followers sang a dirge. At each corner the procession halted, the table was put on the ground, and the coffin placed on it. The priest, with his face toward the deceased, then chanted in a sonorous musical voice, the people responding. The sky was black with an approaching storm, the thunder's distant peal mingling its deep tones with theirs, like a note from the grand organ of the Supreme Being. After each prayer the priest sprinkled the corpse with holy water. Thus they slowly wended their way to the church. At the door the prayers were again repeated; the body was then carried in, the bell tolling while the funeral service was performed.

From the church to the grave the coffin was at the head of the procession, priest and mourners following with the musicians, who played a slow march. Before lowering the coffin into the earth, the lid was nailed on, and a bottle of rum passed round among those present — a parting cup, to wish the lamented friend godspeed on his long journey."

In 1885, The US Fish Commission sent an expedition to Cozumel. The photographer, N. B. Miller, wrote a newspaper article about the trip that appeared in the New York Times. Below is a portion of that article:

"Off the narrow, sandy beach, which at that point breaks the continuity of the "ironbound" coast recorded by Stephens, a few small merchant vessels were anchored. In the small boatyard of the village a couple of little sloops were in process of construction and repair. Along shore we saw numerous piles of logwood awaiting conveyance to the market in Mérida. The village of San Miguel manifested some forms of life in the swarthy forms of children at play in somewhat scant attire. Occasionally a woman clad in a long and loose-flowing garment with short sleeves appeared in a doorway or a barefooted man in light cotton clothing and a straw hat lounged along, smoking a domestic cigar. After *going ashore, we saw a few under-sized horses, some respectable but lean cattle, a lot of hungry and wild-looking pigs, an abundance of chickens, and a horde of mangy dogs, including some with staring white eyes. The village probably contains several hundred people, embracing Indians, Mexicans, and Spaniards, besides some of mixed origin.*

The dwellings now straggle along a street facing the channel, but are principally collected about a small central plaza adjacent to the beach. Some of the houses are enclosed in plastered stone walls and cement floors. There are several cottages built entirely of poles and thatched with palm. There are no chimneys, and the smoke escapes diffusely through the loosely constructed roof and doorways. Red and blue colors are occasionally employed in ornamentation. Tumbled-down houses of comparatively recent construction are not infrequent. Windows are not numerous, and the thatched dwellings are destitute of them.

There are several large plantations on the island devoted to the cultivation of the usual tropical fruits and vegetables. The vanilla bean is one of the products. Near San Miguel there was once a sugar estate, the machinery of which now lies unused. A very good quality of tobacco is produced, and there is quite an industry in the manufacture of cigars, which, though very cheap, are of fair quality."

Of Caleta, Miller had this to say: *"On the west side, about four miles distant from San Miguel, a narrow deep channel leads into a small harbor in which vessels drawing eight or ten feet of water may safely lie alongside. At this place there is a small collection of Indian thatched cottages."*

Mr. George F. Ganmer of Lawrence, Kansas, also visited Cozumel in 1885 with his wife and young son. He wrote a letter home on July 23, 1885 that later was published in the *Lawrence Gazette*. A part of the letter reads: *"Like most other Yucatan towns, it* [San Miguel] *is built mostly of palm leaves and poles with probably half a dozen stone houses. It has about 500 of the laziest inhabitants that ever populated a tropical island, besides the town there are many ranchos all over the island, and one large pine apple orchard and a large cocoa nut estate at the southern extremity. Cozumel is pre-eminently an island of fruit. Thousands of acres have been planted to cocoa nuts, and everywhere* the air is fragrant with the orange blossom. Limes and lemons by tons are decaying every day, because there is no market for them. It is estimated that ten thousand bunches of bananas go to loss in the island every week. One orchard of pine apples that used to furnish 800 dozen per week, is now cultivated as an ornament only, and this is only one of many of the same kind. That Mexico is doing everything needful to annihilate herself as a government is well demonstrated here. Until two years ago and for nearly a century, American vessels came to Cozumel to load with fruits, and since the Central American Mail Steamship line was established, the impetus given to the planting and cultivation of fruits has been enormous, so that today Cozumel alone could load a steamer daily with fruits, but the Mexican government, under the pretext that some smuggling was going on, has passed a law prohibiting any foreign vessel from landing in Cozumel. This law has been in force but two years, but the time has been sufficient to almost ruin the island. The fruit gatherers who were not capitalists, but working men, are nearly all broken up already, and many of them have left the island, and many more are leaving as fast as they can make money enough to pay their passage to another place. An American steamer passes within speaking distance of us every week, bound to New Orleans, and yet dares not stop."

William Henry Holmes came to Cozumel on the Allison V. Armour expedition when he was curator of anthropology of the Field Museum of Chicago in 1894. He made a few short notes regarding the island, and took three photographs of the ruin at Santa Pilar where that *"mujer parturienta"* column once stood before it was removed and taken to the Museo de la Isla in the 1950s. Holmes also painted a wonderful watercolor of the San Miguel waterfront, which now resides in the Smithsonian Museum.

The expedition later traveled to Chichen Itzá, which was at the time the private property of Edward Herbert Thompson, who had purchased the land containing the ruins with funds provided to him by Armour in 1894.

Above: 1894 watercolor of San Miguel by William Henry Holmes

In 1907, Channing Arnold and Frederick J. Tabor Frost visited Cozumel and wrote the following lines about Cozumel in their 1909 book, <u>The American Egypt: A Record of Travel in Yucatan</u>:

"As we anchor some five hundred yards from the shore, the little island town of San Miguel rings the bay. A few palm-thatched huts, a wooden store, an open space, a custom house with a flagstaff, a few small boat-shelters of palm-leaves to save boats from cracking in the sun, and a jetty, three feet wide, running out into water waist-deep. Northward a grove of palm trees; southward stretches, as far as the eye can see, the rocky coral beach. Now there are but two villages, San Miguel and, ten miles southward, El Cedral; and only around these and along the western coast is the land cultivated. There gardens and ranches are rich with oranges and limes, pineapples and sugar-cane, bananas and banana-apples, grape-fruit and the delicious soapy-fleshed guanabana, with groves of cocoanut palms, with figs, with the white starry flowers

of tobacco, with the fluffy bursting pods of cotton, and vari-coloured spicebushes.

At El Cedral we were told that there were ruins intact, and we made arrangements at once to ride over there. The road is just the winding coast-path which girdles the island. At no part more than a yard or two wide, it leads at first over the flattened ledges of coral which divide the beach from the woods. Then as the woods thicken to the water edge, you ride through tunnels of greenery, where the road traverses the wooded bases of the triangles of coral which at intervals jut out from the shore like the spikes on a dog's collar, to emerge again on to level stretches of golden sand, the palms bending rustlingly over its glittering surface. Don Luis Villanueva, whose name had been mentioned to us in reference to his alleged discovery of a temple in the bush, owns the little rancho of San Francisco, some six miles north of El Cedral. We arrived there about midday, very hot and very hungry. Don Luis proved to be a wiry little sallow-faced man, small-featured, with keen small eyes, short grizzled hair, drooping straggly moustache, and one long tuft of grey growing from the extreme end of his chin like the beard of a billygoat. His farmhouse was simplicity itself, formed of wood-stake palisading thatched with palm-leaves. Within, the only furniture were string hammocks, two or three low raw-hide-seated stools, a trestle-like table formed of unhewn poles bound together, raft fashion, with lianas, supported on four small unbarked tree trunks. The floor was just the natural earth, and in one corner of the hut a fire burnt. Every Yucatecan builds his fire on the floor inside his house in this way, with no arrangements for chimney, and the wonder is the huts are not oftener burnt down. In the further corner were piled bales of tobacco-leaf and sacks of rough cotton. From the rafters hung open baskets filled with tortillas, green and red peppers, onions and fruits, and here and there hung a bunch of bananas ripening. Don Luis is a widower and his housekeeping was done by his daughter, a pretty brown-skinned girl of about twenty, whose single thin garment of cotton only accentuated the plump attractiveness of her figure. As all Yucatecan women always are, she was at the metate or tortilla-tray when we entered, but left her work and came forward prettily to greet us. The other inhabitants of the hut were Don Luis's two grandsons, healthy, black-eyed, intelligent-

looking little rascals, and a host of terribly emaciated dogs and puppies, melancholy half-fed brindled cats, so thin that they looked as if they had not got a purr in them, and the inevitable chickens and pigs. We reached the village while the sun was still blazing high. A cluster of palm-thatched huts grouped round a square of wiry grass—these Yucatecan hamlets are as like as peas in a pod. The male villagers streamed out to welcome us with a cordiality which was quite overwhelming. We really thought that at last we had found the exception which proved the rule of Yucatecan avarice and inhospitality. El Cedral received us with open arms. El Cedral walked behind us in its fifties, applauding our attempts at Spanish civilities, laughing when we laughed, grave when we were grave. El Cedral begged us to stay with it; indeed would take no refusal. El Cedral insisted that to us should be paid the meed of honour due to such distinguished visitors, namely that our hammocks should be slung for the night in the Casa Municipal, the village town hall; a distinction much as if London's Lord Mayor gave you leave to sling your hammocks in the Guildhall between Gog and Magog. And El Cedral developed an inordinate interest in procuring for supper just what might tickle our palates. But we were doomed to disillusionment.

First, we started to inspect the ruins. They were singularly disappointing. The chief one was a two-roomed house standing on a mound some 20 feet square. There were no statues, no bas-reliefs, no hieroglyphics. It was desolate enough, but it had had, we learnt, its modern uses; for five years back when a terrible hurricane had swept the island the whole village had been blown away, and this Indian ruin was for days the only shelter of the disconsolate villagers. It was quite Arcadian, this little village, with the homely lights streaming out from the white-faced huts, the merry laughter of the youngsters, the caressing warmth of the night air, and the blackness of the rustling trees flashing into a myriad ever-shifting points of light as the fireflies flew from bough to bough. We slept well in the town hall, the village clock of large American make, brightest jewel in the municipal crown, ticking in homely fashion behind us. But with the dawn we were disillusioned as to the hospitality of Arcady, for we found we had to "foot" quite a large bill for our entertainment. This is really one of the most difficult problems in Yucatan. You never know whether you are a paying guest or not. The head of a village orders your meals, accompanies you to them, and sees that you lack for nothing. You naturally regard him as your host; but if he is a Yucatecan this is the last thing he intends. We steered first to the east coast. An Indian trail leads thither to where, some few miles from the beach, is a spring of fresh water and the relics of an Indian town. Attracted by the water supply, an attempt had been made in recent years to clear the ground there. But vegetation in Cozumel is luxuriant, and the space cleared one season is by the next four feet high in undergrowth. This well was known as San Benito. We rechristened it San Mosquito, for the fury of the Cancun insects paled before the winged inhabitants of this spot which we chose for our headquarters for the next three weeks.... There were two or three old palm-thatched huts at San Benito, and we slung our hammocks in the best-preserved one. If we lived a century we should never forget our nights there. It is ridiculous to call them nights. They were not nights at all; they were orgies of blood and death. The mosquitoes flew at us, shrieking like rockets; and we hammered them to death on one cheek or wiped them off from the other."

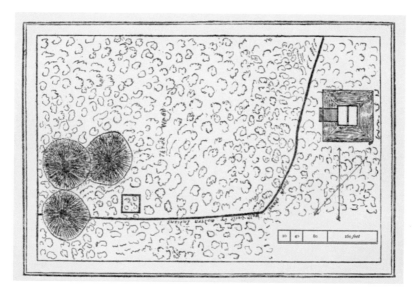

Above: Channing's sketch of a portion of San Gervasio.

Of Cozumel's Carnaval celebrations, Channing had this to say: *"...to San Miguel. There, the carnival was at its height. Little the Yucatecans reckoned of ruined temples and Mayan problems. It was enough for them that the sun shone, that they had habanero and anise to drink, and that there were girls to dance with and make love to. Tin-tray music and a charivari of drum and horn fought for mastery over wild whistlings and cat-callings and the 'loud laugh which spoke the vacant mind.' The few horses of the island had been requisitioned to carry ludicrously drunk Yucatecans in paper caps and masks up and down the beach and round the plaza. Those who could not ride found satisfaction sufficient for their senseless mirth in running behind and shouting. We were hungry to escape from this very unsatisfying gaiety, and we wanted to cross to the mainland."*

In April of 1913, American archaeologists Jesse Nusbaum and Sylvanus G. Morley visited Cozumel and took several photographs of the island.

Above: San Miguel as seen from near Punta Langosta in 1913.

On November 15, 1915, an interesting article accompanied by photographs appeared in the *Lehi Banner*, the newspaper of Lehi, Utah. An excerpt from the article follows:

"The present population of Cozumel numbers some fourteen hundred souls. The capital, San Miguel, is credited with 900 and the village of Cedral has about 150; the remainder are scattered among the numerous ranches. San Miguel is quite a thriving, well-formed town. It has several wide, clean streets; a plaza, a very presentable little church, one large general store and several small ones, an inn, and municipal offices and customhouse; it also boasts assort of esplanade running along the entire

sea front, at one end of which there is a lighthouse and at the other end of which there is a jetty. Although most of the buildings are palm-thatched cottages, there are several strongly built stone houses and the main street has a two-story brick house and a modern bungalow.

The only regular communication with the outside world is by government transport. These steamers call twice each month to leave and collect mail when en route with troops and supplies to and from Veracruz and the military stations of Quintana Roo. Health conditions in Cozumel are extremely good, when the tropical climate of the island is taken into account. The normal rate of mortality averages 14 per 1,000. Epidemics are very rare, indeed, practically unknown. The great majority of the Cozumel Islanders are poor, so far as possessing a surplus of this world's goods is concerned, being satisfied with a hand-to-mouth existence. Among the very few articles exported from the island are sponges, but the quality not very fine. More than one attempt has been made by foreigners to fully exploit the sponge business here, but all efforts to make it profitable on a large scale have failed."

In 1924, Thomas Gann published his book, <u>In an Unknown Land</u>, which contained a description of his 1918 visit to Cozumel:

"About 1am the next morning, we made San Miguel, the capital of the island of Cozumel. Pandemonium seemed to have broken loose on the island, singing, howling, shouting, drums beating, bands braying, guns exploding, dogs barking, all tortured the quiet night, and proclaimed the strenuous observance of the last day of Carnival. The noise was so terrific that we did not go to sleep, and so lay on and off some distance from the shore until about 7am, when we landed for an interview with the Administrador del Aduana, or Chief of Customs, an educated Mexican, dressed in nicely-pressed grey silk suit, tight, highly-polished grey kid boots, with silk stockings to match, a grey figured shirt, and – no collar or tie. The little plaza, or public square, facing the sea contains a pretentious statue of President Juares, and a fine stone clock tower, but is neglected and overgrown with rank vegetation. These two - the Administrador and the plaza – epitomize in themselves what may be termed the Neo Mexican culture, the keynote of which is meretriciousness – a constant striving after the grandiose and

impressive in architecture, institutions, and culture, a lamentable falling short, and the attainment only of the ridiculous.

The next day, with true Mexican hospitality, our new friends refused to let us go till we had attended a dance they were getting up in our honor that night. We pointed out that the night of Ash Wednesday was no good time for good Catolicos *to get up a dance; they replied that, having had a hot time during Carnival, they felt like keeping it up a little while longer, for which our presence offered an excellent excuse. Messengers were sent round to warn the señoritas of the pueblo, and around 8pm, a considerable crowd had collected in the dance house on the plaza, open on all sides to the winds of heaven, and to which various* mirones, *or unlookers without whom no Yucatecan dance is complete. These consist of dogs, children, loafers, the aged female relatives of the performers, and, indeed, all of the inhabitants of the pueblo with nothing particular to do. Most of the guests, in deference to the day, had a smear of ashes on their heads or foreheads; later on, however, as in response to the stimulus to the vino del pais, things became more lively, Held (whose abilities at quick-fire portraiture and caricature proved of inestimable assistance to us throughout the trip) with the aid of a little charcoal, red ochre, and grease, transformed them into a company of demons. Like all Spaniards both men and women were excellent dancers, and performed* danza, danzon, *and Spanish quadrilles as if their hearts were in the business. The island ladies are fine, slummocky, upstanding young women, perhaps not so slim, graceful and alluring as the mestizas on the mainland."*

Two years later, in 1920, Sweden's Prince William visited Cozumel and wrote about the island in his book that was published in 1922: <u>Between Two Continents: Notes from a journey in Central America</u>. It was published first in Swedish and then later translated into English. The prince was singularly unimpressed with the island: *"Gradually Cozumel showed up out of the mist — not precisely on the quarter we had expected, but that was a detail; the main thing was that it was there. We altered our course accordingly, and just as dark was falling, the miniature city of San Miguel came in sight. And soon the Spellman lay at anchor, resting after a fatiguing day. The little place looked quite picturesque, lying there spread along the shore, in a setting of luxuriant green and swelling coco-nut palms. The houses showed clear white in the gloom, the clock in a slender belfry struck six. And at that moment, as if by magic, a row of guttering lights flashed out. 'Impossible! You don't mean to say they've electric light in this little hole?'*

The landing stage was in darkness. 'Attention, señor!' And care, indeed, was needed, for about every third plank was missing, and we had to balance our way along those that remained. Close at hand the power-house motor was coughing in its hiding place. At whose expense this piece of luxury had been installed was never quite determined, it is said, however, that the cost was written off as for charitable purposes."

The prince had arrived on the last night of Carnaval, and was invited by the Cozumel authorities to come ashore and join the festivities. He did so, but his disdain for the fiesta is clearly displayed in his description of the affair:

"Outside the ball-room all was life and movement. Tiny stalls with coloured paper lanterns stood in a long row, inviting purchases of sweetmeats, paper flowers and Chinese crackers. There was also a lottery, where one could try one's luck for a maximum stake of five cents. It was the younger generation mostly, which gave way to this reckless gambling; the boys stood in a double queue, chattering all at once, and getting up a little fight now and then over the winnings. Inside, the hall was a blaze of light. Long strings of greenish white paper flags hung from the roof, each flag cut to the shape of a short pair of drawers, while the walls were hung with a series of portraits, representing the presidents of the republic. As these change pretty frequently, the gallery was extensive and impressive. The orchestra was set up on a raised platform, and consisted of a fiddle, a concertina and a drum. The musicians had been playing and drinking hard for three days, so it was not surprising that they dropped off to sleep regularly between the dances. The atmosphere was saturated with perfume, mixed exhalations, and the odour of garlic, in about equal parts. And here were assembled all that the little community could boast of rank and aristocracy. Here sat the Mayor and his fat señora, with the local grocer between them, conversing excitedly on a bench; there was the local

policeman, with a pretty girl on his arm. A little farther off was the innkeeper with his quiver full, holding the youngest in his arms while his lady danced. In one corner stood an individual who, as we were informed, combined the functions of tailor, schoolmaster and lighthouse-keeper, delivering what, from his excited gestures, appeared to be a political harangue, while immediately opposite, a semi-intoxicated customs official mumbled a maudlin song, offering improper post-cards to all who cared to look. For the rest, the sexes appeared to keep to themselves during the intervals; then, when the music struck up, there was a sort of general post, and a rush for partners. The step-dancing was as regular as ever one sees it at home, giving place now and again to a more rhythmical, gliding dance, called simply danzano, *and said to originate from Cuba. The women moved very gracefully. Their features were regular, though coarse. They wore a huge comb stuck in the hair and an orange-blossom behind one ear. Neck and arms were loaded with a mass of imitation pearls and equally genuine precious stones. The costumes were many-coloured and gaudy, covered with sequins or cheap lace stitched on anyhow. As for the men, their appearance was more or less in accordance with the general idea of a Mexican; small of stature, dark-hued and dirty. Their dress, by no means clean, was cut according to the European fashion, all the colour in which they so delight being concentrated in a single feature, the neckcloth, which was of a glaring red, a venomous green or a blazing yellow — or all three together for choice.*

We stood for a while uncertain as to what would be expected of four strangers from the north in this company, where we knew no one, and where all had evidently made up their parties for the evening. This state of things, however, lasted only till the next dance, when the lighthouse-keeper — himself a cavalier in obvious high favour, resolutely grasped a dark-eyed beauty by the arm, and dragging her unwillingly across the floor, signed to us that we were to dance. According to the strict Spanish etiquette of the ball-room, it was impossible to refuse; it only remained to dash headlong in among the whirling couples and endeavour as far as possible to make a Swedish step dance fit in with the San Miguel trot. Choreographically, the attempt was perhaps not altogether a success, but as a sudorific, it was all that could be desired. One could almost have sworn there must be a pool around us when we finally stopped and stood looking foolishly at one another's heated faces.

Fortunately, an angel of deliverance appeared in the person of the mayor, who, with a glance at our wet handkerchiefs, sympathetically suggested: 'Whisky?' Here at least was a word of international significance. Acting on his hint, we went through into an adjoining room, which turned out to be the saloon bar and ladies' toilet in one. And here, surely enough, we found whisky in plenty — but water — Never! It was not long before we had made the acquaintance of half the city. The fun increased every minute, as did the number of intoxicated gentlemen. We judged it best to make for our waiting dinghy before the inevitable free fight, with which every respectable baile properly concludes. But long after the lights were out in our cabin we could hear the laughter and shouting and music from the shore, the festival continuing until cockcrow.

Next day the whole city was suffering from a bad head. An oppressive dullness hung over the entire community. The streets were deserted; only the pigs and fowls walked at their ease on the pavements, grunting and strutting as if the place belonged to them alone. If by chance one encountered a passer-by, he would mutter something unintelligible, and put his hand with a meaning gesture to his brow.

The great plaza fronting towards the sea lay dry and baking in the sun. In the centre stood an old gentleman in plaster-of-Paris, on a wooden pedestal; some Mexican general it was supposed to be, but the rain had washed the name away, so that we were unable to make his further acquaintance. Instead of plants, rows of shells and bottle-ends were drawn about here and there. Flowers were so common everywhere that it would hardly have seemed proper to plant them in the principal square of the town. They were relegated to the back yards. Every house had its enclosure, away from the street, filled with a marvelous wealth of hues, orchids, bougainvillea, alternating with yellow orange and red-flecked papayas. All this, however, grows of its own sweet will, without the least complicity on the part of the owner; it would never occur to a Mexican to care for a plant or protect a fine tree.

At one corner of the plaza was the store. Armed with a letter of introduction, we turned our steps towards the entrance, which was guarded by a couple of sleeping dogs. Senor Coldwell and his partner Bonastre sat on the counter smoking cigarettes; full-faced, amiable and loquacious gentlemen, having, moreover, some knowledge of English. The former especially was later to prove the one true worthy of the place, and most helpful and useful to ourselves. The store, it should be explained, was likewise a saloon and reading-room — being the only place on the island where Spanish newspapers could be found. Accordingly, the matter was settled over a drink of whisky — without water, as before — among the sacks of meal and packages of sugar that lined the place. The house kindly placed at our disposal was in a side street. It consisted of four pale-blue walls, a bare floor, and a corrugated iron roof. In the centre was a wooden partition, dividing the place into two rooms. The sole furniture consisted of a row of rough iron hooks in the walls, to sling the hammocks — beds being altogether unknown in this province. In the yard behind the house was the kitchen, situated in a hut to itself, built of dry palm leaves and with a flat slab of stone for a stove; the well was dug beneath a lemon tree heavy with yellow fruit.

All this looked well as could be wished. From to-day we might consider ourselves residents of San Miguel, starting housekeeping on our own. All we lacked was a pig and a few fowls. These, however, soon came wandering in from our neighbours, paid their respects and made themselves at home. The girls' school in particular, which was next door, generally furnished a little troop of piglets, which did scavenger work all round to mutual satisfaction. Soon, also, the girls themselves ventured to look in and beg for sweetmeats, and we found an opportunity of practicing our Spanish with the lady teachers over the garden wall. Both Dona Aurora and Dona Julia were somewhat shy and reserved at first, but thawed after a while, when they found that our stores included drinkable tea and English biscuits.

The five hundred inhabitants of the city vouchsafed us during the first few days an attention which was certainly flattering, though somewhat inconvenient. A handful of loafers constantly hanging about, observing how one eats, dresses and sleeps, becomes a nuisance after a while.

Soon, however, the public interest in our movements dwindled, to the advantage of both parties, and the idyll was complete. For the rest, the inhabitants were kindly folk, and not without a touch of true Spanish grandeza on occasion. In matters of business, however, and agreements, they were hopeless, their motto apparently being to promise anything and fulfil as much as might suit them. They had a way of flourishing about and answering just what they imagined would seem most agreeable to the inquirer, without in the least considering whether it was true ; whether the matter were feasible at all or entirely out of the question. It is so easy and pleasant, after all, to spread one's arms wide and with a winning smile declare that it shall be done in a moment. The ultimate result is invariably the same; mañana — tomorrow. And tomorrow brings a new mañana in an avalanche of progression ending somewhere in infinity. Heaven knows if they can even manage to die properly when their time comes, or whether here too they put off this last business of life with a shrug of the shoulders and a mañana that may prolong their existence a day or so. And as to their daily occupation, this consists of doing nothing. Regular work is as unheard-of a thing as a snowstorm in these regions. Everything is put off, postponed indefinitely. Morning, noon and night make one prolonged siesta, broken, maybe, by a game of billiards or a chat on the steps outside the house at sunset, with a black, straw-scented cigarette as if glued to one corner of the mouth. How they ever care to sleep their eight hours after such a day's work is a marvel. But they ask so little of life, and life itself perhaps would hardly ask much of these remote islanders of the south. The island exists for their sake, not they for the island's. And sufficient unto the day is the siesta thereof. To-morrow's time enough to think of the day after — and after that there is always — mañana.

School goes on all the year round. In addition to our neighbours with the little girls and the piglets, there is also a boys' school, which proved to be identical with the ball-room of the fiesta. On winter evenings it serves as a theatre. Here and there ragged bits of scenery showed out, and the blackboard just sufficed to hide a sickly sweet rococo idyll from Versailles, somewhat split at the seams. The class-room walls, by the way, were covered with pictures in fantastic colouring, at a distance resembling a futurist exhibition, but on closer inspection found to *represent merely the interior anatomy of a cow, or the back view of a serpent-like crocodile in the act of swallowing a human being. This unpleasant motive occurred in every conceivable variation, doubtless calculated to inculcate a wholesome fear in the youthful mind of over-familiarity with the reptiles in question.*

Church there was none. There was a clock-tower, however, but minus the hands of the clock. There were also seven or eight drinking saloons, each with its rickety billiard table. The balls were rather square than round, the cloth for the most part worn away, and the cues warped to an 'S' shape, but trifles of this sort did not seem to affect the local players. The game is evidently a national pastime of the Mexicans, in the widest sense of the word, for the marking indicators, hung from long cords by the ceiling, clattered all day long, worked by old and young. Among the sights of the town there was finally a cinema show, fitted up in a dried fish store. And when, twice a week, the pictures reeled off their shaky second-hand films from the beginning of the century, all the remaining lights of the town went out, the motor being incapable of providing power for both. Between the acts small boys from the audience would turn somersaults on the stage, and an orchestra consisting of fiddle and drum provided ear-splitting music, all turns being equally appreciated. The ladies wept their due quota of tears and emitted odours of patchouli, the gentlemen clapped their hands or whistled as the occasion demanded. The children of the south are easily moved, whether to laughter or tears, but to the credit of the inhabitants be it said that their feelings only exceptionally found vent in blows."

Gregory Mason visited Cozumel in February of 1928. It was his second trip to the island, the first having been made two years earlier on the Mason-Spinden Expedition. He spent most of his time on Cozumel exploring the Maya ruins on the northern end of the island, but he did stay a couple of days in San Miguel. He was not very complimentary in the article he wrote about the island in *MotorBoating Magazine* in October, 1929:

"It was a relief to say good bye to Cozumel. That place always interests me and just as surely gives me the blues. There is something horribly depressing about the people, particularly the half Indian society girls

who go about the street with half an inch of white powder on their brown faces. They do this in towns all over Mexico, but the girls of Cozumel are stunted, anemic creatures, in whom this unintelligent attempt at self-beautification seems particularly grotesque."

Above: Photo taken by Gregory Mason showing San Miguel looking south from the wooden municipal pier. The town had only 1,600 people then, according to the 1930 census.

Mason returned to Cozumel in 1930 during University of Pennsylvania's Central American Aerial Expedition. In his 1940 book, South of Yesterday, he described the water landing of the expeditions' Sikorsky seaplane in Laguna Ciega in Cozumel: *"In a few minutes the ship hits the lagoon at Cozumel and bounces along between two great, curling bow waves, until it subsides into a more even position and taxies up to the landing beach. Mexican laborers rush knee-deep into the water. Some of them bend a hawser onto the ship's bow, while others adjust a gangplank against our forward deck. We walk ashore, to be greeted by a torrent of hospitable Spanish from General Trevino, commanding the Mexican troops on Cozumel. He is accompanied by my old friend, Señor Caldwell, who runs the chief store in San Miguel, and who is the rich man and first citizen of the sleepy, friendly island.*

It was Mason who was responsible for the unfortunate changing the Maya village of Polé's name to Xcaret. Prior to 1926, everybody called it Ppoole, Ppolé, or Polé, from the Mayan root word *p'ol*, meaning "merchandise" or "trade" in Yucatec Mayan. The village was first reported by Juan Grijalva, who sighted by the buildings in 1518.

Francisco Montejo *el Adelantado* spent several weeks there in 1527 and 1528. He too referred to the Mayan town as Polé. Polé was listed on the 1549 tax census and again in a report by Padre Cristóbal Asencio in 1570. In 1571, the name Polé is recorded once more when several Maya from the town testified in the trial of the French corsair Pierre de Sanfroy. In 1582, Polé was listed as having one of only five churches of the entire coast of Quintana Roo. In 1590, documents list the *batab* of Polé as Diego Malah. In 1601, the *batab* of Polé was listed as Juan Ye. The first map showing the location of Polé was the Juan de Dios Gonzalez map of 1766. The name Polé remained on maps through the 1829 Lapie map, the 1843 Catherwood map, the 1864 Malte-Brun map, the 1874 García Cuba map, and the 1878 Berendt map. This last map, however, contained a serious error; all the towns along the coast were shifted 35 kilometers north of their actual positions. Unfortunately, it was this 1878 map of Berendt's that Gregory Mason and Herbert Spinden used on their 1926 Mason-Spinden Expedition, when they travelled for two months along the Quintana Roo Coast, recording Mayan ruin sites and collecting bird specimens for the Smithsonian Institution. When they came across the ruins at Polé, the 1878 Berendt map they had showed the town of Polé was 35 kilometers to the <u>north</u> of its <u>actual</u> location. The map indicated nothing of note where they were standing. Unaware they were looking at the ruins of the same buildings that the Montejos and others had called Polé, they christened the "new" site Xcaret, after a small ranch nearby. The name stuck like glue. For many years after Mason and Spinden published the map of their expedition showing Polé and the Xcaret in two different places, other cartographers followed suite, locating the same town, now with two different names, in two different locations, miles apart from each other. It has only been since the 1960s that the two locations of the same town have been rejoined and repositioned in the correct place, but now with the wrong name; Xcaret.

In 1927, the account of the Mason-Spinden expedition was published in a popular book by Gregory Mason, entitled *"Silver cities of Yucatan."* In 2012, a documentary by the same name about the expedition was released.

CHAPTER 14

Remains of the 16th Century San Miguel Church

In 1830, an article appeared in the popular series The Modern Traveller, a travel atlas written and published by Josiah Conder. In the article, Conder stated: *"The ruins of European edifices in the island of Cozumel, in the midst of a grove of palm trees, indicate the island, now uninhabited, was, at the commencement of the conquest, peopled by Spanish colonists."*

Josiah Condor attributed this passage to Alexander von Humboldt. Searching through von Humboldt's puplications, I found the almost word-for-word origin of the Josiah Condor's lines about Cozumel in the following passage in volume 2 of *Political Essay on the Kingdom of New Spain,* which is the 1814 English translation of von Humboldt's 1808 book, *Essai politique sur le royaume de la Nouvelle Espagne.* The english translation reads:

"The ruins of European buildings, discoverable in the island of Cosumel, in the midst of a grove of palm trees, indicate that this island, which is now uninhabited, was at the comencement of the conquest peopled by Spanish colonists. Since the settlement of the English between Omo and Rio Hondo, the government, to diminish the contraband trade, concentrated the Spanish and Indian population in the part of the peninsula west from the mountains of Yucatán."

Although von Humboldt included much more detailed information about Yucatán in his book, it turns out that he never visited the penisula (or Cozumel) personally. He revealed in a footnote that the information about Cozumel contained in his book came from *"M. Gilbert,"* who had visited the Yucatán prior to being shipwrecked in Cuba in 1801. Von Humboldt went on to mention: *"This enlightened observer went over a great part of the Spanish colonies. He had the misfortune to lose in a shipwreck south from the island of Cuba, amoung the shallows of the Jardines del Rey, of which I determined the astronomical position, the statistical materials collected by him.... Mr. Gilbert, by estimating himself the number of villages and their population, concluded that Yucatán contained, in 1801, nearly half a million of inhabitants of all casts and colours."* That means, if Humbolt's hearsay statement that Cozumel was *"now uninhabited"* is to be believed, *"now"* refers to sometime before the year 1801, and not 1830.

The next mention of the church is in the account written by John Lloyd Stephens in his book, Incidents of Travel in Yucatán, published in 1843 and describing his visit to the island in 1841. Stephens wrote that he had been intrigued by the article in the The Modern Traveller, a guide book for 19th-century travelers, which was an old standby of Stephens. In his earlier book, *Incidents of Travel in Egypt, Arabia, Petra, and The Holy Land*, published in 1838, the writer/explorer mentions how he never left home without a copy: *"Over the head of my bed were my gun and pistols, and at the foot was a little swinging shelf, containing my Library, which consisted of the Modern Traveller on Egypt, Volney's Travels, and an Italian grammar and dictionary."*

On his visit to Cozumel, Stephens managed to examine the ruins that Josiah Condor mentioned. He describes them thusly: *"The whole island was overgrown with trees, and, except along the shore or within the clearing around the hut, it was impossible to move in any direction without cutting a path. We had only our two sailors, and if we should cut by the compass through the heart of the island, we might pass within a few feet of a building without perceiving it. Fortunately, however, on the borders of the clearing there were vestiges of ancient population, which, from the directions of Don Vicente Albino, we had no difficulty in finding. One of them, standing about two hundred feet distance from the sea, and even now visible above the tops of the trees to vessels sailing by, is represented in the engraving that follows.*

It stands on a terrace, and has steps on all four of its sides. The building measures sixteen feet square; it had four doors facing the cardinal points, and, as will be seen by the figure of a man sitting on the steps, it is very low. The exterior is of plain stone, but was forerly stuccoed and painted, traces of which are still visable. The doorways open into a narrow corridor only twenty inches wide, which encompasses a small room eight feet six inches long and five feet wide, having a doorway opening to the centre.

Above: An engraving of Catherwoods sketch of the Maya temple on Cozumel.

South-southeast from this, near an opposite angle of the clearing, and five or six hundred feet from the sea, stands another building raised upon a terrace, consisting of a single apartment, twenty feet front and six feet ten inches deep, having two doorways and a back wall seven feet thick. The height is ten feet, the arch is triangular, and on the walls are the remains of paintings.

These were the only buildings in the clearing, and though, doubtless, many more lie buried in the woods, we saw no other on the island; but to us these were pregnant with instruction. The building presented in the engraving, standing close to the sea, answers, in all its general features, the decription of the "towers" seen by Grijalva and his companions as they sailed along the coast... Perhaps it is the same temple from which Bernal Díaz and his companions rolled the idols down the steps."

"At the rear of the last building, buried in the woods, so that we should never have found it but for our patron, is another memorial, perhaps equal in interest to any now existing on the island of Cozumel. It is the ruins of a Spanish church, sixty or seventy feet front and two hundred *deep. The front wall has almost wholly fallen, but the side walls are standing to the height of about twenty feet. The plastering remains, and along the base is a line of painted ornaments. The interior is encumbered with the ruins of the fallen roof, overgrown with bushes; a tree is growing out of the great altar, and the whole a scene of irrecoverable distruction."*

Stephens goes on in his book to describe an earlier visit he made to an octogenarian monk at the Church of the Mejorada in Mérida, where he saw a cross fixed to the wall over the first altar to the left, just as one enters the church. Stephens says the old priest told him that he had dug up the cross in the ruins of Cozumel many years before. Stephens wrote, *"It is of stone, has a venerable apperance of antiquity, and has extended on it in half relief an image of the Saviour, made of plaster, with the hands and feet nailed. At the first glance we were satisfied that, whatever might be the truth in regard to its early history, it was at least, wrought into its present shape under the direction of monks. And though, at the time, we did not expect ever to know anything more about it, the ruins of this church* [on Cozumel] *cleared up in our minds all possible mystery connected with its existence.*

In front of the building [on Cozumel] *is a cemented platform, broken and uprooted by trees, but still preserving its form; and on this stand two square pillars, which, we supposed on the spot, had once supported crosses, and we were immediately impressed with the belief that one of these missing symbols was that now known as the 'Cozumel Cross,' and that it had probably been carried away by some pious monk at or about the time when the church became a ruin and the island depopulated."*

Another description of the ruins of the Church on Cozumel turns up later on May 10, 1874, on page 6 of the *Morning Star and Catholic Registar*, a newspaper published in New Orleans, Louisiana. The article states: *"The foundation and walls are yet partially preserved; each side has an elevation of some ten feet in places. The altar is covered with an almost impenetrable growth of chaparal; and all about and even inside these ruins are ancient and modern tombs, where patriarchs rest. The wild flowers bloom over them in great profusion, and even the birds carol sweet songs morning and evening. A paved walk extends from the portal several hundred yards westward, but is now almost burried from sight in the sod. Excavations are seen, where searchers after hidden treasures have delved. There is a fine field yet there for the curious to explore. But the natives of the locality allow it to rest so quietly that the dense shrubbery almost buries it."*

In 1874, Claude Luther Goodrich published a small pamphlet about Cozumel in which he mentions the ruins of the 16th century church of San Miguel de Xamancab: *"Cortes... erected the first church ever built on or near the continent of North America! The ruins of which are still in existence. This is an item of some importance in this progressive age because no historian I believe has mentioned it, and very few persons in the United States have ever heard of this church spoken of. The stone walls of the old edifice, though ten or twelve feet high in places, are of course much broken down, and the explorer finds them surrounded and grown over with trees and thick foliage, impenetrable chaparral and wild flowers. Birds enliven the morning with their songs, otherwise the solitude is majestic, and within and all about the old relic are numerous tombs where patriarchs sleep their long sleep."*

In December 1876, Alice and Agustus LePlongeon arrived in Cozumel after having excavated the Chac Mool at Chichen Itzá a few weeks earlier. Later, in 1877 and 1878, Alice wrote several newspaper and magazine articles about their visit to the island and in 1879 she wrote *"Notes on Yucatan"* which was published in the Proceedings of the American Antiquarian Society. She subsequently re-crafted these articles into a book, Here and there in Yucatan, which she published in 1889. She wrote another article about Cozumel in the *New York Times* in 1898, entitled *'Beautiful Cozumel."* When LePlongeon wrote about her 1876-7 trip to Cozumel, she mentions the church: *"...in the island of Cozumel, is the spot where Cortez is said to have left a cross for the adoration of the Indians and near by a church was built, whose walls still remain."*

On January 19, 1883, a nun on the US steamship *City of Dallas* passed by Cozumel on the way to Belize, and she later wrote in *The Irish Monthy* *"the ruins of a church, said to be the oldest in America, were pointed out to us, and we clearly discerned a fair village peeping through numberless palm and cocoa-nut trees... Along this enchanted isle, which remained in sight for several hours, the water was smooth as glass and greener than the emerald."*

In 1885, in volume 20 of *Frank Leslie's Popular Monthly Magazine*, there appeared the illustration that follows, described as "Cemetery at Cozumel."

Above: The illustration of the remains of the church in volume 20, 1885, of Frank Leslie's Popular Monthly Magazine.

The half-barrel shaped tomb in the left side of the image, set close to the stone wall, is shown intact. A second tomb is visible just behind it. Note the two small crosses marking graves in the center of the image just below the palm tree. These graves are INSIDE the confines of the walls of the church. In a later 1910 photograph and a 1924 sketch of the floor plan of the church, both of these tombs are shown. In the description that accompanied the 1924 sketch, they are further described as being shaped like *"an inverted bath-tub"* and had been broken open by treasure-hunters. The 1910 photograph also shows the tombs broken open. Only one cross is shown in the 1924 sketch and the 1910 photo, where two crosses are shown in the 1885 engraving.

On July 28, 1888, on page 7, the *Sacramento Daily Record-Union* newspaper published an article by Fannie B. Ward, recording her visit to Cozumel. Fanny wrote: *"Escorted by a couple of natives our party went a little way into the forest to view a Spanish church, whose history, though comparativly modern, is as obscure as the oldest temples whose worship it suplanted. It is two hundred feet deep by seventy feet front. Bits of plastering still adhere to its crumbling walls and along the base runs a line of painted ornaments. The great altar yet stands, but is covered with creepers..."*

What happened to the Maya ruins that Stephens described next to the church can be understood by the observation made by Channing Arnold and Frederick J. Tabor Frost in their book, <u>The American Egypt; a record of travel in Yucatan</u>, which describes their visit to Cozumel in 1908. They wrote:

"Of these temples not a trace now remains around San Miguel save at the north end, where a path through a plantation of cocoanuts leads to such a scene of vandalism as might be calculated to rouse the indignation of even the Conservator of Monuments, if he remained awake long enough to reach the spot. Here what had obviously been a minor temple has been broken and converted into a quarry. Heaps of stones, broken past recognition, lie in a confused heap with smashed Indian pottery. The largest stones have been carted into the village, and formed a pathetic hotch-potch in a garden close to our hut. One of these was a remarkable carving representing a figure of a god seated cross-legged, in true Buddhist attitude, in a niche."

In July 1910, Henry A. Case published a photograph of the remaining walls of the church in his book, <u>Views on and of Yucatan: besides notes upon parts of the state of Campeche and the territory of Quintana Roo</u>.

In the photo (shownbelow) note the stone wall to the left of the image, the two plundered, convex-roofed tombs behind the figure and the wooden cross directly in front of the palm tree. This is a photo taken from the path leading up to the front of the church and shows what would have been the interior of the church. In his book, Case states: *"In the outskirts of the town [San Miguel], are the ruined walls of an old Spanish church, which measures sixty or seventy feet in front, and runs about two hundred feet in depth, evidently constructed for a good sized assemblage, and undoubtedly had been built to take place of an older building. The history of the Roman Catholic Church of Cozumel is as obscure as that of the ruined pagan temples in the neighbourhood, when it was built can be conjectured to within a hundred years or so, but why it lost its importance, or where its numerous congregation vanished, are questions to which history does not refer, nor has a carved inscription or tablet been found alluding to the foundation of the edifice."*

Above: A photo appearing in **Views on and of Yucatán: besides notes upon parts of the state of Campeche and the territory of Quintana Roo** *by Henry A. Case, 1910, Mérida de Yucatán, México.*

In January 1913, archaeologists Jesse L. Nusbaum and Sylvanus G. Morely traveled to Yucatán to make a silent film to be shown later at the Panamá-California Exposition in 1915. They first visited Chichen Itzá and then later sailed to Cozumel and Tulum. During the Cozumel portion of their trip, they were out of contact with their friends, which led to a big misunderstanding in the US press.

On April 15, 1913, *The Santa Fe New Mexican* published a front-page article entitled *"Two Santa Feans Visit Bad Men on Cozumel Isle."* The article mentioned that the island was noted for its cannibals. Two days later, another front-page article appeared, with the headline: *"Grave Danger in Visiting Isle of Cozumel. Peril of Morley-Nusbaum-Lis Expedition Facing Cannibals Who Have Eaten Other Explorers. Mrs. Morley Alarmed over Husband's Fate."* There was a photo of Nusbaum, with a caption suggesting he may have met his end at the hands of the Cozumel cannibals. The story quickly went national, and the *Boston Globe* published an article on April 18, with the ominous headline: *"Alarm Felt for Them. S. G. Morley, a Harvard Student, and J. H. Nusbaum May Have Died on Visit to Cozumel Island."* The account mentioned that Morley's wife, Alice, was prostrate with concern for the men, since there were reports that two Englishmen who visited the island of Cozumel recently were eaten by cannibals or killed by hostile Indians. Nusbaum and Morley of course were not eaten while they were on the island. Though they did not stay in Cozumel very long, Nusbaum made five glass-plate negatives of scenes on the island, three were of the church.

AMERICA'S OLDEST CHURCH.

Scientists Discover Ruins on Small Island Off the Yucatan Coast.

New Orleans, Aug. 15.—The ruins of the oldest Christian church in America have been discovered on the Island of Cozumel, off Yucatan, by Prof. Morley and Jesse Nusbaum, of the Harvard San Diego expedition. Cozumel has not been visited by white men for almost a century and Morley and Nusbaum had thrilling adventures, but deny that its people are cannibals. The scientists were equipped with a moving picture outfit, but in leaving the island for the mainland their canoe was upset and much of the photograph material was spoiled. While Cozumel is only thirty by seven miles in extent, it was found extraordinarily rich in monumental and architectural remains. It was here that Cortez had a fierce battle with the natives and erected what is declared to have been the first Christian church in America.

Above: August 15, 1913 article in the **Fort Wayne Indiana Sentinel** *about the Nusbaum and the church.*

Above: Two of Nusbaum's photos of the church spliced together.

Above: Close-up, cropped section of the third image of the two vandalized tombs. The north wall of the church is on the left.

When Sweden's Prince William visited Cozumel in 1920, he too visited the ruins of the church. In his 1922 book, <u>Between Two Continents</u>, he wrote: *"From this time date the ruins of a great church which Cortez had built immediately to the north of San Miguel. The jungle has dealt hardly with this monument, leaving barely one stone on another. Lianas twine about the remains of the walls, and three stately coco-nut palms stand where the main altar lights were wont to burn. Four masonry sepulchers above ground bear witness to the perishable nature of humanity; two of them have been plundered, and through the breaches one can still discern the skulls of some Spaniards who lost their lives in the struggle with the Indians. Who they are that lie there no one knows; neither the graves nor the skulls bear any inscription."*

Dr. Thomas Gann was a medical doctor living in Belize, but was also a keen amateur archaeologist who spent a good amount of his time searching for Maya ruins in Yucatán and Belize. He participated in expeditions to Yucatán in 1917 and 1918 that were sponsored by the Museum of the American Indian and another to Chichen Itzá in 1924 that was sponsored by the Carnegie Institute.

In 1924, Thomas Gann published his book, In an Unknown Land, which contained a description of his 1918 visit to the ruins of the church on Cozumel: *"Next morning, after a bathe and tea, we started for the ruins of the ancient church situated about a mile from the village, and now buried in the bush. We were particularly anxious to see this venerable building, which is generally regarded as the first Christian church erected upon the American continent, as it stands upon the traditional site of the chapel erected by Cortez on his way to the conquest of Mexico in 1519."*

After arriving at the ruins of the church, Gann described them: *"The ruins of the church, measuring 98ft. in length and 36ft. 2in. in breadth, face east and west. The roof has entirely fallen in, while the west wall has completely disappeared. Stucco-covered remains of the other walls still stand, varying in height from two to ten feet. Inside we discovered six large and one small overground vaults, built of stone and mortar, shaped something like an inverted iron bath-tub. These had all been opened, probably by treasure seekers. Inside one we found the complete skeleton of a young Mestisa woman which had been buried from sixty to eighty years. This secondary use of the chapel as a burial place has taken place since Stephen's visit in 1841, as he makes no mention of these vaults and states that the island was at that time entirely uninhabited. The altar, probably the identical one which Cortez erected in 1519 is now in ruins; just to the west of it the floor of the church has been dug up, doubtless by treasure-hunters, exposing a row of seven small, stone-lined chambers, possibly the burial place of successive heads of the church in the island."*

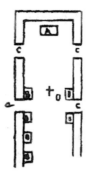

Ground plan of ruins of
Ancient Church on the
Island of Cozumel.

A. Altar.
B. B. B. Overground Vaults.
C. C. C. windows.

Above: Gann's 1918 drawing of the ruins of the church on Cozumel.

In the *Proceedings of the American Philosophical Society*, 1937, H.G. Richards reported: "*... I arrived at Cozumel on the afternoon of April 17, 1936, after a three and one-half hour flight from Havana, Cuba. ... [land] mollusks were especially abundant near the ruins of the old Spanish Church (built about 1519) and nearby a dried swamp yielded some 250.*"

In 1946, Alberto Escalona Ramos wrote about his archaeological investigations on Cozumel during his participation in the *Expedición Científica Mexicana de 1937,* in his article *"Algunas ruinas prehispánicas en Quintana Roo,"* published in the *Boletín de la Sociedad de Geografia y Estadistica de la Republica.* In the article, Escalona reported *"The ruins of San Miguel [Xamancab] are spread along a 600 meter long stretch running north from the fourth city block of the town of Cozumel (San Miguel). These ruins have been destroyed, first, in the 16th century when the stones were used to build the first town and church (later abandoned) and later, during the 19th and 20th century to construct the present town and pier. The level of destruction is extraordinary and little or nothing could be saved."* In a footnote on page 561 of the bulletin, Escalona notes: *"La primera iglesia colonial, de que quedan fragmentos de una espeso muro, está a unos 500 metros del reloj [the* plaza's clock tower] *y cerca de la playa, donde está la estación de gasolina de El Águila; hoy la cubre la vegetación."*

Archaeologists Anthony P. Andrews and Grant Jones, writing in their article *"Asentamientos colonials en la costa de Quintana Roo,"* published in Vol 23, number 1 of *Temas antropológicos: Revista científica de investigaciones regionales,* stated: *"A fines de los años 50 aún quedaba en pie una sección de uno de los muros de la capilla, que formaba parte de la albarrada trasera del patio de una estación Pemex al sur de la entrada al antiguo aeropuerto."*

When I read this mention by Andrews of the church being near a Pemex station, I contacted him to verify the information. As it turned out, he said he was a boy of 10 when he first visited Cozumel with his father, E. Wyllys Andrews IV, another well-known archaeologist who specialized in lowland Maya civilization and who had been good friends with Alberto Escalona Ramos. Escalona had apparently told the elder Andrews that the remains of the church were near the *"gasolinera."* However, in 1937, when Escalona visited Cozumel and saw what he described as a "thick section of the old church wall," Pemex did not yet exist. It was not until 1938 that President Lázaro Cárdenas nationalized the El Águila Oil Company and the newly resulting entity was branded Petróleos Mexicanos (Pemex). The *"estación de gasolina de El Águila"* Escalona described was the old El Aguila storage facility run by Casa Coldwell on the north side of Calle 12 between the malecon and Avenida 5 in the 1930s, and not the Pemex station that Andrews took his young son to visit in the 1950s.

After speaking with Andrews, I interviewed 72-year-old Cozumel native Adolfo Gracia Aguilar. Sr. Gracia told me that he had never seen the walls of the church ruins, but when he was a youngster he was told by two older women, Sras. Rufita and Mechita Rivero that the church had been situated at or near the intersection of Avenida 5 and Calle 12 Norte. Sr. Gracia drew a sketch map and circled the area indicated by the sisters. In the sketch below, **"B.J."** represents the city block occupied by the Benito Juárez primary school, built in the 1970s. The arrow indicates the direction of travel on Calle 12 Norte and the concentric circles mark the church site, as described by the sisters. The sketch map is orientated with northeast to the top, as a concession to the street orientation.

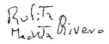

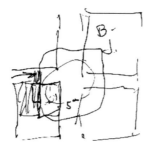

Above: Adolfo Gracia Aguilar's sketch map

Further interviews with older Cozumel natives revealed a rich mythology surrounding this area. On the northeast corner of the intersection, on the present-day property of the Benito Juárez School, a very massive *sacahua* tree stood until toppled by a recent hurricane. This tree was believed by many islanders to be the hangout of the *Xtabay*, or the Maya equivalent of *La Llorona*, a malevolent spirit intent on bewitching men and leading astray, often taking them deep into the forest before abandoning them. Other old-timers say the secluded area near the tree was often used for trysts by the young folks of the island. Still others said that the tree marked the site of an ancient Maya cemetery. One thing they all agreed on was that when the Benito Juárez School was built, dozens of human skeletons were unearthed near there.

To see how the intersection's location coincided with the directions given to the church by John Lloyd Stephens in his book <u>Incidents of Travel in Yucatán</u>, I made a map of the streets and overlayed the directions and distance indicated in the pertinate passages. With the starting point at the beach, I ran a line 200 feet inland to the first temple site Stephens described, then continued the line 550 feet (he wrote *"500 or 600 feet"*) southeast to the described site of the second temple. Stephens then said the church was located "behind" that second temple, and later reports indicated it was orientated east-west. The measurements coincided with the intersection's location, however, Alberto Escalona Ramos' description of the church wall being *"cerca de la playa, donde está la estación de gasolina de El Águila;"* would place the church slightly more to the north by about 100 feet.

On October 5, 2012, with the kind permission of Don Nassim Joaquín Ibarra, I began surveying a piece of land where he keeps a herd of deer on the southwest corner of 5 Avenida and Calle 12 Norte, in San Miguel de Cozumel. The area has been cleared of weeds and brush by the grazing deer and the ground is strewn with ceramic shards dating to the post classic period. The remains of several Maya stone structures are clearly visible, as well as what appear to be a *mampostería bebedero* (animal drinking trough), two wells, and some *mampostería* walls of later vintage. The property includes a stone ridge that is higher than the surrounding areas and most of the structures shown below are located on the top of this ridge.

Above: Foundations of several Maya temples are located on the site.

Above: A multitude of hewn limestone blocks are found on the property, some in their original alignment, and some obviously relocated at some point in the past.

Above: One of the many stone foundations on the property.

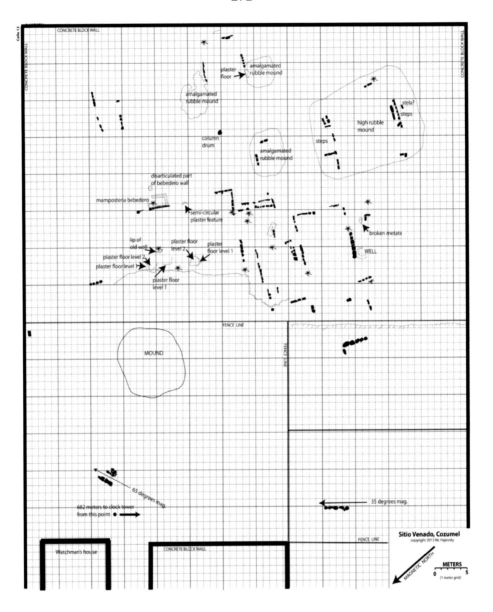

Above: The site plan of the archaeological site I named "Sitio Venado," a ceremonial center of the postclassic Maya city of Xamancab, where Juan de Grijalva met the Batab of Cozumel in 1518 and Hernán Cortés erected a wooden cross in 1519. The first Catholic church of Cozumel was erected adjacent to this site in the 1550s.

Pemex Station
(later Scaramouche disco)

Clock
Tower

Hotel Playa

Chicle warehouse (now Cinco Soles)

Port Captain

Married men's housing

Mr. Roody's beach where the fishing boats unloaded

Mr. Roody's lobster and turtle cannery and ice plant

AeroFoto, S. A.   Cozumel 1951

Avenida 5

Avenida 10

El Aguila Gas Station

Extension of Avenida 5

(Perhaps the old entrance to the airstrip in 1930s, when there was only one runway?)

Single men's barracks

Gym

Road to Tamsa terminal

Airstrip

Airstrip

Above: 1951 aerial photo of San Miguel and the area where the 16th century church once stood, "behind the El Águila gas station."

There is a persistent rumor that a "Maya cemetery" was discovered near the intersection of Avenida 5 and Calle 12 Norte when the Las Ventanas Condominiums were built. The condominiums occupy the entire city block bounded by Avenida 5, Calle 10 norte, Calle 12 norte, and Avenida 10, just across the street from Sitio Venado. On July 1, 2013 I met with Jack Cooper, the architect/developer of the Las Ventanas to ask about this rumor. Mr. Cooper told me that although there were around ten *metates* on the property as well as many shards of broken pottery, he saw no signs of any stone walls or stone foundations. He told me that the only architectural feature he saw on the property was an old, hand-dug well near the center of the property, close to where the swimming pool now lies. Mr. Cooper said that as they were digging the foundations for the first building, archeologists from INAH showed up and stopped the work, because they were told (erroneously) that there was a Maya cemetery on the property and the construction workers were turning up human skeletons. To appease the archaeologists, the crew dug six 40-foot-long trenches with a back-hoe, from which the INAH crew removed several bags of ceramic shards. The archaeologists saw no signs of structures or bones on the site and took the shards back to their office in Cancun, but apparently produced no report of the work they performed and the construction of Las Ventanas resumed unimpeded.

To date, no remains of the 16th century church have been positively identified. It is entirely possible that the remaining *mampostería* walls were demolished and the rubble used as fill for the seawall and municipal pier that were built immediately after Alberto Escalona Ramos' 1937 visit. The fact that no later sighting has been reported since then seems to lend support to this theory.

CHAPTER 15

Five more myths debunked

1. The Spirit of St. Louis never landed in Cozumel

Lindbergh made his first flight into México on December 13, 1927, when he flew non-stop from Washington DC to Mexico City in his plane *Spirit of St. Louis,* tail number NX211. He was received by Mexican President Calles and toured the city for a few days before returning to Balbuena Field, where he made several flights over Mexico City in a Mexican Armed Forces' Morane Saulnier M.S. registration number 31A128. On December 20, he made several more flights in a *Compania Mexicana de Aviación* Fairchild FC-2 (registration number M-SCOE), during one of which he gave President Calles his first-ever airplane ride. On December 22, Lindbergh flew the *Spirit of St. Louis* for a few shorts flights in and out of Balbuena over Mexico City. On December 28, he flew the *Spirit of St. Louis* <u>non-stop</u> from Mexico City to Guatemala City.

After visiting Guatemala City, he flew the *Spirit of St. Louis* on to Belize, El Salvador, Honduras, Nicaragua, Costa Rica, Panama, Colombia, and Venezuela. His return to Washington took him through the Virgin Islands, Puerto Rico, Dominican Republic, Haiti, and Cuba, but he <u>did not pass back through México</u> on the northward leg of his trip.

The *Spirit of St. Louis* was turned over to the National Museum in Washington on April 30, 1928 and <u>it never flew again</u>. What this means, is that the Spirit of St. Louis <u>never landed</u> in Cozumel. Any pictures of the *Spirit of St. Louis* purportedly taken in Cozumel (like the one in the Museo de la Isla) are actually images that were taken elsewhere.

Lindbergh again visited México in February 1928, but this time flew a Curtis Falcon (registration number NC7455) on a round trip jaunt to Cuernavaca.

On February 3, 1929 Lindbergh made his third trip to México, this time accompanied by John Hambleton and Lt. Christian Schilt in a Sikorsky S-

38 (tail number NC8000). The trip was designed as a survey of possible landing areas Pan American could use on their newly awarded airmail routes (F.A.M. 5, 6, & 9) which were mail routes between Miami, the Caribbean, Central America, and South America.   During this trip, Lindbergh landed in Cozumel for the first time, though not in the *Spirit of St. Louis*, as is the myth, but in the amphibious Sikorsky S-38. It was a short re-fueling stop and he took off as soon as the gas was aboard.

On February 24, of 1928 Lindbergh made another trip to Mexico City in a TravelAir 962 (tail number NR8139).

Lindbergh once again visited Cozumel on October 9, 1929 flying a Pan American Airways Sikorsky S-38 amphibious plane (tail number NC9137).   Landing at 6:12 PM, he was accompanied by his wife, Carnegie Institute's Dr. Ricketson, Dr. Alfred E. Kidder, W. I. Van Deusen, Charles Lorber, and William Ehmer, while preforming an aerial survey of parts of the Yucatán Peninsula, Belize, and northern Guatemala under the sponsorship of Pan-American Airways and the Carnegie Institute. On Cozumel they were the guests of Moisey Adams, agent for the Chicle Development Company. Lindbergh and his party departed Cozumel the next morning, October 10, at 9:56 AM.

Above: Pan Am Sikorsky S-38 in Miami

2. There was no US military base on Cozumel during WWII

Pan American Airways was initially a shell corporation founded by US Army Major Henry "Hap" Arnold in 1927 as a front to keep the German airline SCADTA from winning landing rights in Panamá. The German line had already an established route they had been flying since 1920 that went from Colombia, Roatán, Belize City, Cozumel, Havana, to Miami. Arnold was concerned that SCADTA, operating out of Colombia, was angling to get landing rights in Panamá in order to monitor ship movements through the canal. Even though his new company had no airplanes at the time, Arnold was able use his influence with the US government to win a contract to deliver US mail from Miami to Havana. Later, by joining forces with two other airlines (one company had one plane, but no landing rights, and the other had landing rights in Havana, but no plane) Arnold was able to fulfill the terms of the contract. He next tendered bids for contracts on all the new US Airmail routes (F. A. M. routes) between the States and Central and South America, winning every one of the contracts in 1928, thus denying SCADTA the Panamanian landing rights. In a move to thwart competition and get its hands on more planes, Pan Am then purchased *Compañia Mexicana de Aviación* (for a mere $150,000.00) and spun it off as a subsidiary the same year, allowing *Mexicana* to continue to operate in México under the same name. In January, 1929, Pan Am made its first passenger-carrying flight, from Miami to San Juan via Belize and Nicaragua. In February, 1929, Charles Lindbergh flew the first Pan Am mail flight to Panamá, refueling at Cozumel in a 10-passenger, twin-engine, Sikorsky S-38 flying boat along the way. In October, 1929, Lindbergh again visited the island when he flew several Carnegie Institute archaeologists to Cozumel for the night, after making an aerial reconnaissance of Maya ruins on the mainland.

That same year, Pan-Am began a weekly seaplane service between Miami and Panamá. That route had several fuel stops along the way, including one in Cozumel. A copy of one of Pan Am's old 1929 schedules showed the stop on the island was only 30 minutes, from 1:45 PM to 2:15 PM. Not much time to buy souvenirs.

Above: A Pan Am Sikorsky S-38 coming in for a landing on the water.

Above: A Pan Am Sikorsky S-38 at the seaplane ramp at Calle 3 and the malecon in San Miguel in 1929

Later, between 1929 and 1935, seaplanes used a ramp built by Oscar Coldwell on the seafront near Calle 3 sur. There had been a small airstrip on Cozumel prior to October, 1929, but in April 1930, José R. Juanes Domínguez, the representative of Pan American's subsidiary *Mexicana* in Mérida, announced the purchase of 160 hectares of land north of San Miguel to build their new *Campo de Aterrizaje Cozumel*, where passengers could board a *Mexicana* flight to Mexico City via Mérida. *Mexicana* discontinued the Cozumel stop in July, 1931 and rerouted its flights through Mérida. On April 15, 1932, the Islanders took up a collection to repair the airstrip (total amount donated: $25) and *Mexicana* re-instituted the service. In 1933, *Compania Aeronautica*

Jesus Sarabia S. A. (Sarabia) began to use the island's airstrip for twice-weekly connections to Mérida and Chetumal until the airline suspended operations in 1942. *Sarabia* was sold to *TAMSA* in 1943.

Even before the US was drawn into the war by the Japanese bombing of Pearl Harbor in December, 1941, the American military was worried about how to defend the Panamá Canal from possible attacks by Japanese carrier-based planes. The US had to be able to fly its warplanes south to Panamá as needed and Washington began negotiating with the Mexican government for the rights to fly US military planes through Mexican airspace, refueling them at air bases in Tehuantepec and the Yucatán. Of the several landing fields available in the Yucatán, the *campo de aterrizaje* in San Miguel de Cozumel seemed to be the best option. Permission to improve the strip was requested by the US and granted by México in August, 1941, as well as the rights to use the Pan American Airways' field at Mérida until the work on the Cozumel field was completed, which was expected to take about a year. The US government planned on contracting Pan American Airways to perform the work on the Cozumel airstrip. Pan American, in turn, would sub-contract the work to its Mexican subsidiary *Compañia Mexicana de Aviación*. Consequently, all work was to be done at the proposed San Miguel airbase by a Mexican company utilizing Mexican labor, as required by the agreement with México. The agreement also specified that once the field had been up-graded (with funds to be provided by the US) the field would remain under the control of the Mexican military.

Upon hearing that a contract to begin work on the airport was about to be awarded, Cozumel's *Agrupación Obrera Mixta de Trabajadores Marítimos y Terrestres* (Union of Maritime and Inland Workers) sent Ramon Zapata and Juilio C. Mac to Mexico City in 1941 to lobby for construction jobs for Cozumel's union workers on the project. The lobby effort failed and in 1942 *Compañia Mexicana de Aviación* sub-contracted the work to *Mexicana Constructora Azteca, S. A.*, a Mexican company that had also worked on *Mexicana's* Mérida airport earlier. *Constructora Azteca* then began flying in workers from outside of Cozumel to do the work.

Above: Cozumel's dirt airstrip in 1942.

Above: Cozumel's dirt airstrip in July, 1942

In May, 1942, German submarines sank two Mexican merchant vessels in the Gulf of Mexico. México did not immediately declare war against the Axis Powers, but instead demanded an explanation from the German Embassy. A few days later, they got the German response; a U-Boat sank two more Mexican merchant vessels. The *Fuerzas Áreas Militares (FAM)* was at the time a poorly equipped branch of the Mexican military and did not have the aircraft with which to mount anti-submarine patrols, so they requested help from the US under the "Lend/Lease" program that the US congress had enacted, for cases just like this. The US responded by immediately delivering a group of

Vought Kingfisher OS2Us to *FAM* so they could begin patrols and followed up shortly thereafter with the delivery of a group of North American AT-6s, Beech AT-11s, and Douglas A24s. In addition to the planes, the US also gave México funds to operate the aircraft together with the supplies and parts to maintain them. In June, 1942, *FAM* General Roberto Fierro Villalobos, Chief of Mexican Military Air Operations, designated Colonel Alfonso Cruz Rivera the new Commander of the 2nd Air Regiment and put him in charge of the Gulf Region, which included the Gulf of Mexico, the Caribbean, and the Isthmus of Tehuantepec. Colonel Cruz then sent the 3rd, 4th, and 5th squadrons of the 2nd Air Regiment to begin flying the Voughts and some old, outdated, Consolidated 21-M bi-planes (planes that *FAM* had on hand from before the war) on anti-submarine patrols from the air strips in Tampico, Veracruz, Mérida, Ixtepec, and Cozumel. In July, 1942, the US requested that in return for the planes it had given to México, US forces be allowed to use the air strip at Cozumel as a base to carry out their own anti-submarine operations in the Caribbean. The request was granted, but before the plan could be acted upon, things changed.

In November 1942, W. L Morrison, the manager and director of *Compañia Mexicana de Aviación's* construction projects at Tehuantepec and Cozumel, was summoned to the office of México's Secretary of Defense, ex-President Lázaro Cárdenas, the very man who had nationalized the foreign oil companies and ended US and other foreign oil company operations in México in 1938. Morrison was told to bring to the meeting the plans for the improvements scheduled to be installed at the two fields. When Cárdenas was shown the plans, which included a number of buildings *Mexicana* was going to build in addition to improving the runways, he wanted to know why all the structures were needed, since México had never agreed to allow American servicemen to actually <u>stay</u> in either Cozumel or Tehuantepec. Cárdenas said the agreement was only that they could use the air strips <u>in transit</u>. After the meeting, Morrison reported back to Pan American that México was worried that these planned buildings indicated the US intended to station US servicemen at the two bases, and that the Mexican government was opposed to that. The Mexican government's position was that <u>no</u> foreign troops, even if they were Allied troops, would be allowed to man bases on Mexican soil. US technicians would only be allowed to operate and service radar emplacements along the West Coast as they taught Mexicans how to do the job, but only if they came in very small numbers and dressed in civilian clothing. This unsettling news was passed on to the US War Department, and they were still trying to understand what was going on when, two weeks later, Mexican Secretary of Defense Cárdenas told *Compañia Mexicana de Aviación* they were forbidden to build any lodgings, commissaries, or other buildings in either Tehuantepec or Cozumel, and that they were only allowed to improve the existing runways there, nothing more. Cárdenas then informed his US counterpart that he had halted construction of the two bases, claiming it was only a temporary interruption while they studied the matter. However, the authorization to continue construction never came. In order to protect the Yucatán Channel from German submarines, the US began flying anti-submarine missions out of Cuba and the Cayman Islands, countries which welcomed the presence and protection of US military.

By December, 1942, the tide of the war was turning in favor of the Allies. The Japanese threat to Panama was gone and the German U-boats had been recalled by Berlin from the Western Atlantic so they could help protect North Africa. Consequently, the Mexican airbases were no longer important as before, and the work stoppage at the Cozumel airfield was not contested by the US. In a memo to the chief of staff dated February 11, 1943, the situation concerning the Mexican Secretary of Defense's opposition to the planned airbase on Cozumel was summarized thusly:

"The general strategic situation in the Pacific underwent a decided change as a result of our successes in the South Seas. This and other considerations made it appear more and more questionable whether the War Department should proceed further along these lines [of building airbases in México]. Among the considerations was the naming of Cárdenas as Minister of National Defense of Mexico and the full realization by representatives of the War Department that at no time except in dire emergency would units of US air or ground forces be

permitted to use such defense facilities as might be constructed in Mexican territory."

By 1944, one runway of the Cozumel airfield was being maintained by Pan Am only for use in emergency landings. The other runway was occupied by the Mexican military. After the end of the war, *Transportes Aeros Mexicanos (TAMSA)* began flying from the civilian runway on Cozumel to Isla Mujeres, Carrillo Puerto, Chetumal, Mérida and Belize six days a week, beginning in October, 1945. The Mexican military continued to use the other runway.

Above: Cozumel's dirt airstrip in late 1940s or early 1950s.

3. The US Military did not destroy any Maya ruins on Cozumel or have a submarine base on the island

In Cozumel, there is an oft-quoted story that tells of a Maya city north of the downtown area of San Miguel that was bulldozed into oblivion by the Americans when they built a military base on the island. Sometimes the villain is the US Navy, sometimes it is the US Army, sometimes it is the US Air Force, and sometimes it is the US Marines. Occasionally, it is blamed on the Seabees or the US Corps of Engineers. Regardless of the branch of service these evil-doers belonged, they were always described as American. Sometimes they were supposed to have built a submarine base. Sometimes it was an airbase to launch anti-submarine sorties over the Caribbean. Sometimes it was a base to train WWII Frogmen. Multiple variations and permutations of this story have been printed and reprinted in guide books, web-pages, and magazine articles so many times that they are too numerous to count. A few of the most typical versions are:

The largest Maya ruins on the island were bulldozed to make way for an airplane runway during World War II. **Cozumel Sights**

During World War II, the United States built an airstrip on Cozumel and operated a submarine base. **Diving Cozumel**

During World War II, the US army built an airstrip and maintained a submarine base on the island. Unfortunately they also dismantled some of the larger Maya ruins, not realizing what they were destroying. **Fodors**

During World War II, the Americans built an airstrip and a submarine base on the island, where Marine Corps divers trained for upcoming events in Europe and the Pacific. **The Caribbean Dive Guide**

The American Army Corps of Engineers built an airstrip on Cozumel where the Allies also maintained a submarine base. **Guide to the Yucatán Peninsula**

A US submarine base was maintained there during World War II. **Encyclopedia Americana**

And my personal favorite: *"Thanks to Uncle Sam, Cozumel became a sort of X-rated movie production capital of the Americas [when the] Air Force stationed a Hollywood-trained movie crew on the island [during] ...the construction of an American air base (during which some more of Ixchel's temples bit the dust) on Cozumel."* **Huffington Post**

Obviously, the writers of these misleading stories made no effort to actually research the facts, they just copied and recycled the mistakes and misunderstandings printed in previous guide books. While the truth is that the US may have <u>wanted</u> to fly anti-submarine missions out of Cozumel, the Mexican government never allowed them to use the island as a base for submarine chase/spotter planes, let alone allow them to build any submarine pens with which to dock and service allied submarines.

So, just who was it that improved the old *Campo de Aterrizaje Cozumel* in 1942? *Grupo Aeroportuario del Sureste S.A. de C.V. (ASUR)* is a holding company that, through its subsidiaries, is engaged in the operation, maintenance, and development of nine airports in southeastern México. *ASUR* states that *"during the 1940s, the federal government* [the Mexican Federal Government] *built a number of others* [runways] *with World War II aid from the United States. Those in ASUR's future territory were in Campeche, Chetumal, Ciudad del Carmen, Cozumel, Itxtepec, Mérida, and Veracruz."* The Cozumel runway was significantly lengthened in the 1960s, and paved for the first time. Up until then, the runway had been dirt.

Above: Sign at entrance to Cozumel's FAM Base Area in the 1950s.

But, what about the story of the bulldozing of the Maya ruins to make an airstrip? While it is possible that some vestige of the outskirts of Xamancab (the Maya village that Grijalva, Cortés, and others reported visiting in the early 1500s) was destroyed in 1942 when the *Campo de Aterrizaje Cozumel* was improved, it is obvious the Americans could not have been the ones responsible, since the Mexican government was so adamantly firm in their position that all work to be done under the agreement covering the airstrips in Tehuantepec and Cozumel be carried out by Mexican laborers and employed by a Mexican company, in this case *Compañia Mexicana de Aviación* and *Mexicana Constructora Azteca, S. A.* But, even if either one of these Mexican companies had destroyed of a few ruins north of the city of San Miguel in 1942, that loss would seem insignificant when compared to what the Cozumeleños themselves did to the remains of the Maya buildings and temples that comprised of the bulk of Xamancab.

There are plenty of eyewitness accounts detailing the plethora of Maya and Spanish Colonial ruins that were once standing within the boundaries of what is today's downtown San Miguel. In 1831, James Bell wrote about the island, stating *"The ruins of European edifices on the island of Cozumel, in the midst of a grove of palm trees, indicate that the island, now uninhabited, was, at the commencement of the conquest, peopled by Spanish colonists."*

Above: Etching of ruin at San Miguel, Cozumel, 1842, after Stephens and Catherwood.

Above is an etching made after one drawn by Frederic Catherwood of a temple that was located in the town when he and John Lloyd Stephens visited the island in 1842. Why is there no sign left of this temple today?

The ruins of the old Spanish church were also described by Stephens in the book Incidents of Travel in the Yucatán. In the chapter on Cozumel, Stephens says they saw "...the ruins of a Spanish church, sixty or seventy feet front and two hundred deep. The front wall has almost wholly fallen, but the side walls are standing to the height of about twenty feet. The plastering remains, and along the base is a line of painted ornaments. The interior is encumbered with the ruins of the fallen roof, overgrown with bushes; a tree is growing out of the great altar, and the whole is a scene of irrecoverable destruction." Again, what happened to these ruins?

In 1895, William Henry Holmes also visited the island. He later wrote: "there were large masses of shapeless ruins and mounds around the area of the old church." Holmes went on to say: "The intact ruins mentioned by Stephens, were not to be found. In front of the ruins of the ancient Spanish church of which he speaks at length there is only a shapeless mound to represent the temple at that point." After walking about a mile north of the village of San Miguel, Holmes described a shrine he found at a location called Miramar, which had a doorway supported by a column bearing a bas-relieve carving of a female giving birth. He sketched and photographed the nearly intact temple, which is a good thing for us, since it has since been dismantled and the main column carried away. It is now in the town's museum. Holmes went on to describe another temple nearby and then observed it was "in an advanced state of ruin. The ready-cut stone of these buildings is so much more easily utilized for fences and building purposes by the present residents than is the rock in place — though the limestones are all soft and easily quarried along the natural exposures everywhere occurring — that it is surprising to find even these remnants left."

When Channing Arnold wrote about his 1908 trip to Cozumel, he specifically mentions the destruction of the Maya temples being perpetrated by the Cozumeleños. He says of the shrines and temples mentioned by John Lloyd Stephens: *"Of these temples not a trace now remains around San Miguel save the north end, where a path through a plantation of cocoanuts leads to such a scene of vandalism as might be calculated to rouse the indignation of even the Conservator of Monuments, if he remained awake long enough to reach this spot. Here what had obviously been a minor temple has been broken up and converted into a quarry. Heaps of stones, broken past recognition, lie in a confused heap with smashed Indian pottery. The largest stones have been carted into the village, and formed a pathetic hotch-potch in a garden close to our hut."*

In 1940, prior to any significant improvements to the original 1929 Pan Am air strip on Cozumel, Henry Raup Wagner visited the island while researching his book *The Discovery of New Spain in 1518*. Wagner postulated that the Maya village of Xamancab and its temples reported by the early Spanish explorers were located exactly where the town San Miguel lay. He further theorized that was why no ruins have been found in that location; that since the construction of the streets and buildings of this rather large town would have consumed far more than the limestone blocks than could be easily quarried, the Cozumeleños simply re-utilized stones from the ruins of the houses, halls, and temples reported by Grijalva, Cortés, and the others.

I have witnessed this re-purposing of the stones and columns from Maya temples myself. In the early 1980s, I leased an old Cozumeleño home from Pedro Gual at the corner of Avenida 5 and Calle 8. I intended to use the building to house an offset printing shop, but when it came time to bring in the presses, the doorways proved too narrow. I had to ask the owner for permission to widen one of the building's doorways in order to get the presses inside. When the *albaniles* began swinging their sledges and tearing into the two-foot thick wall, it turned out the stones used to build the house had been scavenged from Maya structures. Round columns, dressed square stones, lintels, and *metates* were stacked up one on top of another like so many concrete blocks. Multiply the size of that opening we made by the volume of the rest of the house's standing walls, and you are talking about enough scavenged archaeological material to construct all the buildings in the main plaza of San Gervasio. Multiply the amount of re-used Maya building material in that whole house by the number of other houses of the same age and construction in the immediate area, and you are talking about enough dressed stones to build an entire Maya village.

4. Jacques-Yves Cousteau did not film an underwater documentary at Palancar Reef in the early 1960s

In 1955, Jacques-Yves Cousteau and Louis Malle made a 1 hour and 23 minute documentary entitled *Le Monde du Silence* (the same title as the book published by Cousteau and Frédéric Dumas in 1953) which contained underwater scenes.

The film debuted in Cannes in 1956 and won a *Palme d'Or*. In 1957 it won an Oscar for the Best Documentary at the American Academy Awards. Many people over the years have come to believe that this film contained scenes of Palancar Reef, but that is most definitely not true. All the scenes in this documentary were shot in the Eastern Hemisphere. All the underwater shots were made in the

Mediterranean, Red Sea, Persian Gulf, and Indian Ocean. None were filmed in México.

Many websites and guidebooks state that the diving related tourism industry on Cozumel began due to a TV documentary Cousteau made underwater at Palancar Reef. Some sites and guides state this was in 1959; others 1960; still others 1961. In fact, the Cousteau Society themselves state that no such TV documentary ever existed.

The source of this rumor of how a TV special launched Cozumel's diving industry most probably springs from confusion with the 1957 movie *Un Mundo Nuevo* with the 1956 movie *Le Monde du Silence*. Cinematographer Lamar Boden, (who would later be the cinematographer for the movie *Flipper* and the *Sea Hunt* TV series starring Lloyd Bridges) filmed *Un Mundo Nuevo* in Cozumel's waters in 1956, under the direction of René Cardona. The reef where the filming took place was later re-named Cardona Reef, after the film's director. However, the story that it was Cousteau who put Cozumel on the map has been repeated so often and published so frequently by authors plagiarizing each other that now the public accepts it as fact.

Above: Movie posters advertising the 1957 film "Un Mundo Nuevo."

In a way, Cousteau's 1956 film *Le Monde du Silence* did impact Cozumel, as it was the inspiration for Cardona's 94-minute movie *Un Mundo Nuevo*. However, it was Cardona's film that put Cozumel on the map. Released in Mexico City on August 7, 1957, the film starred the director's son, René Cardona Jr., along with Antonio Raxel, José Pulido, John Kelly, Manuel Dondé, Rafael Alcayde, Angel Di Stefani, Lorena Velázquez, Arturo Arias, and René Cardona Sr. The script is not anything to write home about; the film was basically a vehicle to showcase Cozumel's underwater scenes and cash in on the popularity of Cousteau's award winning documentary *Le Monde du Silence*.

Cardona's film was dubbed in English and released in the United States in 1958 as a TV movie under the name *A New World*. After that, Americans began to be more aware of the island and its underwater beauty. That same year, in the May issue of *Holiday Magazine* (at the time, a Curtis publication for the American Automobile Association), an article about Cozumel appeared, written by John R. Humphreys and entitled *"Bargain Paradise Revisited."* The rush for paradise was on.

While Jacques Cousteau did produce several TV series and documentaries, his very first TV series broadcast, *The World of Jacques-Yves Cousteau* was not made until 1966. No Cousteau-made documentaries, TV specials, or series that contained footage shot under waters anywhere near Cozumel were aired until the 1970s. The Cousteau Society themselves admit there has never been a Cousteau documentary about Cozumel. Cozumelenos should be proud of their compatriot film producer, René Cardona, and give him credit for helping to put Cozumel on the diving and tourist destination map.

René Cardona Jr., one of the stars in the movie *Un Mundo Nuevo* and the son of René Cardona Sr., also made two films in Cozumel; one was the 1978 action-thriller, *El triángulo diabólico de las Bermudas* and the other was the 1978 disaster movie *Cíclón*. However, *Cyclone* (as it was named when it released in English) probably did not do as much for Cozumel tourism as his father's movie did. The plot was about a sudden storm that caused a plane to crash in the sea near a glass-bottom boat full of tourists from Cozumel. Drifting on the currents, out of gas, the survivors eventually resorted to cannibalism and then some of them were eaten by sharks before the rest were rescued.

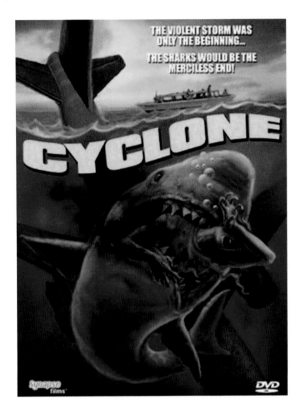

In 1976, Cardona Jr. had just finished his film *Survive,* filmed in the mountains near Mexico City. He went on to film *El triángulo diabólico de las Bermudas* in Cozumel with John Huston and Carol Baker playing bit parts in January of 1977. He filmed *Cyclone* on the island a month later; the movie was not named *Survive II,* as reported by many websites and guidebooks.

Cardona Jr. bought the old hulk of the twin-engine plane used in the movie *Cyclone* from the government of Cozumel, filled it with Styrofoam, and dragged it from the Cozumel airport to the water. From there the plane was towed to a spot offshore in front of La Ceiba Hotel and sunk. This plane was a popular dive spot until Hurricanes Gilbert and Wilma strew its parts all over the seafloor.

5. There was never a "giant sea-shell" on top of the El Caracol ruin at Punta Sur, nor was it used as a lighthouse or a hurricane warning system

A persistent and often-repeated myth is that there was once a giant sea shell atop the ruin known variously as *"Ruinas del Islote" "Punta Islote,"* *"Tumba de Caracol,"* or *"El Caracol."* This myth also asserts that the giant shell served as a sort of early-warning system in that it would make whistling sounds when a hurricane was near. This is pure bunk.

The small ruin features a truncated mampostería cone atop its roof that has several normal-sized caracol shells cemented in place in four vertical rows along the cone's axis. The upper portion of the cone is broken off and missing and it is upon this broken top that the legend says the giant shell was located. One version of the myth says a rich American took it away in the 1960s. Another version says it was stolen by people who came to help the island rebuild after the hurricane of 1955. Neither version is true.

On the second of September, 1938, three members of the *Expedición Cientifica Mexicana* went to the site of El Caracol with local guide Ramón Coronado. In the report *Exploraciones Arqueológicas en la Isla Cozumel, Quintana Roo* that archaeologist and expedition member Miguel Angel Fernández published about the visit to the ruin, Fernández stated that near Punta Islote at Punta Sur they found *"a small uniquely shaped santuario that by luck was very well conserved. On the top part of the building, right in the center, was a miniature temple, on top of which was a type of hollow cone that is formed by embedded conch shells, the ends of which protrude, forming a decorative element. This miniature temple on top of the building has four small openings twenty-five by thirty centimeters each, that I imagine were where they burnt incense, with the intent that it spread to the four cardinal points, as well as out of the top opening."*

Fernández included detailed drawings he made of the cone located on top of the small ruin, and the drawings clearly show the cone was intact with no "giant shell" atop it in 1938. All the reports of sightings of this shell in the 1950s and 1960s are pure baloney, the same as the statement that this giant shell made a whistling sound when a hurricane was approaching.

LAMINA 3.

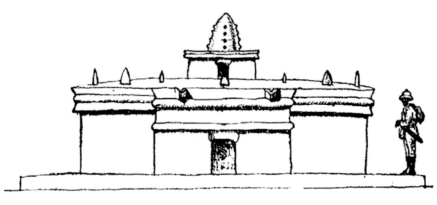

Fachada.

Above: Arq. Miguel Angel Fernández 1938 drawing of El Caracol ruin.

LAMINA 5.

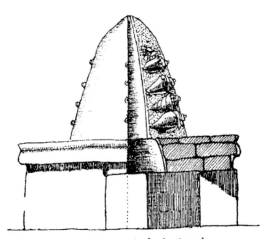

Detalles de la Cúpula de Caracoles.
Ruinas del Islote Celarain.

Above: Arq. Miguel Angel Fernández cut-away detail drawing of how the cone atop El Caracol ruin looked in 1938.

In 1984, Archaeologist Daniel Schávelzon visited El Caracol and made the observation that the upper part of the cone had been destroyed, probably by treasure hunters looking for something of value in the hollow interior.

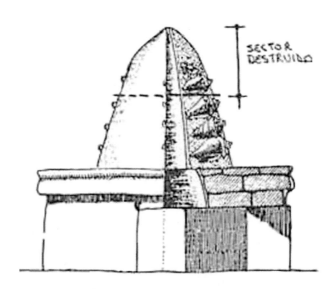

Above: Drawing by Daniel Schávelzon (after Miguel Angel Fernández) showing how the upper section of the cone was missing in 1984.

There is also a theory often floated that the El Caracol ruin was used as a lighthouse by the Maya. This is not true. For one thing, I crawled through the entire interior of the little building on my hands and knees and found no sign of fire damage or soot. If a fire had been built in it to make a beacon light, the soft lime mortar of the walls and ceilings would have been severely damaged by the heat. The other point that makes the whole "Caracol was a lighthouse" idea absurd is the fact that it is such a small, low-to-the-ground structure. The Maya knew how to build tall towers and pyramids. If they were building a lighthouse, why would they make one that would be so low and hard to see? There is one other Maya building visible today that lies to the north of El Caracol (building #2 in the drawing below), but the sand dune that breaks the line of sight from El Caracol (building #1) and the sea hides the ruined remains of three other buildings (#3, #4, and #5) and from what I saw in the 1970s, at least two large, phallic columns. If the low, small building of El Caracol was meant to be a lighthouse, why would the Maya erect these other buildings and phallic columns between it and the sea, blocking the line of sight?

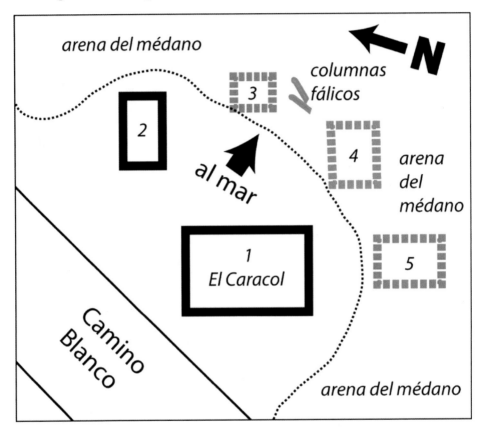

Above: The El Caracol complex of buildings at Parque Punta Sur.

CHAPTER 16

Indiana Jones, German Spies, & Cozumel

When I was investigating Sylvanus Griswold Morley's 1918 visit to Cozumel, I found that while he was working as an archaeologist for the Carnegie Institute, he was also working simultaneously for the US Office of Naval Intelligence. His expedition along the coast of Yucatán and Belize was actually a cover for his main objective: Hunting WWI German spies and sympathizers, or people who might be in a position to help supply German U-boats from secret spots along the Caribbean coast of the Yucatán Peninsula. Some say Morley was the real-life model for Indiana Jones.

Above: Sylvanus Morley, the real Indiana Jones?

As I was reading some declassified letters on-line which Morley had sent back to the State Department via diplomatic pouch from the American Consulate in Progreso, I was amazed to run across the name Ernesto

Kentzler in one of them. Now, I realized it could not have been the Ernesto Kentzler I knew from Cozumel; these letters were written in 1918 and my Ernesto Vera Kentzler is in his 60s. No, this was a different Ernesto; but the name Kentzler is not a common one in México, so I felt they must be related somehow.

The Ernesto Kentzler living in 1918 Progreso was, Morley felt sure, a German sympathizer, if not an out-right operative. In one of the dispatches Morley sent back to the State Department, the archaeologist/intelligence officer indicated that he had copies of at least three telegrams exchanged between Ernesto and Ernesto's father, Emil Kentzler. The American Consul had intercepted and copied them with the implicit understanding of the Mexican Telegraph Office. The telegrams had been sent to Ernesto from Mexico City, where Emil Kentzler had a *botica*, or compounding pharmacy.

Searching the Internet uncovered the address of Emil's *Botica Iturbide*, which back in 1918 was located at #21 Calle de San Francisco (now Avenida Madero) in Mexico City. Then I found where Emil appeared on the American "Black List" of 1918; a list of companies and individuals operating in neutral countries (like México) who were deemed by the US War Trade Board to be complicit in supplying the German war machine under the "Trading with the Enemy Act of December 6, 1917."

In another declassified letter to the State department, the American Consul in Progreso, O. Gaylord Marsh, had reported that Ernesto Kentzler was working in January of 1918 at the *Farmacia Puerto y Correa* in Mérida, but had plans to open his own pharmacy soon, with funds provided by his father, Emil. In an ad in the March 5, 1913 edition of *"La Revista de Mérida,"* it seems that some of the products that *Farmacia Puerto y Correa* was pushing were *"Elixir, Pasta y Polvo Dentifricos,"* or, toothpastes and tooth powders.

Searching deeper into the record of registered brands in México, I found where Emil had registered *"Dr. Buettner's Elixir Balm"* on December 15, 1900. The compound was actually a dentifrice, one of the earliest brands on record. Was there some kind of German spy/toothpaste connection going on here?

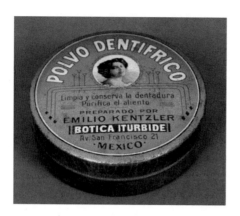

Above: Emilio Kentzler's dentifrice

In addition to his pharmacy job, Ernesto managed to get added on to the payroll of the Progreso *Ayuntamiento* in the department of *Hacienda*. Consul Marsh felt sure that this was a cover for Ernesto to get close to classified information that he could then pass on to his German handlers.

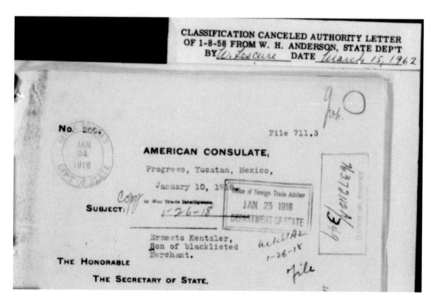

Above: Declassified dispatch regarding Ernesto Kentzler.

When an anonymous letter arrived on Marsh's desk, accusing Ernesto of being a spy, the Consul whipped off a missive to Carlos Castro Morales, the Governor of Yucatán, telling him how the young German had infiltrated the ranks of his government's workers. The Governor sent a letter back to Marsh within the week, saying that they had investigated Ernesto and found his papers were not in order, as he had falsely claimed that he was a Mexican citizen. The Governor had him summarily fired from his job at *Hacienda*. The German Consul in Progreso protested the firing, but the Governor stood his ground. Ernesto was now a *persona non-grata* in Progreso.

Emil Kentzler, Ernesto's father, turns up in several internet archives. His name appears on the May, 1895 passenger manifest (along with his wife and 3-year-old, German-born son, Ernesto) of the *MV Yucatán*, arriving in New York from Veracruz. In another ship's 1903 manifest, he is shown accompanying 10-year-old Ernesto to Germany to enroll him in school there. In a 1908 copy of the *American Druggist and Pharmaceutical Record*, there is an article describing Don Emilio Kentzler as *"a graduate pharmacist of the University of Marburg, Germany. He is a titulado of the Escuela de Medicina y Farmacia, Mexico, who has always had a high reputation as a pharmacist, and his business is mainly devoted to first class prescription trade. From 150 to 200 prescriptions a day are nothing unusual there."*

Running through the entries online for his name in association with pharmacies, I found a few more mentions of his *Botica Iturbide*, but when I tried to cross-check his name with toothpastes, I ran into something odd. There was a *Kentzler-Kaschner Dental GMBH*, in Germany that was today producing dental equipment. What were the odds of that? I decided to ask them if they were related, so I wrote the General Director, Eric P. Kentzler, in Berlin. I got back a very nice email from his daughter, Christine, who unfortunately had to inform me of her father's recent passing. She, however, was a wealth of data about the Emil Kentzler of Mexico City, who was her great-grandfather.

Emil and his wife had five children, Hans (Christina's grandfather), Hilde (whose descendants still live in México), Heimito, Walter, and Ernesto, the oldest. Christine told me the extended Kentzler family all still stay in contact, but none of them ever knew (or could find out) what became of Ernesto and his descendants. The family rumor was that something so bad had happened that no one had wanted to see him anymore or talk about him.   Later, they just lost track.   Christine sent me a wonderful photo of Emil's Family, taken in Mexico City, and there was young Ernesto Kentzler, standing proudly in a straw boater, in the back row between his nanny and his youngest brother.

Above: Emil, his wife had five children: Hans (Christina's grandfather), Hilde (whose descendants still live in México), Heimito, Walter, and Ernesto, the oldest.

Armed with the photo and this new information, I looked up Ernesto Kentzler Vera's phone number and gave him a call.   Did he know his grandfather's first name, I asked him?   Sure, he replied, it was Ernesto.   Eureka!   I gave him a rundown of what I had discovered online, and Christina's email address.   They all had a lot of catching up to do!   Sometimes taking a little detour during an archival investigation can produce surprising results.

Sylvanus Griswold Morley was not the only American who searched for German spies along the coast of the Yucatán Peninsula.   Another was Leicester Hemingway, the younger brother of author Ernest Hemingway.   In the summer of 1940, Leicester and his friend, Anthony Jackson, sailed their schooner, the *Blue Stream*, from New York down to México, Belize, Guatemala, Honduras, Nicaragua, and Costa Rica to search for German U-boat supply depots. During this non-governmental expedition, the two stopped in Cozumel and immediately felt that they had uncovered a huge conspiracy on the island; an organized team of Nazi sympathizers lead by some of the island's leading citizens whose purpose it was to resupply German U-boats with diesel fuel. Hemingway and Jackson wrote a series of newspaper articles about what they believed they found and by using inflammatory words and innuendo in the articles, convinced many readers of the articles that the acusations were true.

The North American Newspaper Alliance (NANA) reprinted the articles all across the US, where the series ran from August 21 to August 27, 1940. *"Nazi Fuel Bases for U-boats and Raiders set up in Caribbean,"* read the headline of the first article. *"Snoopers find Ideal Nazi Base off Mexico"* announced the second. *"Nazi runs island 300 miles from Panama Canal,"* warned the third. *"Oil stored on Cozumel Island near Yucatán believed Awaiting German Use!"* screamed the fourth. The other two articles were about more supposed Nazi bases they found in Nicaragua and Costa Rica. These articles were later combined into one and published in 1940, in volume 37 of *The Reader's Digest* magazine.

The pair of writers reported that the Cozumeleño Oscar Coldwell Fernandez, son of Oscar Coldwell Anduze, was in charge of this nefarious operation. However, they apparently mistook Jacinto Coldwell for his brother Oscar, as Oscar died three years earlier, in 1937. Jacinto was quoted by Hemingway as having said *"Britain never did us any good and when Hitler wins he will bring order to the world."*

Whether or not Jacinto Coldwell really did say these words, we'll never know; they may have been his true sentiments, or they may have been words only attributed to him by the two writers who were determined to find German sympathizers behind every bush. For example, Hemingway and Jackson also accused two other Cozumeleños, Mauricio and Adolfo Grau Klinger, of being Nazis. These were the two Austrian fellows who operated a small hardware store on the south-east corner of the plaza from 1939 until the end of the 1980s, and whose last will and testament donated their life savings to set up and fund the *Fundación Comunitaria Cozumel. "Among Coldwell's associates are two*

'Jewish refugees,' anti-Nazi in name only, who came to Cozumel *recently,"* one of their articles stated, in an attempt to implicate the Grau's in the imaginary plot.

In another of the articles the two writers reported that the Coldwells owned a concrete shed north of town near the waterfront that held 500 drums of diesel. Another 200 drums were supposed to have been stored behind *Casa Coldwell,* on the plaza where *Comercial Joaquín* now stands. In a third article they said they were storing 500 drums in the waterfront shed and another 200 at *Casa Coldwell.* Regardless of the actual number of drums *Casa Coldwell* owned, there was a perfectly good reason for them to have that much: *Casa Coldwell* was the leading commercial establishment on Cozumel and as the sole Pemex concession holder on the island, they supplied all the gas and diesel to ships and planes calling on the port and the Cozumel airstrip. There is no evidence whatsoever that any German submarines ever called on Cozumel, or were ever fueled or provisioned from the island.

After Leicester's adventure cruise, he went to Europe with the US army and later in 1953 wrote his first novel about the experience, *The Sound of the Trumpet,* which was well received by critics. He then wrote a prize-winning biography of his brother, Ernest. However, the most memorable achievement this adventurer-writer managed to pull off was his founding of the micro-nation of the Republic of New Atlantis, on July 4, 1964. On that day, Leicester anchored a 8-foot-wide by 30-foot-long bamboo raft over a shallow reef in international waters just outside of Jamaica's territorial limits and declared it an independent nation by taking advantage of the US Guano Islands Act of 1856.

This piece of US legislation was originally enacted so that US citizens could claim any *"unoccupied island, rock, or key,"* in order to exploit guano (bird droppings) for use in the US and abroad as fertilizer. Since the act had never been repealed, Leicester used it to bolster his claim of independence. After visiting with Jamaican officials and assuring them that his new republic *"would be a peaceful power and would not threaten its Caribbean neighbors,"* Leicester obtained their tacit understanding that they would not interfere with New Atlantis, and he elected himself its first president. The first thing he did as the republic's new leader was to authorize a national flag and to commission the printing of five denominations of postage stamps, which he intend to sell at a huge profit to collectors around the globe.

Above: The National Flag of New Atlantis

Above: A New Atlantis postage stamp.

Unfortunatley, the Universal Postal Union, the Swiss organization in charge of administering the world's postage stamps, refused to recognise the legitimacy of the republic, or its stamps. The scheme flopped, and a few years later the raft was blown away in a storm and Atlantis disappeared below the waves once more.

German submarine sunk on Chinchorro Reef?

The public's interest in sunken WWII German U-boats seems to be unending. There are frequently-heard reports of one being discovered with either a load of mercury, or a ballast of mercury, depending who is spinning the tale. Often, the site where this submarine was found is reported to be Chinchorro Reef, south of Cozumel. But, is there really a sunken U-boat, or German submarine, on Banco Chinchorro, slowly leaking its ballast of mercury onto the seafloor? No. There is no sunken submarine at Chinchorro. No German, American, Russian, Chinese, or even Tibetan sub sank there for that matter. Why, then, do so many folks swear it is true? Their dad, (or uncle, friend, cousin, etc.) told them so. Or, they heard it from a friend, who had a friend, who had a friend, whose cousin saw it. One telling fact is that in all these years, no photographs have ever been taken of the wrecked sub and given the shallow depths of Chinchorro Bank, a sunken German submarine would make a very photogenic subject. But, the truth is, if any diver found a small pool of mercury lying on the bottom in some pocket of the reef, the origin of that liquid metal is much easier to explain that inventing a phantom submarine; it is from a cargo ship carrying the mercury from Europe to the New World to be used in refining gold from gold ore, in a process known as "amalgamation."

Over the centuries, many of these cargo ships sank before they could off-load their cargo of mercury. As mercury is insoluble in water, every last drop lost from one of the wrecks is still as intact as it was the day the ship went down; shimmering, heavy, and poisonous, it still lies nestled in cracks on the bottom of the sea. Many such sunken cargo ships have been found over the years and often their cargo of mercury has been salvaged and sold. Currently mercury sells for about 50 dollars a pound, so it's a lucrative endeavor.

Many other early shipwrecks went down with much smaller amounts of medicinal mercury aboard. In the 15th and 16th centuries, a syringe-load of mercury pumped up the penis of a man infected by syphilis was thought to help combat the disease. Almost all doctors aboard ships at that time carried both the mercury and the syringe to administer it, as syphilis was apparently a common ailment among sailors.

Above: A five-inch-long, 18th century penile syringe used for introducing mercury into the urethra.

As late as 1918, mercury was still employed in the fight against this venereal disease. Sometimes it was used to rub directly onto the penis by a "trained rubber," or a physician. Other times it was injected directly into the flesh or inserted up the rectum as a suppository. In the *Practitioner's Encyclopaedia of Medical Treatment* published by Oxford Medical Publications in 1915, the following description was included to explain how the mercury should be prepared:

"The best method of prescribing mercury is in the form of unctions, but these are useless, except in congenital syphilis, unless carried out by a trained rubber. Mercurial unctions are messy, and cause the patient some inconvenience, owing to the time they take up. More convenient are mercurial injections. The insoluble preparations are more efficacious than the soluble. The strongest compound is the subchloride, but unfortunately its use is so frequently accompanied by pain and occasional abscess formation that some preparation of metallic mercury is better. When a patient cannot get regular medical attendance, mercury should be taken internally in some form; if this method causes depression or sets up gastro-enteritis or diarrhea, a suppository inserted every night just before going to bed will often meet the difficulty."

CHAPTER 17

One person's prison is another person's escape

The Green Hell of Cozumel

During the reign of Emperor Maximiliano I in México (1864-67), the island of Cozumel was used as a sort of "Devil's Island" prison where political prisoners could be banished. The town only had around 400 people living in it at the time. It was so far off the beaten track that the authorities in México City considered anyone stuck on the island to be effectively neutralized. The newspaperman Yanuario Manzanilla and newspaper publisher Eligio Ancona were two of the more famous dissidents that Maxilimiano's government exiled to the island in 1866. Manzanilla later wrote about his experiences on Cozumel in his memoires, which were published in 1888: "*The appearance of the village is poor. Their houses are made of palm; only a very few are made of stone and mortar. They only have two regular streets. Ashore we were guarded by Señor Benjamín Pasos, who had been previously sent by the municipal mayor and military commander to await those who were to be deported and serve as their custodian. This man received us with courtesy and told us that we were at liberty within the population, but we could not leave its perimeter. To be free within the town was a forced concession, because there is no prison in it, and the island is so little frequented by boats that we cannot escape; such that in the more than two months that we stayed in San Miguel, we only saw two in anchorage. So, he who enters here cannot leave at will. He is isolated from the rest of the world. It has walls like China, except they are giant waves produced by the sea.*"

During the term of Mexican President Porfirio Diaz (1876-1911), when Yucatán was termed the *"Infierno Verde"* or "Green Hell," he too used Cozumel as a warehouse to store dissidents. In 1913, Mexican President Victoriano Huerta continued the practice of shipping political enemies to Cozumel.

Although the whole island of Cozumel may have been considered a prison at one time, it later had its own jails. One was located in San Miguel on the main square, where the Plaza del Sol shopping center is today. It had no restroom and the prisoners were allowed to use the bathroom in a house down the street. Cedral also had a jail. The old Maya ruin that stands near its center was retrofitted sometime after 1909 with wooden doors and the occasional drunk was locked up inside for the night. On the left is a photo of what it looked like shortly before it was "restored" in 2003.

Above: Ruin of a Maya oratorio that was used as a jail in Cedral.

From Hell to Cozumel

Like the story of Papillon, (the French prisoner played by Steve McQueen in the movie of the same name) who escaped from Devil's Island off the shores of the French penal colony of French Guiana, other daring escapes from the Iles du Salut have been attempted during the years 1852 to 1946, when the penal colony was in operation. One such story is the account of three different groups of escapees who managed to get away and eventually meet up together on the island of Trinidad.

"I was working in the garden of one of the administration buildings on Royal Island [one of the three islands that make up the Iles du Salut]," wrote Jean Duvernay in 1939, "and had been there for three months when, one day, I was along the beach fishing for shellfish and had the chance to speak with a fisherman from the mainland. This fisherman had a dugout canoe about seven meters long and about a meter and a half wide. At this particular time my friends, three of whom were with me on Royal Island, four on St. Joseph Island, and two on Devil's Island, had turned over to me their savings, telling me they were counting on me to do the necessary. I had two thousand five hundred francs and offered the fisherman five hundred to remain in the passages between the Islands after dark and later turn over the canoe to us. One thousand was agreed upon.

I got the word to my friends and it was agreed that we would meet at a certain spot on my island as soon as it got dark. In spite of the danger of swimming in shark-infested waters between the islands, the bunch gathered as planned. Soon we were aboard after swimming out to the boat off the shore some little distance, as no boats being allowed close in at night. In a very short time we had taken the fisherman ashore, gathered together some food and were at sea, realizing that we might be sacrificing our lives for the sake of the liberty we all loved so much."

Duvernay's group became lost after a few days because of a defective compass and drifted aimlessly until a British freighter gave them water and provisions and pointed them towards Trinidad, their intended goal. They arrived in Trinidad a few days later where they met two other groups of escapees who had managed to get away from the French penal colony as well. The three groups united for the time they were on Trinidad, but later decided to spilt up and reform into three new groups, made up new combinations of the members from each of the three original groups. The first of the reformed groups (made of nine men) sailed to Colombia, where they were quickly recaptured and returned to French Guiana.

The second of the new re-combined groups, made up of 10 men, set sail for Haiti, but ended up wrecking on Curacao 12 days later. The people of Curacao gave them a new boat, but when they set sail for Aruba they wrecked their boat on the rocks of the harbor just as they were leaving. The islanders gave them a <u>third</u> boat, which they sailed to Aruba, then onwards to Colombia. In Colombia, this group also splits up; three of the escapees eventually to be arrested and returned to the French penal colony, and the remaining seven of the group managing to continue on to freedom.

Above: The French convicts' vessel.

The third group managed to find a freighter in Trinidad that took them as far as the coast of Quintana Roo. There, at Punta Herrero, they were given one of the ship's longboats and put adrift. This group of escapees was made up of Jonas Varennes, Pierre Pouillon, Germain Jolion, Fernando Girial, Jean Goutelle, and Louis Kieffer. From Punta Herrero, the six hitched a ride on a Mexican Customs ship, which carried them and their small boat to Cozumel on August 15, 1938. There they sold the boat for around 200 pesos and were allowed to settle on the island, where they used the money to start new lives.

Above: Photo taken in Aruba of Jean Duvernay.

A memo filed with the American Consulate General in México City in 1939 appears below and sheds more light on the situation:

American Consulate General,
Mexico, D. F., Mexico,
April 29, 1939.

MEMORANDUM

Mr. Arthur Falconer, whom I had known some years ago in San Luis Potosí when he was employed with the American Smelting and Refining Company, called this morning and stated that Vice Consul Stephen C. Worster of Mérida, Yucatán, had met him in Cozumel and had informed him of the desire of the Consulate General to obtain information concerning any convicts who may have escaped from French Guiana and come to Mexico.

The inquiry had been made of Vice Consul Worster because of a report that Mr. John Abney and companions had purchased a boat on Cozumel in which certain escaped French convicts had come to that island. Mr. Falconer said that as a matter of fact four or five men had come to Cozumel in the boat in question which was practically unseaworthy and leaking badly. They sold the boat for 150 or 200 pesos to a resident of Cozumel and then remained there because the authorities would not allow them to depart. It seems that at least three of them are still living in the Comandancia in Cozumel and are working for a wage of about three pesos a day on Government projects and seem to be quite content. The one other member of the group seems to have become enamored of a Mexican circus performer in Cozumel some time ago. When she returned to Mérida she sent him two or three hundred pesos and he followed her to Mérida where it is understood he married her and is traveling with her and the circus at the present time.

It would appear from the statements of Mr. Falconer who has spent the last two years in Yucatán and Quintana Roo for a chicle company that the authorities are perfectly well aware that these men are escaped convicts and, in fact, it was common knowledge that one was sent to French Guiana for murder, another for robbery with fire arms and another for some sexual crime. It would appear further that these convicts were received rather sympathetically and that no action against them is contemplated.

Geo. P. Shaw,
American Consul.

813
GPS:acf

CHAPTER 18

How tourism, boa constrictors, and a one-armed statue of Christ came to Cozumel

During his exile in 1869, Mexican General Antonio López de Santa Anna (the Mexican general who defeated the Texians at the Alamo) convinced Thomas Adams of New York to try to develop a product utilizing *chicle*, the gum of the sapodilla tree *(Manilkara zapota)*, a tree found in Yucatán, Guatemala, and Belize. After several failed attempts to make toys, masks, and rain-boots out of the material, Adams finally added flavoring to it and came up with *chicle*-based chewing gum. Chewing gum had been around for a few years already in the US, but up until then it had been based on Spruce gum and had never really caught on. This new concoction did.

Above: Adams first chicle-based chewing gum.

In 1880, William White improved the ability of chewing gum to hold a flavor and launched a new line of gum called "Yucatan Chewing Gum."

Above: William White's chewing gum.

The same year, Henry and Frank Fleer began manufacturing "Chiclets."

Above: Fleer's Chiclets.

In 1891, 29-year-old William Wrigley opened a business selling soap wholesale to grocery stores. As an incentive to his clients to buy more of his soap, he began giving them free baking soda with their follow-up orders. When the popularity of this incentive skyrocketed, Wrigley switched his focus from selling soap, to selling baking powder. To help this new product take off, Wrigley began giving free chewing gum to his clients re-orders.

Above: Wrigley's Soap.

Wrigley soon began to manufacture his own gum and sourced his *chicle* directly from the Yucatán. In 1893 Wrigley's introduced Juicy Fruit Gum and a few months later, Wrigley's Spearmint. These two gums, as well as others being manufactured in the US, became wildly popular and the chewing-gum craze fueled a race to see who could control the *chicle* supply. The Mexican government tried, but since the territory with the most sapodilla trees (also called *chico zapote* trees, in Yucatecan Spanish) were located in lands held by the Maya *Cruzoob* rebels, there was not much they could do about it at first. Later, in the 1910s, after the War of the Castes had wound down, the Mexican Federal government began to enforce concessions, as well as the export of *chicle*.

By the 1920s, Cozumel had become an important port in the *chicle* trade and needed a hotel to house visiting American buyers and Mexican government officials. To this end, Refugio Granados constructed the Gran Hotel Louvre in Cozumel in 1924 at the intersection of Juárez and Zaragoza. In 1932, Felipe Rivero Herrera built the Hotel Yuri, located on Calle 1 Sur between Avenidas 5 and 10. Between 1936 and 1938, the Hotel Playa was built off Avenida Playa Norte (today's Avenida Melgar) by the government of Quintana Roo.

In 1919 synthetic chicle was invented, but it did not become popular with manufacturers until the late 1920s. By World War II, the *chicle* trade had crashed. With no other industry or trade to replace it, Cozumel's economy was in shambles and hard times were had by all. The Hotel Playa closed its doors due to the lack of business travelers. The former hotel is now the *Museo de la Isla*.

The war years were hard for Cozumel. The planned American airbase that the US War Department had assumed it could build and man on Cozumel had been rejected by Mexican Secretary of Defense Lázaro Cárdenas, the ex-president of México who nationalized the Mexican oilfields and expelled the American oil companies. As a result, little of the money, munitions, and supplies the US gave México in exchange for the right to build airbases actually ended up in Cozumel. Some of the US funds were used by *Mexicana de Aviación* (a subsidiary of Pan American Airways at the time) to improve the island's old dirt airstrip, but the American troops and their spending money never appeared. The newly elongated dirt runways were, however, one of the necessary building blocks for the island's tourism infrastructure, and that was a consolation.

In 1948, a nautical mishap occurred which would have the odd result of indirectly causing a large number of American tourists to visit Cozumel. On February 13 of that year, the freighter "Narwhal" was passing by Cozumel on its way from Puerto Barrios, Guatemala to Mobile,

Alabama. The ship was captained by J. Wilson Berringer and carrying 125 tons of bananas when it grounded on the point of the east coast of Cozumel called Ixpalbarco. The ten-member crew managed to get off safely and walked across the island to San Miguel, where Nassim Joaquin opened up the moth-balled Hotel Playa for them. When notified of the wreck, the boat's owner, Charles Fair, flew down to Cozumel from his home in New York to oversee the salvage operation. During his stay, he became impressed with the island and told Carlos Namur Aguilar, the honorary Consul of Honduras in Cozumel, he would recommend it to his friends.

Above: The Narwal

In May, 1951, the Committee for the Betterment of Cozumel met and began to discuss the idea of promoting tourism to the island. A speaker at the meeting, Roberto Sarlat Corrales, urged Cozumel to join forces with the rest of the peninsula in an effort to entice the tourists. Although the suggestion received little attention, tourism was soon to become the island's salvation.

When Mr. Fair, the owner of the stranded freighter, returned to New York in 1948, he was true to his word and told his writer friend, John R. Humphreys, about how pleased he was with his stay on Cozumel. Humphreys, in turn, travelled down to Cozumel to check it out for himself. While staying at the Hotel Playa for only sixty cents a day, he began taking notes for an article. A few months later, he returned for another month-long stay while he finished writing it. The completed product was a glowing story about the island, but he didn't find a publisher for another few years. *Holiday Magazine,* the in-house magazine of the American Automobile Association at the time, finally decided to print the article in its August 1955 issue. Entitled *Cozumel: A new island Paradise,* the article described a scene of an idyllic, inexpensive, tropical Eden. *"Tourists seldom go there,"* wrote Humphreys. *"Visitors from the United States are rarely seen on its shores. Yet you can live on Cozumel in style and even in relative luxury for less than 100 dollars a month."* The airfare to the island was $51.70 one way from Miami to Mérida, then another $10.00 to take TAMSA Airlines's DC-4 on the two-hour flight on to Cozumel.

The island population was only around 2,300 at the time. Streets were still unpaved, life was slow, and travelers could get three meals a day at the Fonda Tropical (later renamed Casa Denis) for seventy-two cents. Humphreys wrote that he hired a sailboat for five dollars a day and sailed to the small village of Playa del Carmen, which he described as *"a semicircle of thatched native houses on the mainland beach."*

The article struck a chord with the American public. The description of a nearby tropical island where steak was twenty cents a pound, custom-tailored suits made for $3.00, five-bedroom houses rented for $30.00 a month, and cooks could be hired for $5.00 a day, caused a huge influx of vacationers that caught the island by surprise.

In 1956, Mexican movie director René Cardona made the film *Un Mundo Nuevo,* which was shot under Cozumel's waters by cinematographer Lamar Boden, who would later be the cameraman for the movie *Flipper* and the *Sea Hunt* TV series starring Lloyd Bridges. It was Cardona's film that brought Cozumel's reefs to the attention of the Mexican public. It also began to elicit the interest of American divers, when *Un Mundo Nuevo* was translated into English and shown on American TV in 1957 as *A New World.*

In 1957, the American scuba diver Robert F. (Bob) Marx showed up in Cozumel along with Mel Fisher and his wife Deo, where they were to film some underwater promo films for Pan American World Airways. After the filming, Bob stayed on in Cozumel and began using Hotel Playa as a base of operations for a tour-guide/diving business, the first commercial operation of its type on the island. He was charging $8.00 USD per day for his services, boat, and equipment, according to an article about Cozumel in a 1959 *Esquire* magazine. Initially, Bob gave the diving lessons and acted as a dive guide for tourists who wished to try the sport, but soon took on a couple of Cozumeleños as interns and trained them to take care of the tourists. A year or so later, Tiburcio García opened El Clavado Dive Shop and Ramon Zapata's opening of Aqua Safari in 1960 with partners Juan Marrufo, Renato Bauche, Antonio Venegas, and Orlando May followed closely thereafter.

In the January 1958 edition of *Travel Magazine* and again in the February 1958 edition, Cozumel got some nice publicity. The articles pointed out that *TAMSA* airline was flying a DC-6 to the island from Mérida for $17.50 USD one-way. Also in 1958, an article headlined *"Cozumel se Acapulquiza"* (or, *"Cozumel is becoming another Acapulco"*) appeared in Volume 15 of *Visión* magazine. This article states that the North-American tourists have been coming to Cozumel for a few years now, due in part to previous US magazine articles. It also laments the fact that it is easier to get to Cozumel from the United States than it is from Mexico City! Some things never change.

During his stay in Cozumel, diver Bob Marx heard about the wreck of the *El Matancero* (officially named *Nuestra Señora de los Milagros*), a Spanish merchant vessel which ran aground on the coral reef near Akumal on February 22, 1741. In 1957, Marx crossed over from Cozumel to check out the wreck. Although a few fishermen knew about it, it still had not been excavated. Returning with two friends of his, Clay Blair (the associate editor of *Saturday Evening Post*) and the magazine's photographer Walter Bennett, Marx began to salvage the wreck. The first effort yielded little, but when they returned a few months later, they began to find and remove hundreds of objects that had gone down with the ship. Blair returned to the US and wrote a short article about the find in the March 1, 1958 *Saturday Evening Post* and the secret was out. When he and Marx returned to the wreck for a third effort at removing the cargo, the Mexican authorities put a stop to their salvage operation and instead granted a permit to Pablo Bush

Romero, who had just formed a brand new organization called *Club de Exploraciones y Deportes Acuáticos de México (CEDAM)* that same year. After a few false starts, Bush and *CEDAM* began to excavate in earnest in 1959. Bush offered Marx the opportunity to participate with *CEDAM*, so the salvage operation eventually consisted of around 25 Americans invited by Marx and another 125 Mexican divers (including Alfonso and Reggie Arnold). Bush later purchased the land near the wreck and made Akumal the club's headquarters, where he later installed the *CEDAM* Museum (since moved). In 1960, Clay Blair published his book, *Diving for Pleasure and Treasure* in the US and then republished it in 1961 in Great Britain. The book detailed Blair and Marx's adventures in Cozumel and added fuel to the blossoming dive industry on the island.

A second article by Humphreys appeared in the May 1959 issue of *Holiday Magazine*, entitled *"Cozumel: Bargain Paradise Revisited."* This new article described the huge differences Humphreys noted that had occurred on the island since his first article was published. For starters, the island was on the verge of being over-run by Americans. The island, Humphreys wrote, *"had been discovered by thousands of Americans in search of a Caribbean paradise."* Humphreys' travel agent in Mérida told him the islanders had found themselves in the middle of a gold-rush style stampede. *"They came and they came, so many people, so suddenly... from New Orleans and Miami, planeload after planeload. They all demanded the way to your island."* The frequency of flights from Mérida to Cozumel had risen from four to nine a week, and they were all fully booked.

Other changes in island life were also noted by Humphreys. The streets in the center of town were now paved. The old Hotel Playa that had been built by the government in the 1930s and left to run down for lack of visitors had been leased by the Joaquín's and renovated. The room rates had risen from the previous sixty-cents to an astronomical $4.00 per day. *"Millionaires,"* wrote Humphreys, *"accompanied by lawyers and construction engineers, arrived and departed, leaving in their wake visions of modern hotels, night-clubs, yacht basins and swarms of cruise-ship visitors."*

Because of *Holiday Magazine's* wide circulation, this second article also had a huge impact on Cozumel's economy; Americans were now ready and able to take Mexican vacations in large numbers, and that they did. After Humphreys' second article appeared, another author wrote (in an article about Cozumel in *Esquire Magazine*, 1965, Vol. 64) about Humphreys' trip, saying that no one in Cozumel would let him pay a bill during his stay!

Two of the tourists drawn to Cozumel by Humphreys' first article were an American born in London to Russian parents, Ilya (sometimes translated as "William") Chamberlain and his American wife, Mary Helen Byrnes, who visited the island for a short two-day stay and fell in love with it. They would return later with some capital and renovate two adjacent houses on Avenida Melgar (one of which Humphreys had rented during his second visit) and turn them into the Hotel Mayaluum in 1955. Located on the southern corner of Avenida Melgar at Calle 8 norte, it sported a nightclub and offered a so-called *"haute cuisine."* Later, in 1960, Chamberlain would add the *Instituto de Arte Cozumel* to his enterprise.

Across the street from the Mayluum, Fernando Barbachano opened the Hotel Caribe Isleño at the corner of Avenida Rafael Melgar and Calle 8 norte, where today Los Cinco Soles now stands. Soon after that, 12 new cottages forming the beginnings of Cabañas del Caribe were built in what would later become the Northern Hotel Zone, on San Juan beach.

In 1959, *Esquire Magazine* writers Louis Renault & Richard Joseph wrote about Cozumel in the travel section of the magazine. Cozumel again made the magazines in 1960 with the article *"Centro Turístico Cozumel: de piratas a buzos,"* when it appeared in *Visión* magazine on October 21 of that year. The island also got a good mention in the 1960 book *The Treasure Diver's Guide*, written by John Stauffer Potter. The same year, Mayaluum Hotel was advertising in the magazine *Saturday Review*.
After the fall of Cuban strongman Fulgencio Batista's government to Fidel Castro's communist rebels in 1959, Castro nationalized the American-owned hotels and casinos on Cuba. Americans then began looking for some other Caribbean destination to visit for vacation.

Cozumel was one of the beneficiaries of this turn of events, as was the Bahamas. The flood gates were now open, and Americans were visiting the island in droves. By 1961 Cozumel was appearing in *Life* magazine as an "unspoiled vacation spot." Hotel construction in Cozumel took off, with a dozen new lodgings opening prior to 1970 and the new vacation destination of Cozumel took its rightful place in the world.

Other visitors take up residence on the island: The boa constrictors arrive

Prior to 1971, Cozumel was an island free of boa constrictors. The island did have a few other non-venomous snakes, such as the Green Vine Snake *(Oxybelis fulgidus)* and the False Fer-de-lance *(Xenodon rabdocephalus),* as well as "slightly" venomous snakes, like the rear-fanged Cat Eye snake *(Leptodeira annulata).* These snakes all fed on lizards, frogs, and toads, but the island was free of any large arboreal snakes that preyed on birds. Consequently, the island was a haven for the Yucatán Parrot *(Amazona xantholora)*, also known as the Yellow-lored Amazon, Yucatán Parrot, or Yellow-lored Parrot. That all began to change in 1971.

In that year, Felipe Cazals made his 112 minute film, *El jardín de tía Isabel*, a movie telling the story of Spanish shipwreck survivors that was filmed at Estudios Churubusco Azteca (in Mexico City) and on location in Cozumel. Part of the filming in Cozumel took place near Xlapac on the northeast end of the island and more scenes were shot at Palancar Beach, on the southwest end. The film crew included an animal wrangler who brought a few collared peccaries, tarantulas, green iguanas, and six boa constrictors to Cozumel to be used in the film as extra scenery. One of the boas actually appears in the film for a total of five seconds. These five seconds turned out to be disastrous for Cozumel, because once the filming was completed in April, 1971, the wrangler turned all the animals free near Palancar Beach.

The boas found the island to be an ideal habitat and began to breed like wild-fire. One female is capable of having 60 live-born offspring every two years, and by 1991, these snakes started showing up all over the island. Growing up to six and a half feet long, the boas began to decimate the rodent and bird population of Cozumel. One of the snake's favorite preys turned out to be the island's parrots. In a few short years, the formerly raucous flocks of yellow-lored parrots that were once one of Cozumel's most visible (and audible) forms wildlife became a rare sight; the boas were wiping them out. Today, the parrots are hanging on, but in much, much lower numbers.

The statue of Christ at Chankanaab Park

Contrary to the popular myth, Jacques Yves Cousteau did not have anything to do with the underwater statue of Christ at Chankanaab Park. In 1984, Ramon Bravo, the famous underwater explorer and cinematographer from Isla Mujeres, approached Quintana Roo's Governor Pedro Joaquín Coldwell with a plan for erecting a statue of Christ underwater on Palancar Reef. Pleased with the idea, the Governor commissioned the artist Enrique Miralda Bulnes to make a statue as a gift for Cozumel on behalf of the state government. When it was delivered to Cozumel by truck from Mexico City, one of the arms had broken off in transit and it had to be reattached in a local island repair shop. The statue, once reunited with its arm, was placed at the "Horseshoe" in Palancar Reef in 1984; I helped pour the concrete for its base in a mold we assembled on the deck of a wooden-hulled boat at Puerto de Abrigo. The finished cement base was placed on the seafloor at Palancar and the statue was lowered down onto the base and secured. However, the statue eventually was removed from Palancar and placed in the water in front of Chankanaab Park. The old base of the statue still remains on the seafloor at Palancar, and occasionally is visible when it is uncovered by storms or currents.

Above: The base of the statue at The Horseshoe in Palancar Reef.

CHAPTER 19

The Cozumel Cross, Casimiro Cárdenas, the Cedral church

The "Cozumel Cross"

For hundreds of years, there have been many different stories that link Cozumel with some kind of special stone cross. Some of these stories have a basis in fact, some are pure flights of fantasy, and some are a mixture of both. For example, there are several versions of an old story about a carved, stone cross found on Cozumel by the first Spanish explorers; a stone crucifix carved by the Maya before the Spanish ever arrived. Sometimes this story of the "Cozumel Cross" merges with the story of Grijalva's visit to Cozumel in 1518 and the "cross" he saw near a temple that was actually an image of the Maya god of the rain and just happened to be shaped somewhat like a cross. Sometimes the cross in this story gets mixed together with the <u>wooden</u> cross Hernán Cortéz erected on Cozumel in 1519.

The origin of the myth that describes a cross found on Cozumel by the first Spaniards to arrive on the island is a line of text in *Primera y segunda parte de la Historia General de las Indias con todo el descubrimiento, y cosas notables que han acaecido donde que se ganaron hasta el año de 1551, con la conquista de México, y de la Nueva España*, (also known as *Historia General de las Indias y conquista de Mexico*) written by Francisco López de Gomara and published in 1552. In that text, Gomara says that on the island of Cozumel *"habia una cruz de cal tan alta como diez palmos, a la cual adoraban por dios de la lluvia."* (there was a stucco cross as high as ten palms [a little higher than one meter] which they adored as the god of the rain.) This god of the rain was the god Chaac, and the carved stone image of the god was somewhat similar to the shape of a cross.

Other early Spanish historians took this description of a cross-shaped Maya god and twisted it into a story falsely stating that prior to the

Spaniards' arrival, the Maya had been worshiping a god who died on the cross and that stone crucifixes were found all over Yucatán. Sometimes the story even described the crucifixes as being made of bronze. Obviously, none of that was true.

Above: A carved stone panel in Palenque showing the adoration of a Maya "cross" that was actually an image of the rain god Chaac.

Bernal Díaz del Castillo, in his 1568 manuscript *La Historia Verdadera de la Conquista de Nueva España,* wrote that on Cozumel in 1519, Hernán Cortés ordered his carpenters, Alonso Yáñez and Alvaro López, to build a wooden cross. Díaz goes on to say this cross was then placed on a pedestal *(humilladero)* next to the Maya temple where Cortés had a Mass said before departing the island. What ever happened to this wooden cross? Pedro Sánchez de Aguilar, in his 1613 *Informe contra idolorum cultores del obispado de Yucatán,* says Cortés: *"puso una Cruz*

*y la mandó adorar, quando pasó a México con su armada, la qual quitó
el Governador don Diego Fernández de Velasco el año de 1604 y la enbio
al Marqués del Valle nieto de Cortés."* (erected a cross and ordered
them to worship it and when he went to México with his navy,
Governor Diego Fernández de Velasco took it away in the year 1604 and
sent it to the Marquis del Valle, grandson of Cortés.) If this is true, the
wooden cross Cortés erected on Cozumel in 1519 is now long gone.

There are other fanciful stories that mix together the wooden cross that
Cortés left on Cozumel with the cross-shaped stone image of the Maya
god of rain and a 16th century stone cross that was supposedly found on
Cozumel in the Colonial period and taken away to Mérida. This colonial-
period stone cross that was removed to Mérida is now known as "The
Cozumel Cross," or the "Cross of the Conquest."

The origin of this story can be found in López de Cogolludo's 1655
manuscript, *Historia de Yucatán*: *"En medio del patio, dice, que hace el
claustro de nuestro convento de la ciudad de Mérida, hay una Cruz de
piedra, que será del grueso de una sexma por cada parte de los lados, y
como una vara de largo, y se echa de var estar su longitud quebrada y
faltarle algún pedazo. Tiene sacado de medio relieve, en la misma
piedra, una figura de un Santo Crucifijo como de media vara de largo.
Entendiéndose haber sido una de las que en el tiempo de la infidelidad
de los indios se hallaron en la isla de Cozumel. Había muchos años, que
estaba en lo superior de la iglesia, y se decía, que desde que pusieron
allí, no daba casi rayo alguno, y que de antes solían caer muchos en el
convento. Cayóse con algún temporal, y la bajaron a la iglesia, donde
algún tiempo la vimos arrimada al pié del altar de la capilla del capitán
Alonso Carrio de Valdés, con poco decencia. Habiendo sido electo
Provincial el R. Padre Fr. Antonio Ramírez, por decirse lo que se decía de
esta Santa Cruz, y colocarla más decentemente, hizo labrar un asiento
de piedra de sillería, y sobre él unas gradas, en medio una columna de
altura competente, en cuyo remate hizo fijar el de la Cruz, quedando
derecha, y la efigie del Santo Crucifijo á la parte oriental; dorados los
remates de la Cruz, que son labrados de vistosas molduras. Por la voz
común así de religiosos como de seculares, y por no afirmar cosa de que
no hay total certidumbre, se puso á las espaldas de ella un rótulo que*

dice: 'Esta Cruz se halló en Cozumel, sin tradición.' Habiendo sabido D. Eugenio de Alcántara (que murió beneficiado de Hoctun, y fue de los ministros doctrineros que más lengua ha sabido de estos indios; curiosísimo en averiguar antiguayas suyas, grande eclesiástico y celosísimo de que fuesen verdaderamente cristianos), que andaba yo ocupado en estos escritos (de la Historia de Yucatan), me dijo, no una vez sola, que podría escribir con seguridad que esta santa Cruz la tenían los indios en Cozumel en tiempo de su infidelidad, y que había años que se llevó á Mérida, porque habiendo oído á muchos lo que se decía de ella, había hecho particular inquisición con indios muy viejos de por allá, y se le habían afirmado así." (In the middle of the courtyard that is the cloister of our convent [the Franciscan convent] in the city of Mérida, there is a stone cross, which is of the thickness of a sixth part of a yard on each part of its sides and **a vara [2.8 feet] long, but its length is broken off and it is missing a piece. It has in bas relief, in the same stone, a figure of the Holy Crucifix a half *vara* long [1.4 feet].** It is understood to have been one of the crosses found on the island of Cozumel at the time of the infidelity of the Indians. Many years ago it was on the top of the church, and they say, that after they put it there, no lightning struck, although previously, it used to strike the convent frequently. Once, a storm came and it fell, so it was lowered from the church, where for some time we saw it close to the foot of the altar of the chapel of the captain Alonso Carrió de Valdés [*Procurador General de Yucatan*], with little dignity. After Reverend Father Antonio Ramírez was elected *provincal*, he had a base made of stone with a few steps and on top a column of adequate height, and on top of that he placed the cross facing straight with its face to the east to place it more decently because of what they said about this cross; **he gilded the finials** of the cross, which are ornately carved moldings. And though it was commonly said by secular as well as religious persons, but because there was no way to be sure, they placed a sign on the back that said: 'This cross was found in Cozumel, without tradition.' Having known Don Eugenio de Alcántara (who was the *benificio* of Hoctun when he died, and was the teaching minister who had the most grasp of the language of these Indians; curious to ascertain the old story of this, keen that they were truly Christians) that when was I busy in these writings (of the history of Yucatan), he told me, not only once, that I could safely write that the Indians in Cozumel at time of their infidelity had this Holy Cross and that it had been years since it was brought to Mérida, because after listening to what many had said of it, he had made particular inquiry with very old Indians from there and they had confirmed this as well.)

In Cogolludo's text we can see that he still clings to that old myth that the Maya were worshiping stone crucifixes before the Spanish ever arrived and tries to tie that myth to the stone crucifix that was in the courtyard of the Franciscan convent in Mérida in the mid-1600s by saying that it was found on Cozumel. Who found it, when it was found, or where this information came from, Cogolludo does not say. He does however, give a good description of the cross taken down from the roof of the Mérida convent and placed in the courtyard, a description which does not square at all with the one given by later eyewitnesses of the cross in the Mérida museum, which was purported to be one and the same. Cogolludo also gives an accounting of the movement of the crucifix from the roof to the chapel of the captain Alonso Carrió de Valdés, and afterwards to the courtyard. He then details the alterations made to the cross by Father Antonio Ramírez: the finials were gilded and the cross (which he says had lost a portion of its length when it broke off) was cemented to a pedestal. This description is also at odds with later photographs of what has been purported to be the actual cross that Cogolludo said he saw in the courtyard of the convent.

Justo Sierra O'Reilly published an article in 1841 in the magazine *Museo Yucateco* that stated the cross that Cogolludo wrote about in 1655 was removed from the Franciscan convent by Father Vicente Velázquez in 1820 when the troops of Juan Rivas Vertiz destroyed the interior of the church. O'Reilly says that after that, Father Velázquez placed the cross in the sacristy of the San Juan Bautista church in Mérida. From there, say historians Michel Antochiw and Cézar Dachary, Father Vicente Arnaldo moved it the the the Church of the Mejorada in Mérida.

John Lloyd Stephens visited the old Rancho San Miguel in 1842 and wrote about the ruins of the Spanish church he found just to the north of it in his 1843 book <u>Incidents of Travel in Yucatan</u>. Stephens stated: *"It is a notion, or, rather, a principle, pervading all the old Spanish writers, that at some early day Christianity had been preached to the*

Indians, and connected with this is the belief that the cross was found by the first conquerors in the province of Yucatan as a symbol of Christian worship. Prophecies are recorded supposed to show a traditionary knowledge of its former existence, and foretelling that from the rising of the sun should come a bearded people and white, who should carry aloft the sign of the cross, which their gods could not reach, and from which they should fly away. The same vague idea exists to this day; and, in general, when the padres pay any attention to the antiquities of the country, they are always quick in discovering some real or imaginary resemblance to the cross. A strong support of this belief is advanced in the "Cozumel Cross" at Mérida, found on the island of Cozumel, and in the time of Cogolludo, as at this day, supposed to have been an object of reverence among the Indians before their conversion to Christianity.

*Until the destruction of that edifice it stood on a pedestal in the patio of the Franciscan convent, and, as we were told, from the time when it was placed there, no lightning had ever struck the building, as had often happened before. **It is now in the Church of the Mejorada**, and in looking for it at that place, Mr. Catherwood and myself were invited into the cell of an octogenarian monk then lying in his hammock, for many years unable to cross the threshold of his door, but in the full exercise of his mental powers, who told us, in a tone which seemed to indicate that he had done what would procure him a remission from many sins, **that he had himself dug it up from among the ruins, and had it set up where it is now seen.** It is fixed in the wall of the first altar on the left; and is almost the first object that arrests the eye of one entering the church. It is of stone, has a venerable appearance of antiquity, and **has extended on it in half relief an image of the Saviour, made of plaster, with the hands and feet nailed.** At the first glance we were satisfied that, whatever might be the truth in regard to its early history, it was at least, wrought into its present shape under the direction of the monks. And though, at that time, we did not expect ever to know anything more about it, the ruins of this church cleared up in our minds all possible mystery connected with its existence.*

In front of the building [on Cozumel] is a cemented platform, broken and uprooted by trees, but still preserving its form; and on this stand two square pillars, which, as we supposed on the spot, had once supported crosses, and we were immediately impressed with the belief that one of these missing symbols was that now known as the "Cozumel Cross," and that it had probably been carried away by some pious monk at or about the time when the church became a ruin and the island depopulated. For myself, I have no doubt of the fact; and I regard it as important, for, even though crosses may have been found in Yucatan, the connecting of the "Cozumel Cross" with the ruined church on the island completely invalidates the strongest proof offered at this day that the cross was ever recognised by the Indians as a symbol of worship."

Clearly, the cross John Lloyd Stephens described in 1842 was not the same cross that Cogolludo described. For one, there is the octogenerian priest who told Stephens that he had dug the cross up himself on Cozumel; if you subtract the priest's age from the year 1842 (the year Stephens spoke to him), it is obvious that it could not be the same cross that was in the Franciscan courtyard in the 1650s, nearly 190 years earlier. For another, Cogolludo stated that the Christ on the cross in the courtyard was *"in bas relief, in the same stone."* Stephens, on the other hand, says the crucifix in the Church of the Mejorada *"has extended on it in half relief an image of the Saviour, made of plaster, with the hands and feet nailed."*

In 1903, the interim director of the Museo Yucateco in Mérida, Miguel Gamboa, issued a report regarding recent acquisitions of the Museum, which included the *"Cruz de Cozumel."* In his report, he stated: *"El eminente Dr. D. Justo Sierra, escribió las siguientes palabras en el año de 1845, en su periódico El Museo Yucateco, acerca de la cruz de Cozumel, que entonces se guardaba en la sacristía de la Iglesia de San Juan de esta capital: 'A nuestro amigo el padre Aranda, capellán de aquella Ermita, recomendamos el especial cuidado de conservarla, mientras que Dios mejora sus obras y se consigue la formación de un museo de antigüedades yucatecas, en que seguramente tendrá un lugar preferente esta celebre cruz de piedra.' Al colocar, pues, como últimamente hemos colocado, este celebre monumento histórico en nuestro Museo de antigüedades, dejamos cumplidos los deseos de aquel esclarecido yucateco."* (The eminent Dr. D. Justo Sierra wrote the following words in the year of 1845, in his newspaper, El Museo Yucateco, about the Cross of Cozumel, which was then kept in the sacristy of the Church of San Juan in this capital: 'We recommend our friend Padre Aranda, Chaplain of the Chapel [San Juan] of this capital, keep it in special care while God improves his works and we achieve the establishment of a Museum of Yucatán antiquities, that surely will have a preferential place for this famous stone cross.' By placing this cross, as we just have placed it, in our Museum of antiquities, we have completed the desires of that enlightened Yucatecan.)

So, here we have Miguel Gamboa, the director of the Yucatecan Museum in Mérida, stating that in 1903 they had just acquired the "Cozumel Cross" that once had been in the San Juan church. It would seem that the provenance provided would prove that the cross in the museum was the same one that had been described by Cogolludo in 1655, except that Cogolludo says the Christ on it was in bas relief of the same stone, and Stephens says the Christ on the cross he saw in the Church of the Mejorada was made of plaster. Somewhere along the line, it seems a different cross was introduced.

Five years later, in 1908, Channing Arnold visited Mérida and said that he saw the cross in a dusty exhibit in the museum in Mérida. He wrote in his 1909 book The American Egypt, A record of travel in Yucatan: *"There is a Museum in Mérida, a poor affair and badly housed in three dark rooms; but there were several things we wanted to see specially, so we made our way thither after leaving the prison. With some difficulty (for our driver did not appear, with true Yucatecan stupidity, to know that his city contained such a very unnecessary adjunct) we ran the national treasure house to earth in a back street, where a small brass plate on a decayed-looking doorway announced itself as 'El Museo.' The director, a middle-aged Yucatecan, whose amiability was only equalled by his archaeological ignorance, was routed out of his hammock by his little ten year-old son who opened the door to us, and sleepily proceeded to do the honours of the place. It is a great pity that, with such limitless wealth and such boundless opportunities, Mérida has taken no pains to establish a Museum worthy of her position as the capital city of the Egypt of the New World. What we saw, if it had not been so sad, would* have been really comic. Absolute confusion reigned. There was no catalogue, the smiling director forming a peripatetic one. Exhibits bore numbers which were thus meaningless to everyone but himself. It was Mexico Museum over again on a humbler scale. Wretched pieces of Spanish carved stonework from the interiors of churches or from the facades of seventeenth century houses, were jumbled up with really marvellous pieces of Indian workmanship, figures in bas-relief of gods and animals and warriors in feathered dress. But the good director had not been content with making a hotchpotch such as one sees in the shop of a dealer in marine stores and scrap-iron. He was guilty of archaeological crime, for on the top of a Spanish church pillar he had actually cemented a carved Indian head from one of the temples. In another corner a slab of stone, an eighteenth-century Spanish coat-of arms, had joined forces by means of cement with a wonderful Indian frieze. The result was ludicrous in the extreme: but when we expostulated with him, he smilingly explained that he had done it to 'prevent them from falling about'! There was, as far as quantity is concerned, an excellent display of Indian pottery, incense-burners, water-pots and domestic utensils, and small stone figures of gods. But these were all lying haphazard in a case with Spanish pottery and tile work. One of the most interesting exhibits from the archaeologist's point of view is the much disputed 'Cozumel Cross.' Found on the island of Cozumel in the seventeenth century, it was brought to Mérida and placed first in the patio of the Franciscan Convent, then in the Church of the Mejorada, whence it was removed to its present position. **It is a very ordinary stone cross, standing some three feet high with a two-foot cross-piece. On it, in half relief, is an image of the Saviour, made of plaster, coloured, with the hands and feet nailed.** Chiefly upon this relic has been based a ridiculous theory that at some remote date Christianity had been preached to the Indians and that the worship of the Cross was found to exist in Yucatan by the Spaniards."

Channing Arnold's description of a plaster Christ matches the description of Stephens, but does not match that of Cogolludo. To make things even more confusing, Sra. Carmen de Regil viuda de Molina of the Regil family of Mérida now claims to have possession of the cross, which she says was deaccessioned from the Mérida museum in

1915, and the photographs of the cross she has do not match the descriptions of Cogulludo, Stephens, or Arnold. Here, the story gets even murkier. In their 1991 book, *Historia de Cozumel*, historians Michel Antochiw and Alfredo César Dachary stated that they had been informed that the Regil family had sold the cross to a collector in Puebla, México. However, Raúl Alcalá Erosa interviewed Carmen de Regil in 2000 and was allowed to photograph the cross, which the Regil family still owns. Alcalá included a short recap of the historical mentions of the cross as well as a couple of photographs of it in his 1998 book, *Historia y vestigios de la Ciudadela de San Benito.*

Above: The Regil family's **purported "Cruz de Cozumel,"** *photographed by Raúl Alcalá Erosa and appearing in his 1998 book* <u>Historia y vestigios de la Ciudadela de San Benito</u>.

The stone cross the Regil family has does not match the descriptions made by Stephens or Arnold, who both said the Christ was made of plaster, but neither does it match the description of Cogolludo, who stated the cross was missing its lower portion and that the finials were gilded. Alcalá points out the similarity of the Regils' cross to a drawing of a stone crucifix identified as the *"Cruz de Cozumel"* and appearing in the 1888 edition of the encyclopedia *México a través de los Siglos*, but that illustration has its own profound differences with the photograph of the Regils' cross and the descriptions of the cross made by Cogolludo, Stephens and Arnold.

Above left: The alleged "Cozumel Cross" that appears in México a través de los Siglos. Above Right: The version of this drawing that appears in the 1998 book, Historia y vestigios de la Ciudadela de San Benito, by Raúl Alcalá Erosa.

In his book, which also deals with the convento de San Francisco where the "Cozumel Cross" once resided," Alcalá states that *"Casi al cierre de esta edición y luego de multiples pesquisas en varias localidades, he podido ubicar el paradero de la que considero que sea la legendaria Cruz de Cozumel, cuya fotografía me permitio incluir junto al dibujo que de la misma se presenta en su obra México a traves de los Siglos (pág. 287) donde se hace una breve mención de su origen."* (Almost at the close of this edition and after researching multiple locations, I was able to locate the whereabouts of what I consider to be the legendary cross of Cozumel, whose photograph I was allowed to include next to the drawing of it appearing in *México a traves de los Siglos (page 287)* which makes a brief mention of its origin.)

The drawing Alcalá includes in his book was copied from the illustration in Vicente Riva Palacio's 1884 encyclopedia *México a traves de los Siglos*. Palacio's illustration is nothing more than a drawing of a crucifix with a separate crown motif, both designed to be hung or placed on a wall and not to be freestanding. Although the drawing in the 1884 encyclopedia is entitled *"Cruz de Cozumel,"* the short text about the Cozumel Cross which appears on the same page as the drawing in no way positively identifies the illustration as such; the drawing Palacio used to illustrate the page is of a wall-mounted crucifix, not a free-standing crucifix. Although Alcalá claims the drawing was made by Frederick Catherwood, there is no proof of that and the style in which it was drawn is unlike any other drawing Catherwood produced.

It is true that its upper portion of the Regils' cross looks similar to the wall-mounted crucifix in Palacio's 1884 encyclopedia, but the lower portion of the free-standing cross of the Regils' is completely different and the arms of the Regils' cross lack the small, decorative bands shown on the arms in the drawing. There are other aspects of the Regils' cross that do not match up with historical descriptions. First, Stephens and Arnold both stated clearly that the Christ on the cross was made of plaster; the Christ in Alcalá's photograph is a bas-relief carved into the stone of the cross. Second, there is the fact that Cogolludo testified that Padre Antonio Ramírez gilded the decorative tips of the cross prior to 1655 and there are no signs on the Regils' cross of either gilding or the stucco undercoat that first would have been applied to the stone to give the gilding a smooth surface on which to adhere. Third, Channing Arnold stated the cross he saw in Mérida in 1908 was *"three feet high with a two-foot cross-piece."* The Regils' cross clearly does not fit those proportions. As of 2015, the Regil family still has refused to give anyone from the Instituto Nacional de Antropología e Historia permission to inspect the cross in order to authenticate it.

Above: A recent fabrication of the "Cozumel Cross," atop a monument in Cedral, Cozumel.

In Cozumel's village of Cedral, the government erected a monument with a plaque and a reproduction cross atop, which is a copy of the Regil family's cross made in a workshop in Mérida in 2003 and donated to Cozumel by Raúl Alcalá Erosa that same year. He also donated a twin of this reproduction to the Corpus Cristi Church in San Miguel.

The plaque on the monument also states, erroneously, that the 16th century church in Xamancab was located on top of the hill where the present-day *CAPA* water tower is located. This mislocation happened when the *Cronista de La Isla*, (meaning Island <u>Chronicler</u>, not Island <u>Historian</u>) misidentified the foundations of a 20th century church which was begun in the decades prior to the current church of San Miguel being built by the Maryknolls in 1945. The work on this 20th century hill-top church was abandoned before construction could be completed because there were too many complaints over how difficult it would be for the elderly to climb the hill. The true location of the 16th century church was more than a mile to the north, near Avenida 5 and Calle 12.

Casimiro Cárdenas and the Cedral Mayfair

For some time now, around the first of May the village of Cedral on Cozumel has celebrated the miraculous salvation of Casimiro Cárdenas. The legend at the root of the Cedral Mayfair is the claim by Cárdenas' family that he was saved by miracle during a massacre at the church in Saban, Yucatán, during the War of the Castes. According to the story, he was in the church with a crowd of other residents of Saban when the Maya Cruzoob rebels attacked. Everyone in the church was killed except him, because he was able to hide underneath a pile of dead bodies and evade detection. It is said he attributed his good luck to the fact that he was clutching a small, wooden cross; so he swore that if he escaped Saban alive, he would celebrate his salvation every year with a *novena* (nine consecutive days of prayer) in honor of the cross. And so, says the legend, when Cárdenas found safety in Cozumel with the rest of the *Repobladores de 1848*, he settled in Cedral and began the yearly tradition of holding a *novena* in honor of the cross for his good luck. Sometimes the legend even goes so far as to claim Cárdenas was the actual founder of Cedral.

Today, Cedral's May celebration (now named the *Feria de Cedral*) includes much more than just the *novena* and a religious celebration on the third of May; horseraces, bullfights, drinking and dancing have all been incorporated into the commemoration. One of the most iconic of the dances performed at the Cedral fair is the Dance of the Pig's Head, a bastardized version of the ancient Yucatec Maya ceremony also known as *Pool kekén, Okosta Pool,* or *K'u' Pool,* in which a pig's head has been substituted for a sacrificial deer's head.

A big part of the May celebrations at Cedral is the third of May's Catholic feast day of the "Finding of the Holy Cross," one of several days the Catholic Church once observed in regards to the "True Cross." It was to commemorate the finding by Saint Helena of what she believed to be the "True Cross" in the year 355. This feast day, however, was removed from the liturgical calendar of the Catholic Church by Pope John XXIII in 1960, in order to reduce the number of major feasts and to focus devotion to the Holy Cross on September 14. This abolishment of the "Feast day of the Finding of the Holy Cross" was something that was a long time in coming. As far back as 1691, the Holy Inquisition was expressing its concern over the May 3rd celebration. The religious court in México complained that the celebrations were held in *"indecent locations, and the celebrations with Mass, sermon, and processions were mixed up with farces, bullfights, and masquerades on the pretext of honoring the cross, which results in serious scandal."* Mexicans were loath to give up the feast day, however, and the Mexican bishops pleaded for and received an exception, so now México is the only country in the world where Catholics still celebrate May 3rd as a feast day.

This all makes for a good party, but what are the facts behind the story of Casimiro Cárdenas that this fiesta celebrates?

First, the records show that Casimiro Cárdenas Sanguino was born in 1820 in Tizamín, some 89 miles north of Saban. The records also show that he married Vitoria Tapia Alvarez of Tihosuco, some 20 miles north of Saban. There are no surviving records of any type associating Cárdenas with Saban in any manner.

Second, in the January 1850 *"Padrón que comprende todos los hombres que forman el Pueblo de San Miguel en la Isla de Cozumel"* (Census comprising all the men who formed the village of San Miguel on the island of Cozumel), Casimiro Cárdenas is listed as a 28-year-old male resident of <u>San Miguel</u>. Residents of Cedral and many outlying ranchos do not appear in the census. However, some of these non-San Miguel residents appear in other early letters and documents, such as Luis

Lujan, who shows up in a February 1850 letter from *Alcalde* José Francisco Rosel, listing Lujan as the *"dueño o personero del Rancho Santa María de esta jurisdicción, ubicado en esta misma isla a distancia de unas tres o cuatro leguas"* (owner or representative of Santa María Ranch, located in this same island at a distance of three or four leagues) and Lujan's uncle, Luis Borja. Rosel was complaining in the letter to the governor that some people, like Lujan, were refusing to contribute labor to the village of San Miguel because they said they lived too far away.

Third, the census states that Cárdenas was a laborer from Tihosuco, presumably because that is where he was living with his wife when they moved to San Miguel. He is listed as a *Hidalgo*, which in that day and age meant a Maya or part-Maya who was on the Yucatan Government's side of the War of the Castes and fighting against the *Cruzoob* rebels. Cárdenas' wife, Vitoria, is also listed in the *"Padrón que comprende todos las mugeres que forman el Pueblo de San Miguel en la Isla de Cozumel"* (Census comprising all the women who formed the village of San Miguel on the island of Cozumel), as a 20-year-old, white *molendera* (corn grinder) from Tihosuco.

Fourth, although records show that Saban surrendered to the *Cruzoob* in late 1847, there is no record of a massacre having occurred there at that time. The church at Saban was used later as a redoubt by the Yucatecan government forces from January 17, 1848 until they abandoned Saban to the Maya *Cruzoob* in August, 1848. There is no record of a massacre at Saban prior to the one that happened there in 1853, three years after Cárdenas and his wife appeared as residents of San Miguel on Cozumel.

The Cedral church

Father Cristóbal de Asencio stayed on Cozumel for six months in 1570. In his report of the visit, Asencio mentions the run-down condition of the two *ramada* churches on Cozumel: *"...y asi pase mis doctrinas y escuelas en cada pueblo, reformandose las iglesias que estan como cosa de prestado."* (...and thusly I give my religious instructions and classes in each village [San Miguel de Xamancab and Santa María de Oycib] making alterations to the churches which are like temporary things.)

This is the first mention of a church at Cedral. In his report, Father Asencio also included a census of all the adults living on the western coast of Cozumel (the renegade Maya in the interior and east coast of the island were not counted) and the total came to 159 in San Miguel and 202 in Santa María de Oycib (Cedral).

Today's church in Cedral is not located on the spot where the original 16th century church of Santa María de Oycib was located. Nor is it located where the second Cedral church was situated. The location it now has, next to the Maya ruin known as "La Cárcel," is post-1885. In 1885, there was no church next to that ruin; the Cedral church at that time was abandoned and falling apart and located *"in the village,"* while the Maya ruin was out on the *"edge of the village,"* according to eyewitness reports.

In 1885, N. B. Miller traveled to Cedral while he was a photographer on the U.S. Fisheries Commission's expedition to Cozumel. In his report, Miller said of Cedral: *"Our appearance excited so much curiosity that the entire village turned out, so that I had a good view of them, I found their complexion to be that of a bright mulatto, very dark eyes, and with long, straight, coarse, black hair. The men had scanty black beards, and were in height about 5 feet 4 inches, with features blunt and short. I entered several of their houses, which were huts made of poles, with thatched roofs, the floors being made of cement, raised a foot or more above the ground, and kept very clean. In each case I found but one room in a hut where the entire family lived, cooked, and slept, their hammocks being tied up to the rafters during the day. But everything was very clean, all the women were dressed in loose, comfortable white gowns and the children the same — those that had anything on. Some were engaged in making cigars, some curing tobacco, and others making baskets. The occupation of the men at this time is that of wood-chopping, all being engaged in cutting cross-ties for railroad companies in Yucatan.*

Unlike the other villages of the island, the cattle here are not allowed to run at large about the houses, but are kept in big pens with high stone walls around them. I saw some old Indians that were unable to converse in Spanish, and who knew no language but the original Indian tongue.

They all speak the Indian language somewhat. They have a small Catholic church in the village, but there having occured several remarkable spiritualistic exhibitions among the inhabitants on the island, they have in consequence all turned spiritualists, and their church is neglected and about to fall down. Just on the edge of the village is an old ruin, which, these Indians say, was here at the time of the Spanish conquest, but they know nothing definite about it."

INDIAN VILLAGE ON THE ISLAND
OF COZUMEL

Above: Miller's photograph of Cedral taken in 1885 and made into an etching, which appeared in* Science Magazine *on April 10, 1885.

Later, the townsfolk of Cedral abandoned their "spiritualist" religion, returned to Roman Catholicism, and built a new church of poles and thatch next door to the Maya ruin. In a 1915 photograph of the ruin next to the church in Cedral, the exterior veneer of stone and stucco on the ruin has been removed, as well as the stone lintel over the doorway. This material was re-purposed as construction material by the local population of Cedral sometime after 1885. Later, a wooden doorway was added and the ruin was used as a jail cell for a time. The ruin was a typical two-room Maya building, with arched ceilings. It has one doorway in front and a door in the interior median wall giving access to the back room.

Above: The third incarnation of the Cedral church as it appeared in 1909, when it was located next to the Maya ruin known as "La Cárcel."

Above: The Maya ruin in Cedral as it looked in 1966.

In 2003, the ruin next to the church in Cedral was partially restored. The veneer stones and lintel that had been removed between 1885 and 1909 and re-purposed as construction material were replaced with newly-cut stones around the doorway and lower half of the building.

Above: The Cedral ruin in 2003.

However, the results of the reconstruction efforts left the ruin a far cry from what it looked like when it was photographed in 1885 by N. B. Miller, below:

Above: The ruin in Cedral in 1885, before the veneer was removed.

Selected Bibliography

Pre-1492 documents

Dresden Codex, n.d.

Madrid Codex *(Codex Tro-Cortesianus)*, n.d.

Pizzigano, Giovanni, <u>Pizzigano Portolan chart</u>, 1424

Manuscripts and printed documents 1492-1600

Asencio, Fray Cristóbal de, <u>*Informe sobre Cozumel*</u>, 1570

Benavente, Fray Toribio de, *(Motolinía)* <u>*Historia de los indios de la Nueva España*</u>, 1541

<u>*Capitulación otorgada por don Fernando El Católico a Juan Díaz de Solís y Vicente Yáñez Pinzón en Burgos el 23 de Marzo de 1508*</u>

Cerezada, Andrés de, <u>*Carta de 14 Agosto,*</u> 1536

Colon, Bartolomé, <u>*L'informatione di Bartolomeo Colombo della Navigazione di Ponente et Garbin di Beragna nel Mondo Novo,*</u> 1503

Colón, Fernando, <u>*Historie del S.D. Fernando Colombo; Nelle quali s'ha particolare & vera relatione della vita & de' fatti dell' Ammiraglio D. Christoforo Colombo suo padre,*</u> written between 1537 and 1539, published in 1571

Contreras Duran, Diego, <u>*Relación de los pueblos de Nabalon y Tahcabo y la Isla de Coçumel*</u>, 1579

Cortés, Hernán, <u>*Primera carta de relación,*</u> 1519

Cortés, Hernán, *Interrogatorio*, 1534

Díaz del Castillo, Bernal, *Historia Verdadera de la Conquista de Nueva España*, written prior to 1568, published 1632

Forli, Giovanni Ruffo de, Letter to Francesco Chieregati, March 7, 1520

Gomara, Francisco López de, *Primera y segunda parte de la Historia General de las Indias con todo el descubrimiento, y cosas notables que han acaecido dende que se ganaron hasta el año de 1551, con la conquista de México, y de la Nueva España*, (also known as *Historia General de las Indias y conquista de México)*, 1552

La merced de la isla de Cozumel al Almirante de Flandes por parte del rey don Carlos, 1518

Landa, Fray Diego de, *Relación de las cosas de Yucatán*, (an abstract of the original work that was written around 1566 and is now lost)

Las Casas, Fray Bartolomé de *Apologética historia sumaria de las Indias Occidentales*, written during the period between 1527 and 1559

Las Casas, Fray Bartolomé de, *Historia de la Indias*, written between 1527 and 1561

Las Casas, Fray Bartolomé de, *Extracto del diario de abordo*, 1530s

Martyr d'Anghiera, Peter, *De Orbe Novo*, 1511

Martyr d'Anghiera, Peter, *De Orbe Novo Décadas cum Legatione Babylonica*, 1516

Oviedo y Valdés, Gonzalo Fernández de, *Sumario de la Natural Historia de las Indias*, 1526

Oviedo y Valdés, Gonzalo Fernández de, *Historia General y Natural de las Indias, islas tierra firme y mar océano,* part 1 published in 1535, part 2 in 1852

Pané, Fray Ramón, *Relación acerca de las antigüedades de los indios,* 1498

Proceso contra Pierre Sanfroy, Esteban Gilberto, Juan Luayzel, Jaques Montill, Glaudi Yubli, Guillermo de Ezila, Guillermo Conquerie, Marin Cornu, Issac de Rouet, Guillermo Cutiel, y Guillermo Cocrel, 1572-1572

Ruysch, Johann, *Universalior Cogniti Orbis Tabula Ex recentibus confecta observationibus,* 1507

Sahagún, Fray Bernardino, *Historia general de las cosas de Nueva España,* written during the period between 1540 to 1585

Salazar, Francisco Cervantes de, *Crónica de la Nueva España,* 1558

Santillán, Diego de, *Auto de don Diego de Santillán sobre iglesias en isla de Cozumel,* 1573

Tapia, Andrés de, *Relación de algunas cosas que acaecieron al muy ilustre señor Don Hernando Cortés, Marqués del Valle, desde que se determinó a ir a descubrir tierra en la tierra firme del mar Océano,* 1539

Toral, Fray Francisco de, Letters to the Crown, 15 March 1563 and 3 March 1564

Varthema, Ludovico de, Iltinerario de Ludovico de Varthema, Bolognese nello Egitto, nella Soria nella Arabia deserta y felice, nella Persia, nella la India & nella Ethyopa, 1522

Waldseemüller, Martin, *Cosmographiæ,* 1507

Manuscripts and documents 1601 to 1700

Cogolludo, Diego López de, *Historia de Yucatán*, written circa 1655 and published in 1688

Herrera y Tordesillas, Antonio de, *Descripción de las Indias Occidentales*, 1601

Herrera y Tordesillas, Antonio de *Historia General de los hechos de los Castellanos en las islas y tierra firme del Mar Océano*, 1601-1615

Lizana, Fray Bernardo de, *Historia de Yucatán: devocionario de Ntra. Sra. de Izamal y conquista espiritual*, 1633

Osborne, Philip, Depositions concerning cutting logwood October 29th to 3rd November 1672

Paxbolón, Pablo, *Probanza de Pablo Paxbolón*, 1612

Sánchez de Aguilar, Dean Pedro, *Informe contra idolorum cultores del obispado de Yucatán*, 1613

Solís y Ribadeneyra, Antonio de, *Historia de la conquista de México, población y progresos de la América septentrional, conocida por el nombre de Nueva España*, 1684

Manuscripts and documents 1701 to 1800

Canul, Joan (?), *Ritual de los Bacabes*, post-1779

Descripción y noticias del río Balis, río Nuevo, Isla Cozumel, la de Mujeres, Conttoy y Blanquitta, 1751

Hoil, Juan Josef, *Chilam Balam de Chumayel*, 1782

Ximénez, Francisco, *Popol Vuh*, 1701

Documents and books 1800 to 1930

Adams, Ephriam Douglass, Correspondence from the British Archives concerning Texas, 1837-1846

Ancona, Eligio, *Historia de Yucatán; Desde la época más remota hasta nuestros días*, 1878

Archivo do Conselho Nobiliarchico de Portugal, *Terra dos Corte Reais*, 1928

Baqueiro Prevé, Serapio, *Ensayo histórico sobre las revoluciones en Yucatán*, 1878

Bell, James, A System of Geography, Popular and Scientific, 1831

British Archives, Correspondence concerning Texas, 1837-1846, 1913

Calzadilla, José María de, & Echánove, Bolio, Zuaznavar, *Apuntaciones para la estadística de la provincia de Yucatán que formaban de orden superior en 20 marzo de 1814*, 1871

Canto, E. de, *Carta d'Alberto Cantino, de 1501 ao duque de Ferrara*, 1909

Carillo y Ancona, Crescencio, *Historia Antigua de Yucatán*, 1880-82

Case, Henry A., Views on and of Yucatán, besides notes upon parts of the state of Campeche and the Territory of Quintana Roo, Mérida, Yucatán, 1910

Conder, Josiah, The Modern Traveller, 1830

Correspondencia de la delegación mexicana durante la intervención extranjera, 1860-1868, 1870-92

Dunne, B.B., Two Santa Feans Visit Bad Men on Cozumel Isle, 1913

Dunne, B.B., Grave Danger in Visiting Isle of Cozumel, 1913

Dunne, B.B., May Have Died on Visit to Cozumel Island, 1913

Gamboa, Miguel, *Informe que el c. Presidente de la H. comisión de Instrucción Pública presenta al ejecutivo local, acerca del estado que guarda dicha instrucción en todos sus ramos el año escolar 1902-1903*, 1903

Gann, Thomas, In an Unknown Land, 1924

García Icazbalceta, Joaquín, *Colección de documentos inéditos para la historia de México*, 1858 -1866

Goodrich, Claude L., Cozumel Island: The New Tropical Paradise: Its History, Government, Character, Resources, Climate, Location, Soil, Products, Inhabitants, Etc., 1874

Holmes, William, Archaeological Studies among the Ancient Cities of México, 1895-97

Honduras Almanac, Vessels employed in the Drogging and Coastal Trade, 1829

Humboldt, Alexander von, *Essai politique sur le royaume de la Nouvelle Espagne*, 1808

Irish Monthly, Nuns in Honduras, 1883

Joaquín de Torres, José, *Registro Yucateco: Mas sobre Cozumel*, 1846

Kennedy, James, Essays Ethnological and Linguistic, 1861

LePlongeon, Alice, Notes on Yucatan, 1879

LePlongeon, Alice, Here and there in Yucatan, 1889

LePlongeon, Alice, Beautiful Cozumel, 1898

Leslie, Frank, Cozumel, 1885

Lothrop, Samuel K. Tulum, 1924

MacNutt, Francis Augustus, Fernando Cortés and the Conquest of México, 1909

Mason, Gregory, Silver Cities of Yucatán, 1927

Mason, Gregory, Motor Boating Magazine: Caribbean Blue, 1929

Medina, José Toribio, Juan Díaz de Solís, Estudio Histórico, 1897

Molas, Miguel, Derrotero de la Península de Yucatán desde todas las costas e islas, bajos, puertos, y arrecifes, trabajado por la práctica, y cumplido conocimiento de Don Miguel Molas, en el año 1817, 1817

Molina Solís, Juan Francisco, Historia del descubrimiento y conquista de Yucatán con una reseña de la historia antigua de esta península, 1896

Morley, Sylvanus G., Detailed report of a Coast Reconnaissance of the Peninsula of Yucatán, 1918

Morning Star & Catholic Register, Oldest Church in America, 1874

New Mexico Palace of the Governors Photo Archives, Nusbaum Collection; Cozumel, 1913

O' Reilly, Sierra, El Museo Yucateco; El Cruz de Cozumel, 1841

Palacio, Vicente Riva, México a Través de los Siglos, 1884

Peraza, Martín Francisco, *Registro Yucateco: La Isla de Cozumel*, 1846

Science, Vol. 5, No. 114, The Island of Cozumel, 1885
Stephens, John Lloyd, Incidents of Travel in Yucatán, 1843

Texas Government Archives, Report of Henry L. Thompson, August 29, 1837, 1837

Texas Government Archives, Texas Navy actions off Yucatán 1843

Texas Navy Resources, Report of the Brutus's 1837 trip to Cozumel

Texas Navy Resources, Log of the Schooner of War, Brutus, 1837

Topete, Juan Bautista, *Informe del viaje de la goleta Cristina a la Isla de Cozumel*, 1848

Toribio Medina, José, *Historia del tribunal del Santo oficio de la inquisición en México*, 1903

US Executive Documents, Volume 508, 1848

Vignaud, Henry and Martins & Toscanelli, The Letter and Chart of (Paolo Dal Pozzo) Toscanelli on the Route to the Indies by Way of the West, Sent in 1474 to the Portuguese Fernam Martins, and Later on to Christopher Columbus, 1902

Ward, Fannie B., Cozumel, 1888

William, Prince, Between Two Continents, 1922

Books and articles 1931 to 2015

Aguirre Rosas, Mario, _Gonzalo de Guerrero: Padre del mestizaje iberoamericano_, 1975

Alcalá Erosa, Raul, _Historia y vestigios de la Ciudadela de San Benito_, 1998

Alcalá Erosa, Raul, Origen y recorrido la cruz pétrea de Cozumel, 2003

Andrews, Anthony P., Rural Chapels and Churches of Early Colonial Yucatán and Belize, 1991

Andrews, Anthony P., Maya Salt Production and Trade, 1984

Antochiw, Michel & Alfredo A. Dachary _Historia de Cozumel,_ 1991

Antochiw, Michel, _Cozumel Padrones y poblamiento_, 1998

Aoyama, Kazuo, Classic Maya lithic artifacts from the Main Plaza of Aguateca, Guatemala, 2006

Association internationale d'études du Sud-Est européen, _Actes du premier Congrès international des études balkaniques et sud-est européens, Volume 4 : George Fisher_, 1969

Baedeker's Mexico, Cozumel, 1994

Bagrow, Leo, _Imago Mvndi_, 1964

Bercht, Fatima, Taino: Pre-Columbian Art and Culture from the Caribbean, 1997

Braham, Persephone, _El feliz cautiverio de Gonzalo Guerrero_, 2006

Campos Jara, Salvador, _Gonzalo Guerrero, anotaciones entre la historia y el mito_, 1995

Chamberlain, Robert S., The Conquest and Colonization of Yucatán, 1517 – 1550, 1948

Clark, Alan, Guerrero & Heart's Blood, 1990

Coe, William R., Environmental Limitation on Maya Culture, 1957

Cortesão, Armando, Pizzigano's Chart of 1424, 1970

Escalona Ramos, Alberto, Algunas Ruinas Prehispánicas en Q. Roo, México, 1946

Feliciano Ramos, Héctor R., El contrabando inglés en el Caribe y Golfo de México 1748-1778, 1990

Florida State University Institute for Social Research, Slavic Papers: George Fisher, 1967

Graham, Elizabeth, Archaeology in Cuba, 2002

Hajovsky, Ric, The Lost Kivas of San Lazaro, 2010

Harlow, George E. and Murphy, Hozjan, de Mille, & Levinson, Pre-Columbia Jadeite Axes from Antigua, 2006

Kerchache, Jacques, L'Art Taino: Chefs-d'Oeuvre des Grandes Antilles Precolombiennes, 1994

Kerr, Justin, The Maya Vase Book: A Corpus of Rollout Photographs of Maya Vases, 2000

La Península de Yucatán en el Archivo General de la Nación, 1998

Lincoln, Abraham, Speeches and Writings, 2001

Lindbergh, Charles, Log of the Spirit of St. Louis, 1953

Lindbergh, Charles, The Spirit of St. Louis, 1953

Loriaux, F., *Les Belges et le Mexique: dix contributions à l'histoire des relations Belgique-Mexique*, 1993

Mason, Gregory, South of Yesterday, 1940

Miller, Arthur G., On the edge of the Sea; Mural paintings at Tancah-Tulum, 1982

Morley, Sylvanus G., The Ancient Maya, 1973

Mueller, Roseanna, From Cult to Comics: The Representation of Gonzalo Guerrero as a Cultural Hero in Mexican Popular Culture, 2001

Nusbaum, Rosemary, Tierra Dulce: Reminiscences from the Jesse Nusbaum Papers, 1980

Patel, Shankari, Religious resistance and persistence on Cozumel Island, 2009

Pellicer, Rosa, *El Cautivo Cautivado: Gonzalo Guerrero en la Novela Mexicana del Siglo XX*, 2007

Prem, H. J., *The Canek Manuscript and Other Faked Documents*, 1999

Rathje, William and Jeremy Sabloff, Cozumel, Late Maya Settlement Patterns, 1984

Revelli, Paolo, *Un Cartografo genovese amico a Cristoforo Colombo: Nicolò Caveri*, 1948

Richards, H. G. Land and freshwater mollusks from the island of Cozumel, 1937

Romero, Rolando J., Texts, pre-texts, con-texts: Gonzalo Guerrero in the Chronicles of Indies, 1992

Roys, Ralph L., Political Geography of the Yucatán Maya, 1957

Roys, Ralph L. and Scholes & Adams, Report and Census of the Indians of Cozumel, 1570, 1940

Rubio Mañé, J. Ignacio, ed. *Archivo de la historia de Yucatán, Campeche y Tabasco*, 1942

Sabloff, Jeremy A. and E. Wyllis Andrews (eds.): Late Lowland Maya Civilization: Classic to Postclassic, 1986

Sabloff, Jeremy & William L. Rathje, Changing Pre-Columbian Commercial Systems, 1975

Sainsbury, William Noel, Calender of State Papers: Colonial series, Great Britain, Public Record Office, 1964

Santiago, Juan-Navarro; Theodore Robert Young, A Twice-Told Tale: Reinventing the Encounter in Iberian/Iberian American Literature and Film, 2001

Scholes, France V., and Eleanor Adams, *Don Diego Quijada, alcalde mayor de Yucatán, 1561-1565*, 1938

Scholes, France V., and Carlos Menéndez, *Documentos para la historia de Yucatán*, 1936

Solís Robleda, Gabriel & Pedro Bracamonte y Sosa, *Historias de la conquista del Mayab, 1511-1697 de Fray Joseph de San Buenaventura*, 1994

Sons of Dewitt Colony Texas, Coahuila y Texas-Index; Archival Correspondence: George Fisher, 1997

Thompson, J. Eric S., The moon goddess in middle America, 1939

Thompson, J. Eric S., Maya History and Religion, 1970

Vivas Valdés, Veudi, *Cozumel: Raíces genealógicos*, 2015

Wagner, Henry Raup, The Discovery of New Spain in 1518, 1942

Whitley, David R., Sally's Rockshelter, 1999

Maya-Spanish Dictionaries

Ciudad Real, Fray Antonio de, *Calepino de Motul*, 1570

Coronel, Juan *Arte en lengua de Maya recopilado y enmendado*, 1620

Morán, Fray Francisco *Arte y vocabulario en lengua choltí*, 1695

Pérez Bermón, Juan Pío, *Diccionario de la lengua Maya*, 1866-77

Government Archives

Archivo General de las Indias (Spain)

Archivo General de la Nación (México)

National Archives of Belize (Belize)

National Archives (Great Britain)

National Archives (USA)

Registro Civil (Cozumel)

Texas Government Archives (Texas)

Books by Ric Hajovsky available from Amazon.com and other retail outlets:

The Bizarre Events, Odd Theories, and Offbeat Characters of Tulum: Everything you need to know before you go to the ruins

Cozumel Survival Manual

The Lost Kivas of San Lazaro: The discovery and excavation of two underground ceremonial chambers in the Tano Indian ruin of San Lazaro in the Galisteo Basin of New Mexico

The Adventures of Trader Ric: In Kuna Yala, San Blas Islands, Panama

The Adventures of Trader Ric: On the trail of Cristóbal Colón

The Adventures of Trader Ric: Towards the headwaters of the Tapanahonie River, Suriname

The Adventures of Trader Ric: In the Darién Gap, Panama

Spain: Hidden Secrets and Dirty Tricks; how to travel in Spain in high style, but at a budget price

The Secrets of Xcaret: The surprising history that lies buried under this world famous Mexican theme Park

Guide to the Mayan Ruins of San Gervasio, Cozumel, México

The History of Horseshoes

December 21, 2012: Everything you should know to understand what all the fuss is about

-vale-

Made in the USA
Monee, IL
09 September 2020

41258760R00214